Early Literacy Development in Deaf Children

Perspectives on Deafness

Series Editors
Marc Marschark
Patricia Elizabeth Spencer

Early Literacy Development in Deaf Children

Connie Mayer
Beverly J. Trezek

OXFORD
UNIVERSITY PRESS

OXFORD
UNIVERSITY PRESS

Oxford University Press is a department of the University of
Oxford. It furthers the University's objective of excellence in research,
scholarship, and education by publishing worldwide.

Oxford   New York
Auckland   Cape Town   Dar es Salaam   Hong Kong   Karachi
Kuala Lumpur   Madrid   Melbourne   Mexico City   Nairobi
New Delhi   Shanghai   Taipei   Toronto

With offices in
Argentina   Austria   Brazil   Chile   Czech Republic   France   Greece
Guatemala   Hungary   Italy   Japan   Poland   Portugal   Singapore
South Korea   Switzerland   Thailand   Turkey   Ukraine   Vietnam

Published in the United States of America by
Oxford University Press
198 Madison Avenue, New York, NY 10016

Library of Congress Cataloging-in-Publication Data
Mayer, Connie Christine, 1954–
Early literacy development in deaf children / Connie Mayer, Beverly J. Trezek.
pages cm.—(Perspectives in deafness)
ISBN 978–0–19–996569–4 (hb : alk. paper)   1. Deaf children—Education.
2. Deaf children—Language.   3. Literacy.   4. Reading.   5. Deaf students.
I. Trezek, Beverly J.   II. Title.
HV2430.M444 2015
302.2'2440872—dc23
2014050105

9 8 7 6 5 4 3 2
Printed in the United States of America
on acid-free paper

To the many children, both deaf and hearing, who have informed our thinking about early literacy learning. They have been our best teachers. And to our families, who are always there for us when we need them.

Contents

Introduction

The importance of the early years for later literacy learning is now so widely accepted that it is easy to forget that this focus is relatively new in the field of education. For the better part of the twentieth century, the prevalent view was that (1) learning to read and write was a consequence of development, (2) children needed to be taught a set of prerequisite literacy skills, and (3) there was a point in the developmental trajectory when children were ready for literacy learning (i.e., reading and writing readiness), which generally coincided with school entry and the development of conventional literacy.

The notion that young children begin the process of becoming literate from birth—well before they begin school—marked a profound shift in thinking that would have significant implications for both research and pedagogical practice. With this shift came the birth of the terms *emergent literacy, early literacy, emergent reading*, and *emergent writing.* Clay (1966) is credited with being the first person to use the term *emergent literacy* in her doctoral dissertation to describe reading behaviors in young children who imitate reading and writing activities using books and writing materials, even though they are not yet reading and writing in a conventional sense. She also stressed the importance of the relationship between writing and reading and the fact that, contrary to the thinking at the time, it was not necessary to learn to read before learning to write.

Since then, an extensive body of research has broadened understandings of the concept of emergent literacy, expanding on the view that children are doing significant cognitive work during this period. The emphasis is on the fact that a child's literacy development begins well before formal school entry and can be influenced by environmental factors such as the nature of interactions with adults and meaningful engagement with literacy materials (Allington & Cunningham, 1996; Clay, 1975, 1991; Hall & Moats, 1999; Holdaway, 1979; Snow, Burns, & Griffin, 1998; Sulzby & Teale, 1996; Teale & Sulzby, 1986, 1989; Whitehurst & Lonigan, 2003). Additional definitions and descriptions have also been offered that further describe the developmental precursors (i.e., knowledge, skills, and attitudes) of conventional reading and writing that mark the emergent literacy period (e.g., Teale & Sulzby, 1989).

One of the most widely accepted perspectives is drawn from the work of Whitehurst and Lonigan (1998), who suggested that the components of emergent literacy could be categorized according to two distinct sources: *outside-in* and *inside-out*. Outside-in refers to information other than the printed word (e.g., vocabulary, conceptual knowledge, story structure) that supports children's understanding of the meaning of print. Sources of information more closely associated with the text (e.g., phonological and letter knowledge) that allow children to develop the understanding of the relationship between sounds and print involve inside-out skills. These researchers further suggested that skills related to these two abilities are a consequence of different types of early literacy experiences and appear to have shifting significance and influence at different points in the developmental process.

An additional issue that appears in most discussions of emergent literacy is the age range of the children (Sulzby, 1991), with many taking the view that this time period refers to children from birth through kindergarten, or from birth to age five or six (National Early Literacy Panel, 2008). However, as Teale and Sulzby (1986) point out, "It is not reasonable to point to a time in a child's life when literacy begins. Rather...we see children in the process of becoming literate, as the term emergent indicates" (p. xix). From such a perspective, it may be more useful to refer to the emergent literacy period as the years from birth to the beginning of formal literacy instruction (Neuman & Dickinson, 2011), which may occur as early as age four or as late as age six for most children.

Before going further, it would be useful to make a distinction between the terms *emergent literacy* and *early literacy* and to consider whether there is any substantive semantic difference in their use. In many instances, the terms are used interchangeably, yet for some researchers, there is a clear distinction between them (see Neuman & Roskos, 1998). While the National Early Literacy Panel (2008) used both terms, early literacy is seen as the broader of the two and is used to refer to both the precursor abilities (i.e., predictive, foundational, or emergent) and conventional literacy skills (i.e., more mature, later developing) of preschool and kindergarten children. This is the term that we will use throughout this book.

Perhaps what is most important is that irrespective of the terminology, research and practice with young learners cannot be represented as a unified perspective. Rather, work in the field encompasses a broad range of views, methodological stances, and pedagogical approaches (e.g., Crawford, 1995; Hiebert & Raphael, 1998; Kress, 1997, 2000; Whitehurst & Lonigan, 1998). Despite these varying perspectives, there is "a robust body of knowledge that exists about the first five years of life and the extent to which children's early experiences correlate with their competencies in language and literacy" (Ramey & Ramey, 2006, p. 445).

With respect to research on hearing children, this is certainly true, and even the most cursory literature review reveals thousands of studies employing a range of methodological approaches to investigate the nature of the experiences and interventions that support optimal early literacy development. For example, the authors of *Developing Early Literacy* (National Early Literacy Panel, 2008) identified more than eight thousand potential articles to be screened for inclusion in their analysis. Within this body of research, there is also a robust literature on those learners who may face particular challenges in developing literacy skills, such as children with language impairments and cognitive disabilities (see also Kaiser, Roberts, & McLeod, 2011).

By virtue of their hearing loss, deaf children fall into this at-risk group, yet compared with other groups of learners, there is a relative paucity of direct evidence available with respect to the early literacy development and experiences of deaf children (for reviews, see Williams, 2004; Williams & Mayer, in press). This stands in stark contrast to the vast volume of research and writing on the early reading and writing development of hearing children, a body of work that includes a focus on children with disabilities and those who are second-language learners.

Therefore, the motivation for writing this book was to address this gap in the literature with an eye to (1) summarizing what we know, at least to the extent that we have any evidence from either hearing or deaf contexts to support the claims, (2) considering the ways in which what has been learned about the early literacy development of hearing learners applies to deaf children, and (3) identifying directions for research and practice based on this theoretical and research evidence base. We would argue that this is especially timely given the current focus on the early years as a consequence of Universal Newborn Hearing Screening (UNHS). This initiative, in conjunction with advancements in hearing technologies (e.g., cochlear implants) that have resulted in improved speech and language outcomes for many deaf children, has raised expectations that greater numbers of deaf learners will achieve literacy outcomes commensurate with their hearing age peers.

As noted above, we will be using the term *early literacy* throughout this book to describe the early reading and writing development of deaf and hearing children from birth through implementation of formal literacy instruction (i.e., birth to ages four to six or through kindergarten). We are not using the term to refer to students beyond this age range who are performing significantly below grade level and who have not developed the abilities and skills associated with the early literacy years. We would also emphasize that for the purposes of our discussion, we are confining ourselves to the development of text-based literacy. While we recognize the importance of other literacies (e.g., media, social, cultural, digital), they are not the focus of this book.

It is also important to clarify our use of the term *deaf*. As is the convention in several contexts (e.g., in the United Kingdom), we will use *deaf* to refer to any child identified with a hearing loss, from mild to profound, irrespective of the use of hearing technologies (i.e., children with cochlear implants are deaf learners). With respect to the children, we are not making a distinction between *deaf* and *Deaf*,[1] as we do not view this difference as directly relevant to the development of early literacy. We include a focus on sign bilingualism in chapter 5, but even in this instance, it is not the case that very many deaf children come from culturally Deaf homes. Therefore, we have elected to use the more general term *deaf*. That said, we address issues of communication, hearing technologies, modality, and language in each chapter, with an eye to how they are implicated in the early literacy development of deaf children.

The principal aim of the book is to provide an account of the early literacy development of deaf children, not primarily to serve as a "how-to" guide to early literacy instruction for deaf children. We see this explication of theoretical frameworks and overview of research evidence as serving a dual role: informing directions for instruction and driving a research agenda. With this view in mind, we have included "Implications for Practice" and "Implications for Research" sections at the end of each chapter.

We have written this book with the intention that the chapters together form a coherent whole and have made a conscious effort to make explicit links among the chapters by directing the reader to earlier or subsequent chapters in the narrative of each. This is motivated by our belief that the issues presented inform one another and that each topic is best understood in relationship to the others (i.e., how early writing informs reading, how assessment shapes practice and research across domains). While we would see this as the preferred way to engage with the material in this book, we have also written the chapters so that each can stand alone in providing information on a topic (e.g., as course readings in various fields such as education, linguistics, psychology, etc.), including a reference list at the end of each chapter.

OVERVIEW OF THE BOOK

The primary purpose of chapter 1 is to provide a review of the literature related to early literacy development and deaf learners, in order

---

[1] *Deaf* (with a capital *D*) is used to designate members of a distinct culture and community who are defined in large part by the use of a native sign language (e.g., American Sign Language [ASL], British Sign Language [BSL], or Sign Language of the Netherlands [SLN]). The term *deaf* is a more general term denoting any individuals with hearing loss.

to establish a sense of where we are in the field to date. This will also allow us to consider the findings of this research in order to make recommendations for future inquiries. The knowledge of extant studies gained from this literature review will afford us the opportunity to reflect on gaps in the literature and offer specific suggestions for topics requiring further investigation. The information presented throughout the chapter will serve as a reference point for discussions in subsequent sections of the book, as we explore implications for research and practice in the areas of reading, writing, bilingualism, and assessment.

In chapter 2, we outline a theoretical framework for the development of early literacy in which we describe the relative contributions of language-related and code-related abilities in the process of learning to read and write, making the argument that proficiency in a face-to-face form of the language of the text (including its phonological aspects) is the critical requisite for literacy learning. Our discussion is based on the argument that the developmental process from language to literacy is not different for deaf learners, in that they must develop the same set of knowledge, abilities, and skills as their hearing counterparts if they are ultimately to become proficient readers and writers. In considering implications for practice, we emphasize the importance of making the target language accessible as the first step in any early literacy program, and we argue for instruction for young deaf children that is differentiated based on the needs of the individual learner as opposed to notions of generic interventions for deaf learners as a group.

Chapter 3 is centered on the development of early reading, a topic that has garnered considerable attention in the research literature over the past decade. Drawing on the meta-analytic findings of the National Early Literacy Panel (2008), we provide an in-depth discussion of the essential skills and abilities (i.e., phonological sensitivity, letter and alphabet knowledge, phonemic decoding) that strongly predict later conventional reading achievement. While these precursor skills fall primarily within the code-related domain, we also explore the reciprocity of language-related abilities, and the impact of language delays and deficits, with the development of early reading. Descriptions of effective pedagogical practices and strategies to differentiate instruction for young deaf literacy learners are also presented and discussed.

The focus in chapter 4 is on early writing development, an area that has received relatively less research attention than reading in the contexts of both hearing and deaf early literacy learners. We take the view that learning to write is a developmental process in which all children must come to see that text is a representation of spoken language. This understanding is achieved by uncovering/discovering the systematic and arbitrary relationships in which the spoken language is encoded in the orthographic system of the language to be written. We make the argument that this process for hearing and deaf children depends on both language- and code-related abilities, and we use examples from young deaf and hearing writers to illustrate the stages of early writing development and what needs to be mastered at each stage.

In chapter 5, we take up the issue of bilingualism and how this affects literacy development in both a first (L1) and a second (L2) language, considering this development in terms of the theoretical frameworks that have been widely adopted in the contexts of both hearing and deaf learners (e.g., sequential versus simultaneous acquisition, linguistic interdependence model, threshold hypothesis). We review the available research evidence to determine the ways in which bilingualism can improve or constrain the process of learning to read and write, and what this might mean for developing programs and informing practice. While we acknowledge the complexity of this issue, along with the heterogeneity of the group of young deaf bilinguals, we place particular emphasis on the issue of sign bilingualism (i.e., L1 is a natural sign language, and L2 is a spoken language), as this arguably represents one of the most complex instances of bilingualism and early literacy development.

Utilizing three essential questions (why are we assessing, what are we assessing, and how are we assessing?) as a framework for discussion (see Snow & Oh, 2011), in chapter 6, we explore the subject of assessment. Early literacy constructs discussed in previous chapters are explained in order to understand how they are best measured and to gain insights into the associated instructional activities to foster skill development. Descriptions of various categories of assessment (informal, screening/progress monitoring, diagnostic) will be provided, and research findings germane to discussion of early literacy practices for deaf learners will be reviewed. Finally, we will explicate specific accommodation strategies that can be employed to provide differentiated access to early literacy assessments that maintain the fidelity and validity of measures.

REFERENCES

Allington, R. L., & Cunningham, P. (1996). *Schools that work*. New York, NY: HarperCollins.

Clay, M. (1966). *Emergent reading behaviour*. Unpublished doctoral dissertation, University of Auckland, New Zealand.

Clay, M. (1975). *What did I write?* Auckland, New Zealand: Heinemann.

Clay, M. (1991). *Becoming literate: The construction of inner control*. Portsmouth, NH: Heinemann.

Crawford, P. (1995). Early literacy: Emerging perspectives. *Journal of Research in Childhood Education, 10(1),* 71–86.

Hall, S. L., & Moats, L. C. (1999). *Straight talk about reading: How parents can make a difference during the early years*. Chicago, IL: Contemporary Books.

Hiebert, E. H., & Raphael, T. E. (1998). *Early literacy instruction*. Fort Worth, TX: Harcourt Brace.

Holdaway, D. (1979). *The foundations of literacy*. Sydney, Australia: Ashton Scholastic.

Kaiser, A. P., Roberts, M. Y., & McLeod, R. H. (2011). Young children with language impairments: Challenges in transition to reading. In S. B. Neuman & D. K. Dickinson (Eds.), *Handbook of early literacy research* (Vol. 3, pp. 228–241). New York, NY: Guilford Press.

Kress, G. (1997). *Before writing: Rethinking the paths to literacy*. New York, NY: Routledge.

Kress, G. (2000). *Early spelling: Between convention and creativity*. New York, NY: Routledge.

National Early Literacy Panel. (2008). *Developing early literacy: Report of the National Early Literacy Panel*. Washington, DC: National Institute for Literacy. Available at http://lincs.ed.gov/publications/pdf/NELPReport09.pdf

Neuman, S. B., & Dickinson, D. K. (Eds.). (2011). *Handbook of early literacy research*: (Vol. 3). New York, NY: Guilford Press.

Neuman, S. B., & Roskos, K. (Eds.). (1998). *Children achieving: Best practices in early literacy*. Newark, DE: International Reading Association.

Ramey, S., & Ramey, C. (2006). Early educational interventions: Principles for effective and sustained benefits from targeted early education programs. In D. Dickinson & S. Neuman (Eds.), *Handbook of early literacy research* (Vol. 2, pp. 445–459). New York, NY: Guilford Press.

Snow, C., Burns, S., & Griffin, P. (Eds.). (1998). *Preventing reading difficulties in young children*. Washington, DC: National Academy Press.

Snow, C. E., & Oh, S. S. (2011). Assessment in early literacy research. In S. B. Neuman & D. K. Dickinson (Eds.), *Handbook of early literacy research* (Vol. 3, pp. 228–241). New York, NY: The Guilford Press.

Sulzby, E. (1991). The development of the young child and the emergence of literacy. In J. Flood, J. M. Jensen, D. Lapp, & J. R. Squire (Eds.), *Handbook of research on teaching the English language arts* (pp. 273–285). New York, NY: Macmillan.

Sulzby, E., & Teale, W. (1996). Emergent literacy. In R. Barr, M. L. Kamil, P. B. Mosenthal, & P. D. Pearson (Eds.), *Handbook of reading research* (Vol. 2, pp. 727–757). Mahwah, NJ: Erlbaum.

Teale, W. H., & Sulzby, E. (1986). *Emergent literacy: Writing and reading*. Norwood, NJ: Ablex.

Teale, W., & Sulzby, E. (1989). Emergent literacy: New perspectives. In D. Strickland & L. Morrow (Eds.), *Emerging literacy: Young children learn to read and write* (pp. 1–15). Newark, DE: International Reading Association.

Whitehurst, G., & Lonigan, C. (1998). Child development and emergent literacy. *Child Development*, *68*, 848–872.

Whitehurst, G., & Lonigan, C. (2003). Emergent literacy: Development from prereaders to readers. In S. Neuman & D. Dickinson (Eds.), *Handbook of early literacy research* (Vol. 1, pp. 11–29). New York, NY: Guilford Press.

Williams, C. (2004). Emergent literacy of deaf children. *Journal of Deaf Studies and Deaf Education*, *9*, 352–365.

Williams, C., & Mayer, C. (in press). Writing in young deaf children. *Review of Educational Research*.

1

Review of the Literature

While the notion of early literacy began to emerge in the research literature in the late 1960s (e.g., Clay, 1966), examinations validating this concept as a theoretical construct and means of conceptualizing reading and writing development of young deaf children did not appear until the early 1990s (Rottenberg & Searfoss, 1992; Williams, 1994). In initial studies exploring this phenomenon, researchers observed the literacy behaviors of preschoolers (ages 3.0 to 5.10) to determine if deaf children evidenced similar patterns of emergent literacy behaviors to those documented for hearing children. These investigations revealed that the language delays typically experienced by the population of deaf children did not preclude them from participating in activities that developed early literacy concepts. In addition, findings suggest that written language appeared to be a viable means of further developing children's language and face-to-face communication abilities. Overall, the results of these studies led researchers to confirm the applicability of the early literacy construct to the population of deaf children and suggest that activities fostering the development of these skills and abilities should be purposefully integrated into the early childhood curriculum utilized with these young learners (see Williams, 2004, for review).

In the years that followed, additional investigations of early literacy for deaf children were summarized and published, which subsequently led to two reviews of the literature; one focused on emergent literacy in general (Williams, 2004), the other on early writing specifically (Williams & Mayer, in press). In this chapter, we will provide a brief overview of the conclusions and recommendations drawn from the existing reviews of emergent literacy and early writing and consider additional studies that have been published in these areas. We will also identify studies of early literacy that have been conducted in a variety of categories, including those examining skill development and those evaluating the efficacy of instructional interventions. These reviews will allow us to comment on the overall body of available literature related to early literacy development for deaf learners and offer recommendations for future research in this area. The literature review presented in this chapter will also serve as the basis for reflection in later sections of the book, as we discuss implications for research and practice in the areas of reading, writing, bilingualism, and assessment.

EMERGENT LITERACY LITERATURE REVIEW

In addition to examining studies that explored the applicability of the emergent literacy concept for deaf children, Williams (2004) also summarized the findings of investigations of early reading and writing. In the area of early reading, Williams found that the majority of studies investigated the influence of storybook reading on deaf children's development. More specifically, the interactions between children and their parents during storybook reading (Maxwell, 1984; Rottenberg, 2001), the strategies utilized when implementing this approach in the preschool classroom (Gioia, 2001; Rowe & Allen, 1995; Williams & McLean, 1997), and the impact of specific instructional strategies on the development of early literacy abilities (Andrews & Mason, 1986a, 1986b; Gillespie & Twardosz, 1997) were explored.

Collective findings of these studies led Williams (2004) to recognize the promise of storybook reading as an instructional approach for deaf children, with activities aimed at addressing several early literacy skills, including word recognition, storytelling, and comprehension. She also noted the merits of this strategy in improving deaf children's interest, engagement, and self-confidence related to reading. However, she did indicate that the findings of these studies should be considered with caution, "as not all researchers detailed their data collection or analysis procedures, and the body of work is still rather meager" (p. 359).

Five descriptive studies exploring various aspects of the early writing process were also identified in the review of emergent literacy conducted by Williams (2004). Goals for these investigations included determining the purpose of kindergarten students' writing (Conway, 1985), exploring preschool children's knowledge and use of concepts of print (Ewoldt, 1985), examining the type of metalinguistic strategies employed by a deaf child from three through seven years of age (Ruiz, 1995), investigating the role of signed language in emergent writing development for preschool children (Williams, 1999), and understanding the influence of the instructional context and types of activities provided to kindergarten students (Andrews & Gonzales, 1992).

Unfortunately, there were no studies of writing identified that explored the impact of an instructional approach, strategy, or intervention on specific emergent writing outcomes of young deaf children. However, Williams (2004) noted that the authentic nature of the activities employed and the social interaction provided during the writing process in the reviewed studies supported the children's early writing development. She further indicated that children in these studies evidenced an array of essential writing concepts, understandings, and processes to foster the progression toward conventional writing and suggested that the emergent writing development of young deaf children may be similar to that of hearing children.

In the conclusion of her review, Williams offered several observations and recommendations regarding future research in the area of emergent literacy for the population of deaf children. Given that there were fewer than twenty studies available for the analysis, a call for further research in this area was made. Williams indicated that in-depth, longitudinal case studies involving diverse groups of children and including data from both home and school environments would be beneficial in examining both typical and atypical patterns of development. Furthermore, results of these investigations would provide the data necessary to determine the impact of a variety of demographic (e.g., age, degree of hearing loss) and instructional (e.g., type of instruction, communication mode) variables on performance and achievement. It was also suggested that studies investigating the relationship between emergent reading and writing and also the integration of computer technology to improve the early literacy outcomes of deaf children be conducted.

EARLY WRITING LITERATURE REVIEW

Despite the call for increased research, a recent review of early writing conducted by Williams and Mayer (in press) yielded relatively few empirical studies over a twenty-year period (1990–2010). The reviewers also noted that there continues to be a dearth of direct evidence available with respect to the early literacy experiences of deaf children, particularly studies exploring the implementation of specific pedagogical approaches and strategies. For example, of the seventeen studies identified for review, only three descriptive and qualitative case studies examining writing development (Andrews & Gonzales, 1992; Bustos, 2008; Kim, 2008) were identified in addition to the two previously reviewed by Williams (2004) (Ruiz, 1995; Williams, 1999). Conclusions drawn as result of these studies indicated that deaf children appeared to be exploiting a sign-meaning-print connection (Andrews & Gonzales, 1992) and relying on visual coding strategies (Bustos, 2008) along with other intertextual sources such as word walls and storybooks (Kim, 2008) when generating text.

In contrast to these conclusions, the role of phonology for deaf children surfaced as a point of discussion in a study of parental involvement (Aram, Most, & Simon, 2008) and emerged from a synthesis of existing research in the area of spelling (i.e., Allman, 2002; Kyle & Harris, 2006, 2011; Leybaert & Lechat, 2001; Mayer & Moskos, 1998; Padden, 1993; van Staden & le Roux, 2010). This led Williams and Mayer (in press) to conclude that there are two opposing opinions regarding the application of phonology to deaf children's spelling and writing. One viewpoint was that deaf children could become literate in an alphabetic language such as English without an understanding of the phonological system (e.g., grapheme-phoneme relations) that underpins it. Researchers supporting this view recommended instructional strategies that focused on teaching visual coding and making explicit links among fingerspelling, signed language, and English orthography (Allman, 2002; Andrews & Gonzales, 1992; Bustos, 2008; Padden, 1993; van Staden & le Roux, 2010).

The alternative perspective is that young deaf children, like their hearing peers, need to gain control of phonological requisites (e.g., phonological and phonemic awareness) and acquire an understanding of the relationship between graphemes (letters) and phonemes (sounds) in order to learn to read and write an alphabetic language. These researchers encouraged the use of invented spelling and the implementation of manual systems to represent the phonological aspects of the language (e.g., Cued Speech, Visual Phonics) that support young children's spelling and writing development and subsequent literacy achievement (Leybaert & Lechat, 2001; Mayer & Moskos, 1998; Sirois, Boisclair, & Giasson, 2008; Williams, 2011). The views of the second group of researchers are further reinforced by studies indicating that (1) deaf children's spelling skills appear to be delayed for their chronological age (Kyle & Harris, 2006), (2) there is an overall disparity in the reading and spelling achievement of young deaf children, and (3) deaf children's overall trajectories of development tend to diverge when compared with hearing peers following the early childhood years (Kyle & Harris, 2011; Mayer & Moskos, 1998).

Further evidence of the scant intervention research in these areas is the fact that there were no intervention studies published between 1990 and 2007, with the first study of a spelling intervention for elementary students conducted in 2010 (van Staden & le Roux, 2010). While Williams and Mayer (in press) did identify three studies of writing instruction (Sirois, Boisclair, & Giasson, 2008; Wolbers, 2008; Williams, 2011), only one of the investigations focused exclusively on children in the early literacy learning years (preschool and kindergarten). In this qualitative case study, six deaf kindergarteners received instruction from an adapted interactive writing approach (Williams, 2011). Using this method, the teacher serves as facilitator, scaffolding specific skill instruction within authentic writing activities using techniques such as "share the pen" and instructional strategies such as modeling metacognitive strategies, employing recursive processing, and exploiting the reading-writing connection. Results of this study indicated that while the students learned a variety of writing skills from this intervention (e.g., concepts of print, ability to read and write words), none of them evidenced acquisition of the alphabetic principle (i.e., understanding the relationship between graphemes and phonemes).

Based on their review of the studies of early writing available to date, Williams and Mayer (in press) offered several recommendations for future research in this area. As with the previous review of emergent literacy (Williams, 2004), a general call for additional empirical studies was made. Williams and Mayer suggested that these studies include larger number of participants, including those with additional disabilities, and involve investigations that track students' achievement on multiple measures of literacy (e.g., phonological awareness, word identification, spelling) longitudinally. To increase the number of study participants, collaborative investigations among researchers and replication studies of previous works were also recommended.

In terms of writing development and instruction specifically, Williams and Mayer recommended that researchers analyze children's writing beyond the word level (i.e., spelling) and provide an increased focus on evaluating children's performance and achievement at the language (i.e., English grammar and syntax) level. They also specifically suggested that future studies explore some of the same strategies demonstrated to be efficacious in decoding (i.e., reading) instruction, such as Cued Speech and Visual Phonics, to evaluate the application of these strategies to encoding (i.e., spelling and writing). Investigations that explore the reciprocity of reading, spelling, and writing instruction and achievement among this population of students were also recommended. Finally, based on the results of their review, the authors indicated that additional research in the area of assessment was also warranted.

ADDITIONAL STUDIES OF EARLY LITERACY

To further explore previously conducted research in the area of early literacy for deaf learners, an electronic search of published journal articles was conducted, using various combinations of search terms related to the topic (e.g., *early/emergent literacy, reading, writing, deaf, hard of hearing, hearing impaired*). An examination of the table of contents of the primary research journals in the field (e.g., *American Annals of the Deaf, Journal of Deaf Studies and Deaf Education, Volta Review*) and a perusal of references cited in published articles was also completed. Collectively, these search methods resulted in a list of approximately sixty-five works. Publications not directly associated with deaf learners, ones providing theoretical and descriptive accounts of early literacy themes and instructional strategies without related data reports, and those included in previous reviews of emergent literacy (Williams, 2004) and early writing (Williams & Mayer, in press) were removed. Given our focus on early literacy, we also excluded studies of children beyond kindergarten; however, when investigations began when the children were enrolled in preschool or kindergarten and continued in successive school years or included both kindergarteners and children in subsequent grades (e.g., first and second), these studies were retained.

The resulting exploration yielded twenty-five articles summarizing twenty-seven studies, which we divided into the following seven categorical strands for review purposes: (1) writing, (2) storybook reading, (3) American Sign Language (ASL) videos, (4) parent involvement, (5) skill development, (6) communication mode and school environment, and (7) curricular interventions. While we recognize that we may have inadvertently overlooked some published articles, we feel that the review presented in later sections provides a relatively representative overview of the literature to date related to early literacy and deaf learners.

Writing

The development of early print concepts among thirteen orally educated preschool-age deaf children over a two-year period was the subject of the first study of writing we identified (Watson, 2009). Samples of free writing from both home and school were analyzed to determine whether these deaf children were developing knowledge of written language concepts in a manner similar to those documented for hearing learners. Results of this investigation suggested that many of the same concepts of print (e.g., use of mock writing, strings of letters, cultural symbols, space concepts, phonetic match for initial letter of words) evidenced by hearing readers of this age group were also employed by the majority of children included in this study.

Similar to a previously reviewed study (see Williams & Mayer, in press, for review) investigating the role and impact of mothers' cognitive and emotional mediation of writing activities (see Aram, Most, & Simon, 2008), a second investigation conducted by Aram and colleagues examined the contributions of mother-child storybook telling conducted in collaboration with joint writing activities (Aram, Most, & Mayafit, 2006). Subjects included thirty Israeli kindergarteners with varying degrees of hearing loss and their hearing mothers. Videotapes of storybook telling and writing mediation sessions along with measures of literacy in two broad categories—alphabetic skills (word writing, word recognition, letter knowledge) and linguistic skills (phonological awareness, receptive vocabulary, general knowledge)—provided the data for the analyses. Results of this study indicated that storybook telling was more closely related to the development of linguistic abilities and that writing mediation was aligned with the development of alphabetic skills, leading the authors to conclude that the development of skills among this group of children was similar to that of hearing children of the same age.

Storybook Reading

A total of six studies related to the use of shared storybook reading/ telling conducted with young deaf children were identified in our search. Three of these investigations involved examining the strategies employed by parents during shared reading with their children. For example, one study relied on a parent survey as a source of data (Stobbart & Alant, 2008), and a second utilized observation to compare children's interactions with parents using spoken English versus British Sign Language (Swanwick & Watson, 2007). In a follow-up study, parents' and teachers' views of the children's engagement in literacy activities in the home were also compared (Watson & Swanwick, 2008). Collective findings of these studies illustrated that deaf parents tended to engage children in conversations about the pictures and story content, focusing primarily on language and vocabulary development (i.e., storybook telling). Hearing parents, on the other hand, were inclined to concentrate on the text of the story (i.e., storybook reading) and direct attention to labeling pictures and teaching letter names and sounds, thereby suggesting different goals for shared reading with children based on the hearing status of the parent.

In a related study that also examined parental engagement, Kaderavek and Pakulski (2007) explored the literacy interest or orientation of preschool children during story reading with their hearing mothers. Using the Kaderavek-Sulzby Rating of Orientation to Book Reading scale, interactions of mothers using two different genres (e.g., narrative books or manipulative books with flaps, dials, etc.) with their children were coded based on type. Categories of interaction included (1) following the child's lead/not reading the story, (2) modifying the text to meet the child's language level, and (3) reading the book verbatim and interjecting comments. Results of this study involving twelve preschoolers with a range of hearing loss and using a variety of communication modalities indicated that multiple readings of books, along with the genre of text that included a manipulative feature, appeared to increase children's orientation to book reading experiences.

The impact of mother-and-child interactions during storybook reading on children's phonological and reading skill outcomes over a three-year period was investigated in a study of sixteen children with cochlear implants (DesJardin, Ambrose, & Eisenberg, 2009). Children ranging in age from 2.7 to 6.3 at the onset of the study were assessed using measures of expressive and receptive language at pretest and again three years later using assessments of expressive and receptive language, phonological awareness (rhyming, segmentation, isolation, deletion, substitution, blending, graphemes), and reading skills (word attack, letter-word identification, oral vocabulary, reading vocabulary, passage comprehension). Videotapes of mothers engaging their children in storybook reading at pretest were evaluated to determine the type of facilitative language techniques utilized.

Findings of this investigation revealed that children's early expressive language was positively and significantly associated with later phonological awareness skills in the areas of rhyming, segmentation, isolation, deletion, and blending. In terms of mothers' linguistic interactions, the use of open-ended questions was found to relate to children's rhyming, segmentation, and deletion abilities in addition to letter-word identification and passage comprehension skills. Results also indicated that early expressive language abilities along with later expressive and receptive language skills were related to all reading subskills assessed, with the exception of oral and reading vocabulary. However, mothers' use of the language technique of recasting (restating child's utterance as a question) was positively related to skills in both oral and reading vocabulary. Findings also illustrated that children with expressive language standard scores at or above 70 at pretest generally scored better than average on all literacy measures at posttest.

The final examination of shared storybook reading involved evaluating a technologically based product, the Iowa Signing E-Book, which incorporated parent training in shared reading techniques, access to books with an interactive media format, and the choice of using a signed-language narrator while engaging in storybook reading (Mueller & Hurtig, 2010). Four preschool children with varying degrees of hearing loss and their hearing parents were participants in this single-subject investigation. Results of this study indicated that while there was no clear pattern of parents' use of the training modules and while interaction with the e-books was greater at the onset of the study, all parents and children reportedly demonstrated increased knowledge of signed-language vocabulary as a result of participation.

American Sign Language (ASL) Videos

Through our literature search, we located two studies that also employed technology and examined the association between literacy-related behaviors and the use of signed language. Citing correlations between ASL and English reading skills, the mutually reinforcing relationship of language and literacy abilities, and research on active viewing, Golos (2010) investigated the extent to which preschoolers engaged in literacy-related behaviors while viewing an educational video presented in ASL. Participants of this study included twenty-five deaf children, ages three to six years, enrolled in seven different preschool programs, with eight of the twenty-five children having deaf parents.

A pre- and posttest measure of children's ability to match signs or fingerspelling to pictures and printed words that represented vocabulary emphasized throughout a forty-minute video of a trip to the farm was used in this study. The researcher also monitored and recorded the students' literacy-related behaviors (e.g., fingerspelling and signing the vocabulary, engaging in conversations about the video, etc.) as they viewed the video over a three-day period. Results of this study indicated an overall average increase of 20 percent from pre- to posttest on the vocabulary task along with increases in literacy-related behaviors ranging from 130 percent to 287 percent from day one to day three of the intervention.

In a follow-up investigation, the study was expanded to evaluate differences in the children's level of engagement when teacher facilitation was offered (Golos & Moses, 2011). An interactive guide for teachers was created to accompany the aforementioned farm video, and teachers received a two-hour training to learn to promote active engagement, connections between ASL and English print, vocabulary development, and story comprehension. Results of this study suggested findings similar to those of the previous investigation, in that children's literacy behaviors increased with repeated video viewings. In addition, greater engagement was noted when the teacher mediation was provided.

Parental Involvement

Parental involvement was the primary subject of two studies identified through our search of the literature. In the first investigation, the impact of parental involvement on child-related outcomes, including early reading skills and positive and negative measures of social-emotional development, was measured (Calderon, 2000). Participants in this study included twenty-eight deaf children from English-speaking homes, with no identified additional disabilities, assessed between nine and fifty-three months after graduating from a birth-to-three-year-old early intervention program. The interventionists who had worked with the children provided narrative notes from their intervention sessions, which were subsequently rated for parental involvement. Additional sources of data included a parent information form, a teacher questionnaire regarding parental involvement and children's social-emotional adjustment, ratings of maternal communication from a videotaped parent-child interaction session, and child outcome measures (e.g., language abilities and early reading skills). Overall findings of this study revealed that while parental involvement in a child's school-based education program could positively contribute to academic performance, parental communication skill was a more significant predictor for positive language and academic development.

In order to explore the role of parental mediation in language and literacy skill acquisition in ASL, a case study of one deaf child from a deaf family was conducted over a four-year period (Bailes, Erting, Erting, & Thumann-Prezioso, 2009). Videotapes of monthly home interactions and those collected at three-month intervals in a studio, along with interviews with the parents and field notes, provided the data for this investigation. Framing and discussing the results of this case study using Hart and Risley's (1999) stages of development for learning to talk (i.e., becoming partners, staying and playing, and practicing), the researchers illustrated a developmental trajectory that paralleled these stages. In addition, they observed that the parents engaged the child in components of emergent literacy by making explicit connections between ASL and English print.

Skill Development

As a result of our review, three studies exploring the development of specific early literacy skills were identified. In the first, Harris and Beech (1998) examined the role of implicit phonological awareness on the early reading development of twenty-four deaf children during the first two years of schooling. Participants in this investigation ranged in age from four to six years and had hearing loss from severe to profound. Results obtained on various early literacy measures (e.g., single-word reading comprehension, letter orientation, implicit phonological awareness, familiarity with British Sign Language [BSL] and fingerspelling, oral language[1] abilities, and language comprehension) were evaluated. Findings of the single-word reading and implicit phonological awareness assessments were also compared with those of hearing peers matched based on assessments of nonverbal IQ and reading ability. Results of this investigation indicated that there were differences in gains experienced by the deaf participants as compared with their hearing peers after one year of instruction. While deaf children were found to score significantly lower on the measure of implicit phonological awareness than their hearing peers, this skill was positively correlated with gains in reading for both groups of children, as was nonverbal IQ.

In exploring the variables affecting reading gains for deaf children specifically, the researchers reported positive correlations between gains in reading and language comprehension, reading and oral language abilities, and phonological awareness and oral language abilities. While findings suggested that familiarity with BSL and fingerspelling were positively correlated with each other and also associated with language comprehension, these abilities were not found to correlate with gains in reading. Furthermore, knowledge of BSL and fingerspelling were both negatively correlated with oral language abilities, and signing skills were negatively correlated with implicit phonological

---

[1] When the term *oral language* is used, it reflects the terminology employed in the original source (e.g., NELP, a published study, etc.). This term is often used synonymously with *spoken language* in the broader literature in the field of literacy. It is only in the field of deafness that the distinction between oral and spoken language merits attention.

awareness. After two years of instruction, the correlations among the skills assessed remained relatively stable.

The second study explored the development of emergent literacy skills among children ages three to six years over the course of one school year (Easterbrooks, Lederberg, Miller, Bergeron, & Conner, 2008). Selection criteria ensured that the forty-four participants from various educational backgrounds (e.g., public school, private oral school, state school for the deaf) had (1) pure tone averages greater than 50 decibels (dB), (2) the ability to detect patterns for spoken language, and (3) no additional documented disabilities. In addition to the Early Speech Perception Test used to select participants, measures of vocabulary, letter-word identification, passage comprehension, and multiple aspects of phonological awareness (e.g., rhyming, alliteration, syllable segmentation, blending phonemes) were administered as pre- and posttest assessments, and results were compared with the normative sample for each assessment administered.

The findings of this investigation indicated that the results of early literacy measures used with deaf participants related in ways that have been previously reported for hearing children (e.g., phonological awareness and vocabulary predicted performance on letter-word identification and passage comprehension) and that age significantly correlated with scores on all measures. However, variations in findings were also reported with regard to children's performance relative to the normative sample, with some measures indicating performance similar to that of hearing peers (e.g., letter recognition, matching pictures to rebus symbols, basic word recognition) and others revealing relatively large gaps in achievement (e.g., phonological awareness). In terms of growth across the school year, significant increases were noted for study participants on the majority of measures, with the exception of vocabulary and rhyming. The overall findings of this study led the researchers to conclude not only that the development of study participants was delayed but also that it differed from the normative sample, most notably in the area of rhyming.

The third investigation explored the literacy development of twenty-four deaf and twenty-three hearing children over a two-year period. Children who were considered beginning readers were recruited for participation; therefore, at the onset of the study, the deaf children were in either kindergarten or first grade, whereas their hearing counterparts were all kindergarteners. The deaf participants were drawn from a variety of educational settings and communication backgrounds (e.g., spoken English, signed language, simultaneous communication) and were initially matched with their hearing peers based on measures of word-recognition abilities and nonverbal IQ scores (Kyle & Harris, 2011).

Every twelve months, study participants were administered assessments of word reading, spelling, phonological awareness, vocabulary, speechreading, short-term memory, letter naming, and letter-sound knowledge. In addition to comparing patterns of reading and spelling development of deaf and hearing learners, the researchers were interested in identifying predictors of beginning reading abilities. Results of this study indicated that even though deaf and hearing beginning readers evidenced similar levels of progress at the early stages of the investigation, "their reading trajectories began to diverge after the second year of reading instruction" (p. 299).

Findings of this study also suggested that deaf and hearing children utilized different strategies during the developmental process. For example, the deaf participants initially appeared to employ a whole-word method and then transitioned to a more alphabetic approach after two years of instruction, perhaps as a result of acquiring phonological representations via speechreading. In contrast, the hearing participants evidenced use of an alphabetic strategy from the beginning of the investigation. Interestingly, a strong association between earlier speechreading abilities and later phonological awareness not only emerged for the deaf participants but also appeared to be a strong and consistent predictor of both reading and spelling growth in hearing children. After controlling for nonverbal IQ and earlier ability, abilities and skills in the areas of vocabulary, speechreading, and letter-sound knowledge were found to be the best predictors of beginning reading abilities among the deaf participants in this investigation.

Communication Mode and School Environment

The impact of communication mode and/or school environment on subsequent literacy development was the subject of four studies identified for review. The first investigation explored the impact of varying degrees of Cued Speech experience on the literacy outcomes of eighteen deaf six-year-olds educated in France and Belgium (Colin, Leybaert, Ecalle, & Magnan, 2013). Cued Speech is a manual communication system used to convey a language at the level of the phoneme, which is "the same fundamental level that traditionally spoken languages convey via speech" (LaSasso, Crain, & Leybaert, 2010, p. 8). In the study by Colin and colleagues, children were categorized in three groups based on their level of Cued Speech exposure: (1) at home before attending kindergarten (i.e., Early CS), (2) upon entering kindergarten (Late CS), or (3) during first grade (Beginner CS). Assessments of implicit and explicit phonological awareness, reading, spelling, and vocabulary were administered and compared with results obtained by hearing children in a comparison group.

While there were no significant differences among the three groups of Cued Speech users on the implicit phonological awareness measures administered prior to the introduction of formal reading instruction, the Early CS participants outperformed the other two groups by the beginning of first grade, and this pattern of performance continued through the end of second grade. It is also noteworthy that the achievement of the children characterized as Early CS only differed in one area, receptive vocabulary, when compared with their hearing peers. The researchers surmised that early exposure to Cued Speech allowed the children to develop a phonologically based system prior to the introduction of formal reading instruction that focused on attending to grapheme-phoneme relations. In contrast, the Late CS and Beginner CS participants who had yet to establish this organizational system needed to devote greater attention to developing a system for understanding phonology while simultaneously receiving instruction in applying the system required to read and write.

The second investigation was an in-depth case study of one child's language and literacy development from preschool through sixth grade (Nielsen & Luetke-Stahlman, 2002). Data from multiple formal and informal assessments representing a broad range of literacy-related areas (e.g., listening, speech articulation, English language, reading and writing) provided the data to analyze the influence of the use of Signing Exact English (SEE) and the results of creating a data-driven instructional approach. This investigation began immediately following the child's adoption and move to the United States at the age of four and at a time when the child reportedly did not have a formal language system in place. The researchers credit the child's consistent exposure to grammatically accurate English via SEE, the careful monitoring of the child's language and literacy instruction and development, and use of research-based reading instructional practices throughout her education (e.g., phonological awareness, phonics, multisyllabic decoding, semantic and structural cues, etc.) for the child's grade-level outcomes achieved by sixth grade.

The third study explored the development of early literacy skills among three groups of Israeli kindergarteners (Most, Aram, & Andorn, 2006). The groups included (1) fifteen deaf children educated in an individual inclusion setting (individualized program, child integrated in classroom in local school, support services provided by teacher of the deaf employed by the Ministry of Education Center, primary use of spoken language for instruction), (2) sixteen deaf children involved in a group inclusion program (group program, children integrated into general education kindergarten classroom, special instruction provided by teacher of the deaf for approximately two hours per day and supplemented by speech and language therapy, use of spoken language or simultaneous use of spoken language and sign language), and (3) eleven children with typical hearing. A demographic questionnaire completed by parents and seven assessments of early literacy skills (word writing, word recognition, phonological awareness, letter identification, orthographic awareness, receptive vocabulary, and general knowledge) provided the researchers with the necessary data to compare achievement among the three groups of children and explore relationships between early literacy skills and demographic variables.

Results of this investigation indicated that deaf children enrolled in the individual inclusion setting achieved at higher levels than their deaf peers placed in group programs in the areas of phonological awareness, letter identification, general knowledge, and vocabulary. Findings also indicated that children with typical hearing surpassed both groups of deaf children on these measures. While there were no statistically significant differences reported between the two groups of deaf children on measures of reading, writing, and orthographic awareness, the achievement of hearing children in these areas exceeded that of deaf children enrolled in group settings but did not differ statistically from that of deaf students educated in the individual inclusion placements. In terms of demographic variables, general knowledge, reading, and writing outcomes were correlated with age at onset of rehabilitation, and negative correlations were reported between general knowledge and degree of hearing loss. No correlations were found between socioeconomic status and children's early literacy skills. Overall findings of this study led the researchers to conclude that gaps in literacy achievement between children with and without hearing loss, and those between deaf children enrolled in different educational programs, are apparent even as early as kindergarten.

The fourth and final study in this category explored the literacy environment created by eighteen teachers in ten different settings (e.g., public oral school, private oral school, public school adopting a Total Communication approach, state school for the deaf) that employed a variety of communication modes. Ratings of environment were then compared with the literacy outcomes achieved by forty deaf children in preschool through first grade educated in these settings (Easterbrooks, Lederberg, & Connor, 2010). The Early Language and Literacy Classroom Observation (ELLCO) was employed as a measure of classroom environment, and children's achievement was assessed during the fall and spring using several tests of early literacy (e.g., letter-word identification, picture vocabulary, alliteration, and rhyming).

Findings of this study revealed that differences in classrooms as measured by the ELLCO accounted for more than a third of the variability in vocabulary and rhyming growth and that scores on this assessment of classroom environment predicted growth in letter-word identification and rhyming. On the other hand, the results of the ELLCO did not predict picture vocabulary or alliteration skills achieved by children. According to the researchers, ratings for the classrooms included in this study were similar to those reported in previous studies of Head

Start programs[2] prior to receiving instruction on targeted interventions aimed at improving the environment and achievement outcomes for children.

Curricular Interventions

We identified six publications that reported the results of eight curricular intervention studies. All of the investigations summarized in these articles explored the implementation of phonologically based reading instruction for deaf students, with two being conducted with children at the onset of formal reading instruction (kindergarten and first grade) and the other four completed with preschoolers.

The first study examined the implementation of a scripted beginning reading curriculum, Reading Mastery, over the course of one school year with thirteen kindergarten and first grade students educated in a Total Communication environment (Trezek & Wang, 2006). In order to provide access to the phonological activities (e.g., phonemic awareness, phonics) that form the foundation of the curriculum, a multisensory instructional tool called See-the-Sound Visual Phonics (International Communication Learning Institute, 2011) was employed. Visual Phonics is a system of forty-four hand gestures and written symbols designed to represent the individual phonemes (sounds) of a language. The hand movements in this system were designed to represent phonological information at the sublexical and lexical levels, to supplement speech and/or speechreading, and to provide the learner with information regarding the articulatory features of phonemes (see Morrison, Trezek, & Paul, 2008; Trezek, Wang, & Paul, 2010, for discussions).

A standardized measure of reading achievement was administered to study participants as a pre- and posttest assessment. Based on the guidelines of the assessment used (Wechsler Individual Achievement Test II), kindergarteners were administered a subtest assessing word reading, while first graders completed three subtests: word reading, pseudoword decoding, and reading comprehension. Findings of this study indicated that after one year of instruction, there was a statistically significant difference between pre- and posttest scores on the word reading subtest of the assessment, and the effect size was considered large. While it was not possible to conduct a statistical analysis of the remaining two subtests because of limits in sample size, examining the descriptive statistics indicated growth in these areas as a result of instruction. As with related investigations conducted with older deaf students (see Trezek & Malmgren, 2005; Trezek & Hancock,

---

[2] Head Start is a federally funded preschool program in the United States that promotes school readiness for children from birth to age five from low-income families.

2013), degree of hearing loss was not a factor affecting performance at posttest.

Visual Phonics was also employed as an instructional tool in a second study, which investigated the implementation of a curriculum that included phonologically based beginning reading activities (Trezek, Wang, Woods, Gampp, & Paul, 2007). In this investigation, the progress of twenty deaf children enrolled in kindergarten and first grade, taught using either speech only or simultaneous communication (speech and signed language), were monitored using subtests of the Dominie Reading and Writing Assessment Portfolio. According to test administration procedures, kindergarten children completed three subtests (sentence writing phoneme, sentence writing spelling, and phonemic awareness segmentation), whereas first grade students completed these same subtests and an additional three (phonemic awareness deletion, phonics onsets, and phonics rimes), for a total of six subtests.

Results of this inquiry evidenced statistically significant differences from pre- to posttest and a large effect size for each of the six measures. Findings also indicated that mean scores for both kindergarten and first grade students were in the average range when compared with the normative sample of the assessment at the onset of the study and that kindergarten participants maintained this level of performance at posttest. On the other hand, first grade students evidenced slightly below-average performance on three of the six measures administered at posttest (sentence writing phoneme, phonemic awareness segmentation, and phonics onset) when mean subtest scores were compared with the normative sample. While gains were noted from pre- to posttest, the researchers questioned whether students beyond kindergarten age could acquire skills at a rate relative to the hearing children in the normative sample.

Building on the findings of studies conducted with early elementary students, Smith and Wang (2010) examined the impact of Visual Phonics on the phonological awareness and speech production of a four-year-old child with a cochlear implant who was enrolled in a preschool program at a school for the deaf. According to the researchers, lessons from the Fountas and Pinnell Kindergarten Phonics Curriculum were modified to make them more age-appropriate for a preschooler. Visual Phonics was then used in conjunction with speech throughout the six-week intervention to supplement activities included in the curriculum that focused on teaching the letter names and associated phonemes for five consonants and three vowels and applying this knowledge to the reading of eleven words. Measures of phoneme identification and production in isolation, letter identification, and phoneme identification in the initial and medial positions within words were used as a pre- and posttest assessment of phonological awareness and speech production. Interviews with the child's classroom teacher and speech pathologist and formal and informal observations of classroom instruction were also conducted. Findings revealed significant improvements in the child's phonological awareness and speech production as a result of the intervention. In addition to progress on the curriculum-based measures, the teacher reported that gains experienced as a result of individual instruction appeared to support progress in classroom-based instruction, particularly in the areas of phonemic awareness and initial sound awareness.

In a fourth intervention study identified for review, the effects of implementing a phonics-based intervention package on the early reading skill outcomes of three deaf preschoolers were explored (Wang, Spychala, Harris, & Oetting, 2013). While the participants reportedly had a range of hearing loss and used a variety of communication modes, they were all enrolled in the same classroom within a private preschool program for deaf children. The Reading Mastery curriculum, which was used in a previous investigation conducted with kindergarten and first grade students (Trezek & Wang, 2006), was also used as the core curriculum in this intervention. Children received group instruction from the classroom teacher using simultaneous communication, supplemented by both Visual Phonics and vocabulary instruction, for approximately twenty minutes a day over a forty-to-fifty-week period. The children also received thirty lessons of instruction from the Early Reading Tutor program, individually implemented with each child for approximately an hour every week by a trained graduate assistant.

In order to evaluate the effectiveness of the early intervention package, subtests of the Test of Preschool Early Literacy (print knowledge, definitional vocabulary), Phonological Awareness Literacy Screening (name writing, upper- and lower-case recognition, letter sounds, beginning sound, print, word, rhyme awareness), and the Woodcock-Johnson Test of Achievement III (letter-word identification, spelling, passage comprehension, word attack) were used. These outcome measures were administered four times throughout the study: (1) as a preintervention baseline, (2) after approximately six months of instruction, (3) as a postintervention measure, and (4) as a follow-up in early elementary school. Findings of this investigation indicated that study participants not only evidenced growth in early literacy skills during the direct implementation of the intervention in preschool but also maintained the acquired skills and continued to improve on their foundational reading skills at the onset of formal reading instruction in elementary school.

Two multiple-baseline single-subject studies examining the use of a semantic association strategy for teaching deaf preschoolers the alphabetic principle (phoneme-grapheme relations) were summarized in a fifth publication identified in our search of the literature (Bergeron, Lederberg, Easterbrooks, Miller, & Connor, 2009). Originally developed for children with language disorders, the semantic association strategy involves using pictures and stories to provide a meaningful context for students to learn specific phoneme-grapheme relations. In these investigations, the researchers expanded on this approach and also included a language experience component.

The first investigation evaluating the effect of this method involved five deaf children ages 3.10 to 7.10, while the second was conducted with slightly younger children ages 3.10 to 4.5. Selection criteria ensured that participants had a measured hearing loss of 55 dB or greater, no additional documented disabilities, scores of at least 3 on the Early Speech Perception Test, no previous exposure to the approach, and a lack of knowledge of grapheme-phoneme correspondences. After receiving the intervention for approximately thirty-five minutes per day, four days a week, over a nine-week period, all children were able to reach criteria on the six consonant and three vowel sounds that were the focus of instruction, with an average of one week of lessons required to reach criterion.

The second study embedded the previously described instructional techniques (semantic association strategy, language experience) within a researcher-developed curriculum called Foundations for Literacy and evaluated the specific grapheme-phoneme correspondences taught during a six-week intervention. According to the researchers, it was estimated that fifteen minutes of each hour-long Foundations instructional session was devoted to story reading and phonological tasks. Additional measures of grapheme-phoneme relations, alphabetic knowledge, and ability to read decodable words (some taught, some untaught) were also administered at the onset of the study and again at the end of the school year.

Findings of this investigation replicated those of the first study in terms of reaching criterion on grapheme-phoneme correspondences taught, although the average time to achieve mastery was slightly longer (one to two weeks) in the second study. Results of the additional measures also illustrated that the children in this study continued to acquire alphabetic knowledge during the school year and were able apply this knowledge to accurately read 60 percent of words directly taught in the curriculum and 30 percent of novel words. Overall findings from these two studies led the researchers to conclude that the instructional strategy employed was an effective approach for teaching young deaf children and that age was a potential factor affecting rate of learning.

The sixth and final publication reported the findings of two investigations exploring the implementation of the Foundations for Literacy curriculum supplemented by the Visual Phonics instructional tool (Beal-Alvarez, Lederberg, & Easterbrooks, 2012). In the first, one child received instruction from the curriculum in thirty-minute sessions, four days per week, over a ten-week period. Several literacy-related measures (Early Speech Perception Test, Peabody Picture Vocabulary Test, Expressive One Word Picture Vocabulary Test) were administered in addition to a baseline assessment of grapheme-phoneme correspondences taught within the curriculum. Results of this study provided evidence that a preschool-age child with minimal speech perception abilities could acquire and maintain the correspondences taught when Visual Phonics supplemented instruction from the Foundations for Literacy curriculum.

In a follow-up investigation, the combination of the Foundations for Literacy curriculum and Visual Phonics was again evaluated. Participants in this study were three- and four-year-old deaf children who received instruction throughout one school year, in which a total of eighteen grapheme-phoneme correspondences were taught. In addition to the assessments used in the earlier investigation, researcher-developed measures of letter naming, letter-sound relationships, word decoding, and fluency of identifying grapheme-phoneme correspondences were also administered. Findings indicated that the acquisition of the correspondences taught was similar across all three participants, and increases were also reported on the remaining measures assessing generalization of skills. Collectively, the findings of these studies led the researchers to conclude that employing the Visual Phonics instructional tool provided an effective supplement to instruction from the Foundations for Literacy curriculum for preschool-age children.

IMPLICATIONS

While the implications of our review of the literature will be discussed in greater detail in later chapters, we offer some general comments regarding the research available to date here. In concert with the conclusions drawn from previous reviews of emergent literacy (Williams, 2004) and early writing (Williams & Mayer, in press), we acknowledge that there continues to be a paucity of research examining the early literacy development of, and instructional strategies for, young deaf children. In addition to an overall small number of studies, a corpus of investigations focused on specific areas of early literacy (e.g., reading, writing) is lacking. To illustrate this point, among the twenty-seven studies located in our literature search, seven distinct categories of investigations were identified, and the greatest number of individual investigations summarized in any one area was eight (for curricular interventions). Therefore, the overall dearth of research evidence makes it difficult to draw conclusions both within and across categories of studies. To address this situation, we reiterate the general call for increased research in the area of early literacy that was offered in previous reviews of the literature (Williams, 2004; Williams &

Mayer, in press). While currently fairly limited, studies utilizing multiple-baseline single-subject and case study designs also hold considerable promise for increasing the overall number of research investigations of early literacy conducted with deaf children.

The relatively small number of participants included in many of the investigations also presents a challenge in terms of drawing conclusions from the research conducted to date, as this situation poses limits for the generalizability of study findings. While we recognize that the low incidence of hearing loss presents challenges in conducting research with large numbers of study participants, we echo a previous suggestion (see Williams & Mayer, in press) that collaborative investigations among researchers and replicating previous studies can counter this limitation in the research. Collaborative investigations may also serve to increase the number of studies that (1) include children with a range of hearing loss and educated in a variety of settings, (2) employ experimental and quasi-experimental designs, and (3) involve comparison groups.

Our review of the literature also revealed a limited number of longitudinal studies exploring the effects of programs, instructional strategies, and curricula implemented with young deaf literacy learners. While some studies have tracked children's achievement through the early literacy learning years (kindergarten and first grade), none of them followed children through elementary school and beyond, and consequently, none investigated the impact of the intervention on measures of later conventional literacy skills. In addition to a general recommendation for an increased number of intervention studies that follow children's progress in literacy achievement over time, we also suggest that researchers develop a trajectory of inquiry to create increasingly robust investigations in these areas. For example, studies utilizing rigorous study designs and multiple outcome measures of early literacy should be conducted first to establish the need for specific interventions. Follow-up investigations could then be initiated to longitudinally evaluate the impact of these interventions on both early and later conventional literacy outcomes.

Given the overall scant research exploring the early literacy development of deaf children, it is essential to draw on the extensive body of research evidence from studies of a broad range of hearing learners in order to articulate a theoretical and pedagogical model of early literacy for this population. While there is admittedly less available research focused on hearing second-language learners and those with disabilities, converging evidence from available sources suggests that there is little difference among all groups of hearing learners in terms of the set of skills and abilities needed to develop conventional literacy (e.g., Bialystok, 2001; Kaiser, Roberts, & McLeod, 2011). In chapter 2, we will expand on this position and make an argument for a developmentally similar hypothesis in the early literacy development of deaf children. The case will be made that the stages of early literacy learning do not differ because a learner has a hearing loss. Rather, we will argue that the foundational requisites documented as necessary for reading and writing development in hearing children also apply to the population of young deaf literacy learners (Mayer, 2007; Mayer & Trezek, 2011; 2014; Paul, 2009; Trezek, et al., 2010; Wang, Trezek, Luckner, & Paul, 2008).

REFERENCES

Allman, T. M. (2002). Patterns of spelling in young deaf and hard of hearing students. *American Annals of the Deaf, 147,* 46–64.

Andrews, J. F., & Gonzales, K. (1992). Free writing of deaf children in kindergarten. *Sign Language Studies, 74,* 63–78.

Andrews, J., & Mason, J. (1986a). Childhood deafness and the acquisition of print concepts. In D. Yaden & S. Templeton (Eds.), *Metalinguistic awareness and beginning literacy: Conceptualizing what it means to read and write* (pp. 277–290). Portsmouth, NH: Heinemann.

Andrews, J., & Mason, J. (1986b). What do deaf children know about prereading? *American Annals of the Deaf, 131,* 210–217.

Aram, D., Most, T., & Mayafit, H. (2006). Contributions of mother-child storybook telling and joint writing to literacy development in kindergartners with hearing loss. *Language, Speech, and Hearing Services in Schools, 37,* 209–223.

Aram, D., Most, T., & Simon, A. B. (2008). Early literacy of kindergartners with hearing impairment: The role of mother-child collaborative writing. *Topics in Early Childhood Special Education, 28(1),* 31–41.

Bailes, C. N., Erting, C. J., Erting, L. C., & Thumann-Prezioso, C. (2009). Language and literacy acquisition through parental mediation in American Sign Language. *Sign Language Studies, 9(4),* 417–456.

Beal-Alvarez, J., Lederberg, A. R., & Easterbrooks, S. R. (2012). Grapheme-phoneme acquisition of deaf preschoolers. *Journal of Deaf Studies and Deaf Education, 17,* 39–60. doi:10.1093/deafed/enr030

Bergeron, J., Lederberg, A. R., Easterbrooks, S. R., Miller, E. M., & Connor, C. (2009). Building the alphabetic principle in young children who are deaf or hard of hearing. *Volta Review, 109,* 87–119.

Bialystok, E. (2001). *Bilingualism in development: Language, literacy and cognition.* New York, NY: Cambridge University Press.

Bustos, M. T. (2008). Exploring emergent literacy behaviors of Filipino deaf children. *Asia-Pacific Education Researcher, 16,* 101–110.

Calderon, R. (2000). Parental involvement in deaf children's education programs as a predictor of child's language, early reading, and social-emotional development. *Journal of Deaf Studies and Deaf Education, 5(2),* 140–155.

Clay, Marie. (1966). *Emergent reading behaviour.* Unpublished doctoral dissertation, University of Auckland, New Zealand.

Colin, S., Leybaert, J., Ecalle, J., & Magnan, A. (2013). The development of word recognition, sentence comprehension, word spelling, and vocabulary in children with deafness: A longitudinal study. *Research in Developmental Disabilities, 34(5),* 1781–1793. doi:10.1016/j.ridd.2013.02.001

Conway, D. (1985). Children (re)creating writing: A preliminary look at the purposes of free-choice writing of hearing-impaired kindergarteners. *Volta Review, 87*(5), 91–107.

DesJardin, J. L., Ambrose, S. E., & Eisenberg, L. S. (2009). Maternal involvement in the home literacy environment: Supporting literacy skills in children with cochlear implants. *Communication Disorders Quarterly, 32*(3), 135–150. doi:10.1177/1525740109340916

Easterbrooks, S. R., Lederberg, A. R., & Connor, C. M. (2010). Contributions of the emergent literacy environment to literacy outcomes for young children who are deaf. *American Annals of the Deaf, 155*(4), 467–480.

Easterbrooks, S. R., Lederberg, A. R., Miller, E. M., Bergeron, J. P., & Conner, C. M. (2008). Emergent literacy skills during early childhood in children with hearing loss: Strengths and weaknesses. *Volta Review, 108*(2), 91–114.

Ewoldt, C. (1985). A descriptive study of the developing literacy of young hearing-impaired children. *Volta Review, 87*(5), 109–126.

Gillespie, C. W., & Twardosz, S. (1997). A group storybook-reading intervention with children at a residential school for the deaf. *American Annals of the Deaf, 141*(4), 320–332.

Gioia, B. (2001). The emergent language and literacy experiences of three deaf preschoolers. *International Journal of Disability, Development, and Education, 48*(4), 411–428.

Golos, D. (2010). Literacy behaviors of deaf preschoolers during video viewing. *Sign Language Studies, 11*(1), 76–99. doi:0.1353/sls.2010.0001

Golos, D. B., & Moses, A. M. (2011). How teacher mediation during video viewing facilitates literacy behaviors. *Sign Language Studies, 12*(1), 98–118.

Harris, M., & Beech, J. R. (1998). Implicit phonological awareness and early reading development in prelingually deaf children. *Journal of Deaf Studies and Deaf Education, 3*(3), 205–216.

Hart, B., & Risley, T. R. (1999). *The social world of children learning to talk*. Baltimore, MD: Brookes.

International Communication Learning Institute. (2011). *See-the-Sound Visual Phonics*. Available at http://seethesound.org

Kaderavek, J. N., & Pakulski, L. A. (2007). Facilitating literacy development in young children with hearing loss. *Seminars in Speech and Language, 28*(1), 69–78. doi:10.1055/s-2007-967931.

Kaiser, A. P., Roberts, M. Y., & McLeod, R. H. (2011). Young children with language impairments: Challenges in transition to reading. In S. B. Neuman & D. K. Dickinson (Eds.), *Handbook of early literacy research* (Vol. 3, pp. 228–241). New York, NY: Guilford Press.

Kim, M. (2008). *Early literacy learning of young children with hearing loss: Written narrative development*. Unpublished doctoral dissertation, Ohio State University, Columbus.

Kyle F. E., & Harris, M. (2006). Concurrent correlates and predictors of reading and spelling achievement in deaf and hearing school children. *Journal of Deaf Studies and Deaf Education, 11*(3), 273–288.

Kyle, F. E., & Harris, M. (2011). Longitudinal patterns of emergent literacy in beginning deaf and hearing readers. *Journal of Deaf Studies and Deaf Education, 16*(3), 289–304.

LaSasso, C., Crain, K., & Leybaert, J. (Eds.). (2010). *Cued speech and cued language for deaf and hard of hearing children*. San Diego, CA: Plural.

Leybaert, J., & Lechat, J. (2001). Variability in deaf children's spelling: The effect of language experience. *Journal of Educational Psychology, 93(3),* 554–562.

Maxwell, M. (1984). A deaf child's natural development of literacy. *Sign Language Studies, 44,* 191–224.

Mayer, C. (2007). What matters in the early literacy development of deaf children. *Journal of Deaf Studies and Deaf Education, 12,* 411–431. doi:10.1093/deafed/enm020

Mayer, C., & Moskos, E. (1998). Deaf children learning to spell. *Research in the Teaching of English, 33(2),* 158–180.

Mayer, C., & Trezek, B. J. (2011). New (?) answers to old questions: Literacy development in D/HH learners. In D. Moores (Ed.), *Partners in Education: Issues and Trends from the 21st International Congress on the Education of the Deaf* (pp. 62–74). Washington, DC: Gallaudet University Press.

Mayer, C., & Trezek, B. J. (2014). Is reading different for deaf individuals?: Reexamining the role of phonology. *American Annals of the Deaf, 159(4),* 359-371.

Morrison, D., Trezek, B., & Paul, P. (2008). Can you see that sound? A rationale for a multisensory intervention tool for struggling readers. *Journal of Balanced Reading Instruction, 15,* 11–26.

Most, T., Aram, D., & Andorn, T. (2006). Early literacy in children with hearing loss: A comparison between two educational systems. *Volta Review, 106(1),* 5–28.

Mueller, V., & Hurtig, R. (2010). Technology-enhanced shared reading with deaf and hard of hearing children: The role of a fluent signing narrator. *Journal of Deaf Studies and Deaf Education, 15(1),* 72–101.

Nielsen, D. C., & Luetke-Stahlman, B. (2002). The benefit of assessment-based language and reading instruction: Perspectives from a case study. *Journal of Deaf Studies and Deaf Education, 7(2),* 149–186.

Padden, C. (1993). Lessons to be learned from the young deaf orthographer. *Linguistics and Education, 5(1),* 71–86.

Paul, P. (2009). *Language and deafness* (4th ed.). Sudbury, MA: Jason & Bartlett.

Rottenberg, C. (2001). A deaf child learns to read. *American Annals of the Deaf, 146(3),* 270–275.

Rottenberg, C., & Searfoss, L. (1992). Becoming literate in a preschool class: Literacy development of hearing-impaired children. *Journal of Reading Behavior, 24(4),* 463–479.

Rowe, L., & Allen, B. (1995). Interactive storybook reading with young deaf children in school and home settings. In P. Dreyer (Ed.), *Towards multiple perspectives on literacy: Fifty-ninth Yearbook of the Claremont Reading Conference* (pp. 170–182). Claremont, CA: Claremont Reading Conference.

Ruiz, N. T. (1995). A young deaf child learns to write: Implications for literacy development. *Reading Teacher, 49(3),* 206–217.

Sirois, P., Boisclair, A., & Giasson, J. (2008). Understanding of the alphabetic principle through invented spelling among hearing-impaired children learning to read and write: Experimentation with a pedagogical approach. *Journal of Research in Reading, 31(4),* 339–358.

Smith, A., & Wang, Y. (2010). The impact of Visual Phonics on the phonological awareness and speech production of a student who is deaf: A case study. *American Annals of the Deaf, 155*(2), 124–130.

Stobbart, C., & Alant, E. (2008). Home-based literacy experiences of severely to profoundly deaf preschoolers and their hearing parents. *Journal of Developmental Physical Disabilities, 20*, 139–153. doi:10.1007/s10882-007-9085-1

Swanwick, R., & Watson, L. (2007). Parents sharing books with young deaf children in spoken English and in BSL: The common and diverse features of different language settings. *Journal of Deaf Studies and Deaf Education, 12*(3), 385–405. doi:10.1093/deafed/enm004

Trezek, B. J., & Hancock, G. R. (2013). Implementing instruction in the alphabetic principle within a sign bilingual setting. *Journal of Deaf Studies and Deaf Education, 18*(3), 391–408. doi:10.1093/deafed/ent016

Trezek, B. J., & Malmgren, K. W. (2005). The efficacy of utilizing a phonics treatment package with middle school deaf and hard-of-hearing students. *Journal of Deaf Studies and Deaf Education, 10*(3), 257–271. doi:10.1093/deafed/eni028

Trezek, B. J., & Wang, Y. (2006). Implications of utilizing a phonics-based reading curriculum with children who are deaf or hard of hearing. *Journal of Deaf Studies and Deaf Education, 10*(2), 202–213. doi:10.1093/deafed/enj031

Trezek, B. J., Wang, Y., & Paul, P. V. (2010). *Reading and deafness: Theory, research and practice*. Clifton Park, NY: Cengage Learning.

Trezek, B. J., Wang, Y., Woods, D. G., Gampp, T. L., & Paul, P. (2007). Using Visual Phonics to supplement beginning reading instruction for students who are deaf or hard of hearing. *Journal of Deaf Studies and Deaf Education, 12*(3), 373–384. doi:10.1093/deafed/enm014

Van Staden, A., & le Roux, N. A. (2010). The efficacy of fingerspell coding and visual imaging techniques in improving the spelling proficiency of deaf signing elementary-phase children: A South African case study. *Journal of Developmental Physical Disabilities, 22*, 581–594. doi:10.1007/s10882-010-9196-y

Wang, Y., Spychala, H., Harris, R. S., & Oetting, T. L. (2013). The effectiveness of a phonics-based early intervention for deaf and hard of hearing preschool children and its possible impact on reading skills in elementary school: A case study. *American Annals of the Deaf, 158*(2), 107–120.

Wang, Y., Trezek, B. J., Luckner, J. L., & Paul, P. V. (2008). The role of phonology and phonological-related skills in reading instruction for students who are deaf or hard of hearing. *American Annals of the Deaf, 153*, 396–407.

Watson, L. M. (2009). Early print concepts: Insights from work with young deaf children. *Deafness and Education International 11*(4), 191–209. doi:10.1002/dei.267

Watson, L., & Swanwick, R. (2008). Parents' and teachers' views on deaf children's literacy at home: Do they agree? *Deafness and Education International 10*(1), 22–39. doi:10.1002/dei.235

Williams, C. L. (1994). The language and literacy worlds of three profoundly deaf preschool children. *Reading Research Quarterly, 29*(2), 125–155.

Williams, C. (1999). Preschool deaf children's use of signed language during writing events. *Journal of Literacy Research, 31*(2), 183–212.

Williams, C. (2004). Emergent literacy of deaf children. *Journal of Deaf Studies and Deaf Education, 9*, 352–365.

Williams, C. (2011). Adapted interactive writing instruction with kindergarten children who are deaf or hard of hearing. *American Annals of the Deaf, 156,* 23–34. doi:10.1353/aad.2011.0011

Williams, C. & Mayer, C. (in press). Writing in young deaf children. *Review of Educational Research.*

Williams, C. L., & McLean, M. M. (1997). Young deaf children's response to picture book reading in a preschool setting. *Research in the Teaching of English, 31(3),* 59–88.

Wolbers, K. A. (2008). Using balanced and interactive writing instruction to improve the higher order and lower order writing skills of deaf students. *Journal of Deaf Studies and Deaf Education, 13(2),* 257–277. doi:10.1093/deafed/enm052

2

A Model of Early Literacy Development

In this chapter, we argue that with respect to early literacy development, deaf children must follow the same developmental process from language to literacy as their hearing counterparts if they are ultimately to become proficient readers and writers (Paul & Lee, 2010; Mayer, 2007; Mayer & Trezek, 2011; Trezek, Wang, & Paul, 2010). We would further suggest that if the measure of success is taken as the development of age-appropriate literacy, there is no compelling theoretical argument or body of research evidence to make a convincing case that the early literacy development of deaf children should or does differ from that of their hearing age peers. Such a view is in line with the argument that is made for other subgroups of early literacy learners, including language-minority children, children of low socioeconomic status (SES), and children with learning disabilities. For example, research indicates that language-minority children develop literacy in similar ways to their native English-speaking peers, and approaches to instruction that are effective with the majority are equally effective with these groups (see Ehri, 2009, for discussion).

Although for all of these subgroups there may be differentiation with respect to the nature of the interventions, pedagogical approaches, and instructional strategies employed, there is not a fundamental difference in the substance of what needs to be learned to become a reader and a writer. We would argue that deaf children are not unique in this regard and would underscore the claim that the foundations necessary for learning to read and write in the early years do not change as a consequence of a child's audiogram. Rather, we suggest that the focus of our research and pedagogical attention should be on issues of differentiation that will support young deaf children in the literacy learning process, particularly as they are related to concerns of linguistic access.

In her review of the literature, Williams (2004) noted that the available research evidence appeared to indicate that young deaf children's emergent reading and writing did reflect the developmental sequence of hearing children as described in the research literature. Yet in light of the fact that reported outcomes continue to indicate that 50 percent of deaf students graduate from secondary school with a fourth grade reading level or less (Traxler, 2000) and 30 percent leave school functionally illiterate (Marschark, Lang, & Albertini, 2002), it seems that despite claims for a parallel start, the majority of these early literacy learners did not go on to achieve age-appropriate outcomes. While we acknowledge that in all likelihood, these statistics have changed with the advent of Universal Newborn Hearing Screening (UNHS), cochlear implantation, and other advances in hearing technologies, developing age-appropriate literacy remains a significant concern for the field (Archbold & Mayer, 2012; Spencer, Marschark & Spencer, 2011).

To help in understanding why an apparently similar start often does not lead to age-appropriate proficiency, we will outline the developmental trajectory that has been well documented for hearing readers and writers and argue for how this applies to early literacy development in deaf children. More specifically, we will identify how and at what stages the trajectories of deaf children often diverge from those of their hearing counterparts in ways that have an adverse impact on outcomes. In pinpointing these deviations from typical development, we contend that it may be possible not only to identify reasons for the lack of progress on the part of so many deaf learners, but also to provide insights that inform practice and strengthen our claim that all children must master the same set of foundational linguistic requisites.

THEORETICAL FRAMEWORK

The model of early literacy development that we are proposing is drawn from the work of Mayer and Wells (1996), in which they posit a framework that outlines four overlapping phases in the process of becoming literate for learners with a spoken (e.g., English) or a signed first language (e.g., American Sign Language [ASL], British Sigh Language [BSL]), in which progress depends on having a linguistic bridge or means to mediate development in and between phases (see Table 2.1; see also Mayer, 2007). In this model, they appeal specifically to the work of Vygotsky (1978, 1987) and Halliday (1989, 1993) to describe development from initial language acquisition to the mastery of the written text, including the more formal academic genres, focusing on the relationships between language and literacy development for both hearing and deaf learners, and the ways in which the nature of the first language is implicated in later literacy learning.

This symbiotic relationship between language and literacy is well documented for hearing learners (Bishop & Snowling, 2004; Catts, 1997; Catts & Kamhi, 2005; Dickinson, Golinkoff, & Hirsh-Pasek, 2010; Scarborough, 2001), and an extensive body of evidence indicates that a broadly conceived notion of language skills, encompassing vocabulary, syntax, discourse, and phonology, is fundamental for early and long-term literacy success (see Dickinson, McCabe, & Essex, 2006, for

Table 2.1 Phases in the process of becoming literate

	Spoken L1	Natural Signed Language L1
Phase 1		
Acquiring the language	Spoken L1	Signed L1
Phase 2		
Thinking with language	Egocentric spoken L1	Egocentric signed L1
Phase 3		
Linking language to print	Spoken L1	N/A*
Phase 4		
Beyond the early years	Spoken L1	N/A*

* Since natural signed languages do not have widely accepted written forms, development in phases 3 and 4 is not applicable.

an in-depth discussion). The evidence suggesting that children with stronger language capabilities tend to be more successful at the onset of formal literacy instruction further supports the relationship between language acquisition and subsequent literacy development (see Stanovich, 1986). As Perez (2004) points out, "literacy develops when children have encounters with print, presumably written in a language which the child speaks" (p. 57). This notion has also been extended to deaf children, with some researchers arguing for more studies investigating how the development of spoken and/or signed English is implicated in the literacy learning process (see Paul, 1998, 2009).

We propose a model that weds early literacy development to the development of face-to-face language (spoken, signed, or some combination) and argue that learning to read and write is dependent on this language foundation (see Mayer, 2007, 2009; Mayer & Trezek, 2011). To make this argument and provide the theoretical background for later chapters, we will consider the linguistic prerequisites for developing text-based literacy, how these are acquired, and the consequent implications for deaf children.

Phase 1: Acquiring the Language

The first step in learning to read and write any language is developing a level of communicative competence in the language that is to be read and written (see phase 1 in table 2.1). For hearing children, this prerequisite is taken for granted, and it would be a rare occurrence indeed to meet a child who had not acquired a threshold level of competence in the spoken language of his or her community. As Gee (2001) points out, "barring quite serious disorders all human children acquire the full core grammar of their native language" (p. 32). He defines core grammar as the basic grammatical structure and properties of a language that are instantiated in first-language acquisition (e.g., using a relative clause) (see also Chomsky, 1986, 1995). Gee goes on to argue that every speaker/hearer of English, regardless of dialect and in the absence of any formal teaching, "acquires an equally complex and rule-governed core grammar" (p. 32). With respect to vocabulary, research indicates that the typical six-year-old will have about twenty-six hundred words in his or her expressive vocabulary and between twenty thousand and forty thousand words in his or her receptive vocabulary (Owens, 2012). In other words, irrespective of individual characteristics, SES, or other sociocultural variables, all children have the biological capacity to acquire control of vocabulary and complex rule-governed grammatical structures in their native language. To be clear, we are not making an argument here for a Chomskyan language acquisition device (LAD) theory, a notion of a language organ, or a universal grammar (Chomsky, 1972) but rather for a view that this capacity for language acquisition is a feature of a young child's biological inheritance that is brought to bear on the particular language that is used in the child's community and is affected by the nature of the assistance provided by the interlocutors in the child's world (see Wells, 2009, for an in-depth discussion).

That being said, some children do develop a richer and more robust language for communication than others as a consequence of either their individual capacities (e.g., constrained or heightened by cognitive abilities) or their environmental context (e.g., enhanced by richer opportunities for interaction), which can result in significant individual differences by the time children begin to learn to read and write (Hart & Risley, 1995; Hoff, 2003; Vasilyeva & Waterfall, 2011; Wells, 2009). This is particularly evident with respect to the development of vocabulary in the early years and the striking disparity between children from lower- and higher-income homes, which becomes apparent even before thirty-six months of age (see Neuman, 2011, for discussion). It is also well documented that children with language impairments face particular challenges in transitioning to literacy (Kaiser, Roberts & McLeod, 2011).

However, despite these differences, it would never be the case that a minimum threshold level of language for face-to-face communication was not acquired. This process of language acquisition appears to happen so effortlessly most of the time that there is a tendency to lose sight of the fact that the majority of children are mastering a very complex system in the absence of formal instruction or intervention. It is not beyond the bounds of argument to characterize this accomplishment as singular and unique to the human condition.

While we have acknowledged this unique human biological capacity for language, it is the sociocultural conditions under which the acquisition occurs that plays a pivotal role in shaping the path of language development and accounting for differences in individual trajectories. In order for the process of language acquisition to be realized, it necessary that the following four conditions are in place in the child's environment: (1) adequate exposure in quality and quantity (2) to accessible linguistic input (3) in meaningful interactions (4) with others who are already capable users of the language (Mayer, 2007). In other words, from birth, children must have access to abundant, rich language that is used to mediate activities in which they are interested and that matter to them (e.g., bath time, playing games, going for a walk). In these interactions, parents and others who are already competent users of the language serve as contingently responsive conversational partners, scaffolding, expanding, and building on the child's utterances while they are jointly engaged in tasks of mutual attention (Wells, 1994). In a rather circular fashion, it is in the act of using the language that the language is acquired (Halliday, 1975a, 1993), and if any one of the four necessary acquisition conditions is not met—or is met only minimally—language acquisition can be compromised (Mayer & Wells, 1996; Mayer, 2007; Wells, 2009).

In the case of deaf children acquiring a spoken language, there are obvious challenges with respect to meeting the second condition, making the language input accessible. While full linguistic access is taken for granted in the case of hearing children, the same cannot be said for many deaf children who may not have acquired a face-to-face form of their first language in the unrestricted way that their hearing counterparts have. The vast majority (about 95 percent) are born to hearing parents who typically have no expectation that their child will be deaf (Mitchell & Karchmer, 2004). Therefore, the language acquisition environment in which these children find themselves is usually structured on the assumption that the individuals participating in it can hear. While there are certainly visual-gestural aspects to the communication, the hearing world makes face-to-face linguistic meaning through a system that is primarily auditory-oral in nature. This system for making meaning is not fully accessible to the deaf child, and thus the opportunity for contingently responsive interactions with others is limited. This has significant impact on the child's cognitive and linguistic development, as it is primarily through dialogue and discourse that the language foundation itself is constructed. Therefore, the nature and course of literacy development are subsequently—and often adversely—shaped by the quality of this language foundation. As Geers (2006) argues, "The frequently reported low literacy levels among students with severe to profound hearing impairment are, in part, due to the discrepancy between their incomplete spoken language system and the demands of reading [and writing] a speech-based system" (p. 244).

It would be important at this juncture to make a comment about those deaf children whose parents are fluent users of a natural signed language. First, it is worth noting that this would be a very small cohort, as only about 5 percent of deaf children have at least one deaf parent (Mitchell & Karchmer, 2004), and it would not be the case that all of these deaf parents use a natural signed language for communication. But that being said, for these children, it is the case that all four conditions are in place to acquire the native language of the home (e.g., ASL). These Deaf parents can provide the quality and quantity of access to the signed language that, by its visual-gestural nature, is fully accessible to a deaf child, and research evidence indicates that these children demonstrate age-appropriate development in the target signed language (Baker & Woll, 2008; Schick, Marschark & Spencer, 2006). However, despite age-appropriate development in the signed first language, it is not clear how and whether this linguistic foundation can support early literacy development in a second language (e.g., English) (Mayer, 2009; Mayer & Leigh, 2010; Mayer & Wells, 1996). An in-depth discussion of this question will be provided in chapter 5, where we will be appealing to the framework described here.

However, for all deaf learners, including those whose first language is a natural signed language, it is important to recognize that developing communicative competence in the face-to-face form of the language to be read and written requires some degree of intervention in order to make the spoken language accessible. These avenues are either auditory (e.g., hearing technologies), visual (e.g., signed language, Cued Speech), or some combination of the two. It has been an ongoing challenge in the field to sort out the most efficacious means for providing this access, and historically, there is no overwhelming evidence to suggest that one approach has been more effective than another in developing this spoken language foundation in the early years (see Stredler-Brown, 2010, for discussion). The most that can be said is that there were some children who acquired language via all of these avenues, but no one approach has proved effective for all children. Age-appropriate language development has been reported for children using hearing technologies, Cued Speech, or Signed English or as a consequence of an Auditory Verbal Therapy (AVT), an Auditory Oral (AO), or a Total Communication (TC) approach. More recently, improvements in hearing technologies (e.g., cochlear implants, bilateral implantation, bone conducting hearing implants [BCHIs]) and the possibilities for earlier fitting of amplification as consequence of UNHS have afforded greater numbers of deaf children increased opportunities to meaningfully access spoken language via audition, allowing for enhanced probabilities for developing age-appropriate language skills (Archbold, 2010; Spencer & Marschark, 2006). Yet despite significant progress in this regard, there continue to be concerns that not all deaf children are developing age-appropriate levels as predicted (Belzner & Seal, 2009; Geers, Nicholas, & Moog, 2007; Paatsch, Blaney, Sarant, & Bow, 2006).

For deaf children, the significance of this connection between language and early literacy can have implications in two ways. First, many deaf children have delays in their face-to-face language development that can negatively affect literacy learning. Second, deaf children whose first language is not English (but is, e.g., ASL or some other spoken or signed language) are confronted with developing literacy in a language they may not have yet acquired. In both of these scenarios, in the absence of having acquired competence in a face-to-face form of the language to be read and written, deaf children do not have the essential foundation in place for age-appropriate literacy development to occur.

There is a need to call attention to this point, as arguments have been made in the literature that control of face-to-face language (spoken or signed) is not necessary in the early literacy development of deaf children and that even in its absence, deaf children are able to make "gains in literacy knowledge comparable to those made by hearing children" (Rottenberg & Searfoss, 1992, p. 477), learning to read and write via engagement with only the print form of the language (Mashie, 1995; Small & Mason, 2008). Although there is wide consensus that print can and should be meaningfully introduced to children at a very young age, it would not be the case that for hearing children, engagement with print occurs in the absence of, or in lieu of, contemporaneous spoken language development.

Dyson (2001), referring to Ramsey (1997), contends that "it is difficult to see how children could learn to compose [or read] with written graphics unless they could already use comfortably a natural language [spoken or signed] as a tool to plan, narrate, make queries and even reflect on, and analytically examine speech itself" (p. 128). This would suggest that the first and most fundamental aspect of what needs to be considered in the early literacy development of deaf children is that they have achieved an age-appropriate level of proficiency *in the same language that is to be read and written*, just as is the case for their hearing peers. All following claims made in this chapter and throughout this book with respect to early literacy learning are grounded in this premise.

Phase 2: Thinking with Language

In the first phase of the model, children use language to make meaning with others, but in phase 2, at about three years of age, children begin to differentiate between social language and language for self. What marks development at this stage is the move from the use of language for communicating with others (inter-mental) to language for communication with oneself (intra-mental), as children begin to employ language as a tool for thinking (Vygotsky, 1978). In adopting this perspective, cognition can be viewed as grounded in and shaped by the language that has already been acquired, and children can be said to think in the same language in which they already speak and/or sign.

This is first realized as the child begins to use the linguistic resources learned in social interactions as a means of self-direction and solo reflection in the mode of egocentric speech (Wertsch, 1985). Egocentric speech or sign is self-talk or self-sign that is not adapted for or addressed to a listener. This egocentric spoken or signed language, as an outward manifestation of inner language, affords insights into mental representations, as children are literally using their language to "think out loud" (Rowe & Wertsch, 2002). Over time, the nature of this egocentric speech becomes more and more removed in structure from that of the language used in social interaction with others, and at around six or seven years of age, this overt form of speech for self disappears, to become the mode of intra-mental activity that Vygotsky (1987) referred to as "inner speech."[1] Because no other interlocutor is involved, the topic does not need to be made explicit, and so inner speech tends to consist largely of predications; it also tends to be compressed and idiosyncratic, as multiple dimensions of meaning are handled simultaneously (Mayer & Wells, 1996). In other words, the language of inner speech, while born of the language of face-to-face interaction, takes on an abbreviated form of this language, given that the interlocutor is oneself. As Vygotsky argues, it is in this medium that we engage in individual verbal thinking.

Given the intimate connection between face-to-face language and cognition, it can be argued that the quality of the linguistic interactions that children have experienced in phase 1, and the language that has developed as a result, determines the quality of inner language or inner speech. Simply put, how well a child can communicate in a language in the first place is directly tied to his or her ability to think in that language and ultimately to learn to read and write it (Vygotsky, 1978; Watson, 1996, 2001; Wells, 1981). "While the development of external (i.e., social) speech precedes the development of inner speech, written speech emerges only after the development of the latter. Written speech presupposes the existence of inner speech" (Vygotsky, 1987, p. 203). In this way, inner speech stands in an intermediate position between face-to-face language development (phase 1) and the development of written language (phase 3). The implication is that to learn to read and write, children must not only be able to use the language of the text for face-to-face communication, but also be able to think in the

---

[1] *Speech* in this instance is used in the Vygotskyan sense and refers to language, not to speech as modality. Thus, inner speech can be equated with inner language.

language (i.e., using the language inter-mentally to remember, reflect, consider, plan, predict, hypothesize, etc.).

Much has been written about the nature of cognition in deaf individuals and about young deaf children in particular (see Marschark, 1993; Marschark & Hauser, 2008; Marschark & Wauters, 2011, for overviews), with a focus on a broad range of issues from theory of mind (Spencer, 2010) to working memory (Hall & Bavelier, 2010; Rönnberg, 2011) to children with cochlear implants (Pisoni, Conway, Kronenberger, Henning, & Anaya, 2010). While it is beyond the scope of this chapter to provide an in-depth examination of such an extensive topic, we would argue that for the purposes of our discussion, it must be acknowledged that language is critically implicated no matter which aspect of cognitive functioning and development is being considered. As Nelson (1996) notes, although there are aspects of cognition without language that are powerful and complex, at every point in development, "language amplifies and advances thinking in directions that it would otherwise not be possible to go" (p. 87).

It would also be important to make a distinction here between language and modality. As has been widely acknowledged, although there may be differences in the ways in which signed and spoken languages mediate cognitive development resulting in differences in cognitive functioning between deaf and hearing learners (Marschark & Wauters, 2011), the critical element is that irrespective of mode, the child has a language available to mediate thinking, to develop inner speech.

The consequence for those deaf children who have not developed competence in any face-to-face to language is that they will not have developed inner speech and thus not have a full language to "think with." This will have significant repercussions for all aspects of learning, including the development of reading and writing (Akamatsu, Mayer & Hardy-Braz, 2008). While it is certainly the case that any language, regardless of modality, can serve equally well as a language for "thinking with," in terms of early literacy learning, it is essential that children are *able to think in the same language as the text they will be learning to read and write*. This issue will be further explored in the following section and in chapter 5 as it pertains to children who are raised bilingually.

Phase 3: Linking Language to Print

We would argue that phase 3 is pivotal in this discussion of early literacy development, as it is at this stage that children are asked to make meaning not only in their face-to-face language, but also through print. What had heretofore been spoken, signed, or thought about must now be represented in or understood via text. This is the point at which children are learning to read and write, an activity that requires some explicit instruction for most learners. In fact, we would suggest that although there is a range in this regard, there is no child who learns to read and write in the same unconscious and effortless manner in which he or she learned to speak or sign. As evidence of this, consider the energy and attention educational institutions devote to the teaching of literacy and at increasingly younger ages.

This is a consequence of the fact that becoming literate can be a daunting task for all children as they try to make sense of the relationships between the language they already know and the language of print, encountering "rich conflicts" along the way (Grossi, 1990). The connection between talk and text is not immediately evident, and in languages with deep orthographies (e.g., English), these relationships can be especially challenging to sort out. For young literacy learners, this stage represents "their first encounter with what will appear to them as arbitrarily constructed, unmotivated signs" (Kress, 1994, p. 219).

An instructive way to think about this is to consider the differences in the ways in which meaning is made in the spoken or signed language and in the written language (Vygotsky, 1978). In acquiring a spoken or signed language, the words or signs provide a direct, symbolic representation of the events and objects being referred to. Thus, the child comes to see the spoken word or the sign standing in for the thing directly. For example, in saying or signing the word *umbrella*, the word or sign makes a straight-line reference to the object, a first-order representation.

However, according to Vygotsky (1978), writing is a second-order symbol system that offers a visual representation of the spoken word or sign, rather than directly representing a perceived or imagined object. That is, written words are symbols of spoken words. This is true for all languages, even those that are logographic (Perfetti & Sandak, 2000), but it is particularly evident in alphabetic languages where written words record the sounds of a spoken word, which then elicits an attributable referent or meaning. Therefore, to make sense of the written word *umbrella*, it must first be mapped onto the spoken representation of that word. This involves making connections at the phoneme-grapheme level to decode or encode the word and then calling up that word in the mental lexicon to activate the meaning. This represents more cognitive work, an extra step, a second-order representation. All of this is to say that given the intricacies of making sense of the written representation system, learning to read and write can be a complex activity for any child.

To accomplish this task, hearing children exploit knowledge of their face-to-face language as they come to understand written language through spoken language (Vygotsky, 1978), using this knowledge to talk their way into text. "Children are highly proficient in all aspects of the syntax of speech at this stage. That proficiency provides the linguistic foundation on which they build when they first learn to [read and] write" (Kress, 1994, p. 53). At this stage, the automatic and unconscious use of spoken language is brought into consciousness, and children come to understand that a spoken utterance is a unit of language that can be systematically represented in print. Spoken language becomes an object of reflection as children sort out the relationships between language and text at the syntactic, lexical, and sublexical level. It is at this juncture in the literacy learning process that the commonalities between spoken language and print are more important than the asymmetries, as children rely on these commonalities to decode and encode print (Perfetti, 1987). In sum, the knowledge of the spoken language affords the hearing child commonsensical knowledge of the language to be read and written, which anchors and makes possible the subsequent development of literacy.

That said, it must be noted that even though hearing children generally come to the task of learning to read and write with requisite age-appropriate fluency in the language of the text, there will still be qualitative differences among them as they learn to read and write (Rice, 1989), success being related to factors such as the sophistication of their spoken language, their familiarity with a broad range of narrative text types both oral and written, rich internal representations of the distinctive features of these text types, and interest and confidence in experimenting with text (Hemphill & Snow, 1996). There would be no reason to expect that these factors would not also play a role as deaf children learn to read and write.

However, the fundamental question that arises when thinking about the early literacy development of deaf children is tied up with the fact that many of them lack full control of a primary form (spoken or signed) of the language to be read and written. If children cannot express themselves in a face-to-face form of the language and have not developed an internal representation of the same language (i.e., inner speech), they will not be able to make sense of text, as they lack the requisite linguistic foundation. As we have argued, to learn to read and write requires that a child can sort out how the face-to-face language is represented in the written word, and this is dependent on having first acquired the language in phase 1.

In chapters 3 and 4, we will describe in detail and more specifically the processes of early reading and writing development, but we want to emphasize again that the discussions of development in these chapters are predicated on the fact that children have the necessary language foundation in place. We believe that this issue cannot be overstated: language is the essential factor that underpins literacy. As Dickinson, Golinkoff, and Hirsh-Pasek (2010) argue, "Language is unique among precursor abilities in its pervasiveness for both early and later reading [and writing] competencies and for the duration of its effect on reading comprehension [and writing development] as code breaking turns into meaning making" (p. 308). It is language that affords the initial bridge to learning to read and write, and as we will argue in the following section, it is also through discourse that children develop control of the more complex forms of written texts that are the hallmarks of educational settings.

That being said, it is interesting to note that in the National Early Literacy Panel (NELP) meta-analysis (2008), oral language,[2] or the ability to comprehend and produce spoken language including vocabulary and grammar, was described as only moderately correlated with literacy achievement (see chapter 3 for an in-depth discussion of the NELP). This may be taken as a view that is contrary to our claim; however, we would argue that this finding must be considered in terms of the broader context of literacy learning in which we typically refer to the development of both code- and language-related abilities. It has been shown that code-related (e.g., phonological awareness, phonemic awareness, and word reading skills) and language-related abilities (e.g., semantic and syntactic) assume relatively greater significance at different stages in the developmental trajectory (see Dickinson, Golinkoff & Hirsh-Pasek, 2010; Storch & Whitehurst, 2002, for discussions).

Specifically, the relationships between language and literacy development weaken in kindergarten and first grade, when the emphasis shifts to making sense of the code, but they strengthen again in the later grades. In other words, code-related phonological skills account for much more of the variance in performance in the early stages of learning to read and write than they do in the later years. Therefore, we would recommend caution when interpreting the results of a recent meta-analysis of studies of deaf readers (Mayberry, del Giudice, Lieberman, 2011) that considers the relative influence of code- and language-related skills. The studies included spanned an age range from preschool to postsecondary, raising questions about the applicability of their findings, at least as they relate to the importance of code-related, phonological abilities in the early literacy development of deaf children (see discussion Mayer & Trezek, 2014).

In terms of our model, decoding and encoding abilities are foregrounded in phase 3, when the major focus is learning to make the connections between face-to-face language and print. By the time typically developing children are entering this phase of development, it could be suggested that there is something of a ceiling effect for language.

---

[2] As we said in chapter 1, when the term *oral language* is used, it reflects the terminology employed in the original source (e.g., NELP, a published study, etc.). This term is often used synonymously with *spoken language* in the broader literature in the field of literacy. It is only in the field of deafness that the distinction between oral and spoken language merits attention.

In other words, the majority of children have acquired a requisite language threshold—the implicit phonology, morphology, lexicon, grammar, and syntax of their face-to-face language—that, despite individual variations, does not differ in its basic substance. In some sense, this creates a level playing field in terms of language when most children begin to read and write the simpler texts that are typical of the early years (e.g., decodable texts, pattern books, etc.).

Once children have "cracked the code," language-related abilities assume greater prominence, as the focus turns to the comprehension and production of more complex text. This is not to say that language does not play an ongoing role throughout but rather that it takes a backseat to developing code-related skills until these are established. It should also be acknowledged that while word recognition is critically dependent on phonologically based code-related skills, comprehension of text appears to be much more reliant on language-related skills such as vocabulary knowledge and grammar (Muter, Hulme, Snowling & Stevenson, 2004). However, in the absence of being able to recognize words in the first place, there is little hope for comprehension, illustrating the intimate and necessary link between code- and language-related abilities in the literacy learning process.

For all learners who struggle with literacy development, there is general agreement that a core difficulty in learning to read and write "manifests itself as a deficiency within the language system and, in particular, a deficiency in mastering phonological awareness skills" (Pugh, Sandak, Frost, Moore, & Mencl, 2006, p. 65). We would point out here that phonology is an aspect of acquiring a language in the first place, and most early readers and writers have this in place as part of their linguistic foundation. In this way, language provides a basis for developing phonological awareness and other code-related abilities (Whitehurst & Lonigan, 1998; see also Dickinson, McCabe, Anastasopoulos, Peisner-Feinberg & Poe, 2003 for review). Although we tend to isolate phonological abilities as discrete skills to be taught in the literacy learning process, it is only for the purposes of teaching a print form of the language that we need to make these phonological aspects explicit. In the process, explicit teaching of the code-related skills exploits the implicit phonological knowledge (e.g., sensitivity to rhyme, syllable recognition) that has been established in concert with language acquisition. Therefore, it could be argued that even with respect to the development of the code-related skills, language plays a critical role.

In taking this perspective, we are not arguing against making a distinction between the code- and language-related aspects of learning to read and write, particularly as they are implicated in early literacy instruction. To be sure, we make use of this distinction in later chapters. However, we want to emphasize that even in phase 3, where the attention shifts to uncovering the relationships between talk and text (i.e., the code-related skills), it is the face-to-face language that mediates the process. That said, we would also stress that systematic attention to developing decoding and encoding skills (e.g., phonemic awareness, alphabetic principle) is critical at this stage. This view will be expanded on in the following two chapters, where we will describe the reading and writing development in phase 3 in greater detail.

Phase 4: Beyond the Early Years

Before moving on to a more in-depth examination of early reading and writing, it is important to examine what occurs in phase 4, as this is the stage that is concerned with developing literacy for learning and educational purposes beyond the early years, the goal of literacy education for all learners. This is often construed in the educational litera-ture as the difference between learning to read and write (i.e., early literacy) and using reading and writing as tools for learning (Chall, 1996). Although this is not the primary focus of this book, understand-ing the trajectory of development at this stage provides insights into how the foundations established in phase 3 are critical for later literacy learning.

By the time children have reached phase 4, it is assumed that the connection between face-to-face language and print has been made, that basic decoding and encoding skills have been mastered, and that comprehension and generation of text are possible. With these abilities in place, children are ready to engage with the more complex texts characteristic of this phase. It is in the synoptic written genres of this stage (e.g., expository texts such as essays, arguments, etc.) that discipline-based, educational knowledge is typically constructed and communicated, typified by the use of lower-frequency vocabulary, compound-complex grammatical constructions, and grammatical met-aphor (Halliday, 1993).

This stands in contrast to the ways in which meaning is made in the more dynamic mode of the spoken conversational texts of everyday life, the language that young readers and writers use to initially talk their way into text in phase 3. Meanings foregrounded in the dynamic mode are those of doings and happenings, which are realized lexi-cogrammatically in clauses that are congruent, where processes and attributes are realized as verbs and adjectives/adverbs. In contrast, in the synoptic mode, meanings foregrounded are those of structure and stasis, realized in texts featuring grammatical metaphor (see Mayer & Wells, 1996). This important distinction is perhaps best illustrated with an example.

In the dynamic mode, meaning is typically conveyed via the use of a clause consisting of a noun phrase (an agentive subject) and a verb of process. For example, "Nigel eats Vegemite[3] at every meal." In the synoptic mode, through the process of nominalization typical of grammatical metaphor, the meaning of this entire sentence can be captured in the noun phrase "Nigel's passion for Vegemite." This rewording or nominalization allows the phrase to become the subject of a subsequent sentence in which the main verb and complement encode the consequence of the action (i.e., "Nigel's passion for Vegemite was not understood by his Canadian friends"). This illustrates a new way to use language to make meaning in a manner that is increasingly removed from that of everyday, dynamic discourse. Gaining control of this kind of language in phase 4 is challenging for all children, as they must "learn to construe their experience in two complementary modes: the dynamic mode of everyday commonsense grammar and the synoptic mode of the elaborated written grammar" (Halliday, 1993, p. 112). This requires mastery of the vocabulary and grammar necessary to make meaning in the abstract concepts and categories of grammatical metaphor.

Building on this discussion, it would also be useful to cite the distinction made by Cummins (1979, 1981) between the development of basic interpersonal communication skills (BICS) and cognitive academic language proficiency (CALP), as these terms are also often used to refer to this difference, albeit in terms of acquiring a second language. Cummins (2000) characterizes these as marking the contrast between conversational and academic proficiency. Gaining control of BICS entails mastery of the high-frequency vocabulary and basic grammatical structures of a language that allow for conversational fluency and the ability to communicate easily in face-to-face situations and familiar contexts. Not unlike Halliday's characterization of the dynamic mode, it is reasonable to argue that BICS underpin literacy development in phase 3, when children rely on their spoken everyday language to mediate text.

However, the development of CALP is more closely aligned with phase 4 and the synoptic genre. This characterization of language denotes the ability to use language to read and write about more abstract topics, employing low-frequency vocabulary and more complex sentence structure and grammar. Again, an example can be informative here. In talking about a family tradition such as the Sunday roast in BICS, we might say, "His family had a roast every Sunday." Contrast this with the more CALP-like utterance, "He knew what to expect for dinner, as the Sunday roast had become an enduring tradition in his family."

---

[3] Vegemite is an Australian food that is a popular spread for sandwiches and toast. Vegemite is similar to British, New Zealand, and South African Marmite. Many North Americans do not favor its slightly bitter, malty, and salty taste.

These differences also align with Halliday's (1973) hierarchical categorization of the functions of language that provide a description of development from the earliest-developing instrumental (e.g., requesting) and regulatory (e.g., directing behavior) functions of language, which are linked to BICS and readily accomplished in the dynamic mode, to the later-developing informative (e.g., explaining, comparing, discussing) and heuristic (e.g., predicting, solving, clarifying) functions that are more closely tied to CALP and realized in the synoptic mode. We would argue that it is the use of language to accomplish these later functions that marks development in phase 4 and is the level of literacy necessary for school-based learning. Competence at this stage goes far beyond a functional level of literacy (i.e., sixth grade level), is necessary for advanced academic study, and is the standard by which success as a literacy learner is often measured, a standard that many deaf learners often fail to meet.

As we have already pointed out, developing this level of reading and writing is a challenge for all children, as this is when written language becomes even more removed from the face-to-face form. But even in phase 3, as they are learning how to decode and encode, children face the challenges of capturing the auditory and visual-gestural aspects of spoken or signed language in written text. They must deal with the inherent tension in representing both the propositional content and illocutionary force of the face-to-face utterance in their writing (Olson, 1977, 1993). In addition to this, they must learn to make inter-mental meaning in the absence of a physically present interlocutor.

"Dialogue presupposes visual perception of the interlocutor (of his mimics and gestures), as well as an acoustic [visual] perception of speech [sign] intonation. This allows the understanding of thought through hints and allusions" (Vygotsky, 1987, p. 271). In both reading and writing, establishing intersubjectivity and understanding relies solely on the appropriate choice of words and their syntactic organization. Making meaning with text requires an elaboration and expansion of thought and a preciseness of expression not needed in face-to-face communication, necessitating the use of a larger vocabulary and a greater number of words. As Vygotsky puts it, the "transition from maximally contracted inner speech (i.e., speech for oneself) to a maximally expanded written speech (i.e., speech for the other) requires a child who is capable of extremely complex operations in the voluntary construction of the fabric of meaning.... Written speech forces the child to act more intellectually. It requires conscious awareness of the very process of speaking [or signing]" (1987, p. 204).

While these challenges of using written versus spoken or signed language are present from the outset of learning to read and write, they become more pronounced in phase 4, when, as we discussed above, the language used is more removed from the everyday conversational language that has been acquired in phase 1. However, just as in phase 3, this move to the use of the synoptic genre and academic proficiency is also mediated by the child's spoken or signed language. Those children who have acquired a richer, more fulsome vocabulary and have used their spoken or signed language to accomplish the more complex informative and heuristic functions are better placed to make sense of this use of language when they encounter it in print. This is where the value of rich conversational encounters from the earliest days cannot be underestimated. This is also when the impact of being read to becomes very evident, as it is through the language of books that children will engage with vocabulary and grammar that are not features of face-to-face communication (Halliday 1975b; Wells, 2001). Even a phrase as simple as *once upon a time* is one that a child meets in print, not in conversation. Many hearing children who face challenges in literacy development beyond the early stages do so as a consequence of not having this robust language in place, even though in most cases, they have established basic communicative competence.

For deaf children, the challenges can be even more profound. They are often in a situation in which they are being expected to work with academic, school-based texts (phase 4) without full control of the dynamic mode or BICS of the language they are meant to read and write (Mayer, 2007; Mayer & Trezek, 2011; Paul, 1998, 2009, 2011). In the absence of this foundation, it becomes very demanding to master the more complex lexicogrammar of phase 4. For those deaf children who, like their hearing age peers, have established a level of competence in the face-to-face form of the language (e.g., hard-of-hearing learners, children with cochlear implants), it is in this phase that literacy development may be negatively affected as a consequence of compromised listening environments and the challenge of accessing complex language in noisy educational settings (Archbold, 2010).

IMPLICATIONS FOR PRACTICE

As has been emphasized throughout this chapter, there is "no indication that these [deaf] children bypass or do not need to acquire the same understandings (e.g., a knowledge of the language to be written, phonological processing skills) as all other young literacy learners" (Mayer, 2007, p. 427). This premise informs the implications for practice presented below.

1. **Making face-to-face language accessible is paramount. It is the key factor in allowing for the language input that is critical for the development of literacy.**

As Neuman and Dwyer (2009) argue, "Talk may be cheap but it is priceless for young developing minds" (p. 384). The relationships between sheer volume of *language input* and its relationship to *language output* in home, child care, and early school settings has been well established (see Harris, Golinkoff & Hirsh-Pasek, 2011, for discussion). For example, one of the main findings of the Effective Provision of Pre-School Education (EPPE) project in the United Kingdom was the "enduring and interacting effects of family and pre-school influences on children's literacy development from age 3 to 11" (Sylva, Melhuish, Sammons, Siraj-Blatchford, & Taggart, 2011, p. 98). The significance of this language input extends beyond the language directed specifically to the child and also to the language that the child overhears (incidental exposure) (Akhtar, 2005). Providing this volume of language input has been an ongoing challenge for deaf children, as access to a spoken language (i.e., the language underpinning literacy) is compromised to varying degrees (Moeller, Tomblin, Yoshinaga-Itano, Connor & Jerger, 2007). Even when children may have meaningful access in an optimal listening environment, this access can be significantly reduced in a more demanding listening environment (e.g., a noisy preschool classroom), interfering with the overhearing that is such an important aspect of early language development.

Therefore, for deaf learners, some level of intervention is necessary to provide access to the spoken language of the text. This access can be accomplished via the auditory channel (e.g., hearing technologies such as hearing aids, cochlear implants, BCHIs, and group amplification systems), the visual channel (e.g., speechreading, Cued Speech, signed forms of the spoken language), or some combination of the two. In other words, access to a spoken language, achieved most easily via ear, can also be achieved via eye, when the visual input enhances the input from the auditory channel. Ensuring this access not only differs from child to child but can also vary at different ages and stages of a child's early life. For example, some children may not be able to access language only through listening when they first get a cochlear implant, especially when they are implanted later. Other children may need access to spoken language via alternative routes before they get their implants or if they have additional learning needs. Or children may need additional support to access spoken language when they have to cope with more challenging listening environments such as childcare centers and preschool settings. Therefore, we would argue that *ensuring access to the face-to-face language of the text is the indispensable first step* if deaf children are to learn to read and write. This requires that educators and other professionals abandon their biases with respect to modality and focus on making the language for communication accessible, by whatever means are necessary for that child. This also means ensuring that hearing technologies are worn and working and that parents and children learn how to manage the equipment. And finally, it means knowing how to appropriately support the auditory input with visual input when ears alone are not enough.

2. **Given that an unresolved early language delay puts children at risk for difficulties in learning to read and write, specific and targeted interventions and remediation may be needed if language development is not developing at an age-appropriate level**.

As we have argued, in the normal course of development, children acquire language as an outcome of their explorations of the world in a rich social setting mediated via contingently responsive interactions with more capable others. As Rice (1989) emphasizes, it is generally the case that explicit teaching from adults is not necessary, and "if adults try to structure and direct a child's language learning, the outcome may be interference with, instead of enhancement of, a child's language skill" (p. 24). However, we know that there are deaf children who, for a range of reasons (e.g., late identified, additional disabilities, no access to language in the environment), have not developed language for basic communication, that control of common-sense, everyday vocabulary and grammar. Therefore, we need to think about interventions and strategies for teaching language to those children who have not acquired it.

While we would never recommend that natural interactions be abandoned in favor of a remedial curriculum, more structured approaches can be used in concert with a focus on language in meaningful use. This requires a careful assessment of a child's language development to identify gaps and causal factors so that interventions can be targeted appropriately and implemented efficaciously. Deaf children in this situation have much in common with hearing children who have language delays, impairments, or disabilities, sometimes as a secondary consequence of having another disability (e.g., cognitive impairments) and sometimes as the only significant developmental issue (see Kaiser, Roberts & McLeod, 2011, for discussion). Therefore, we would suggest that remedial approaches designed for these children would also be appropriate for deaf learners who are evidencing a language delay (see chapter 3 for discussion of NELP findings related to language enhancement interventions).

3. **An efficacious early literacy program achieves an appropriate balance between language- and code-related abilities.**

We have been clear that the development and teaching of code-related abilities are a necessary focus in early literacy education. However, because the set of code-related skills (e.g., alphabetic knowledge, print knowledge) is more discrete and constrained, more teachable, and more easily assessed, there can be a temptation to focus on these at the expense of an emphasis on experiences that focus more globally on language development (Paris, 2011). That being said, along with Paris (2009), we signal a caution that attending to these code-related skills should not be the exclusive pedagogical focus in the early years, but rather that the aim should be for balance, being mindful of the complementary contributions that code and language play in the early literacy learning process for both deaf and hearing children.

We would also suggest that there are many well-designed early literacy curricula that have been developed with this balance in mind, and we see these as efficacious and appropriate for young deaf learners. We question whether there is a need for curricula designed specifically for deaf children, as the foundational skills and requisites that must be developed in these children do not differ from those of their hearing peers, and given the fact that the overwhelming majority of deaf children are now educated in inclusive, general education settings using mainstream curricula. Therefore, for purposes of our discussions throughout this book, we refer to instruction as *differentiated* (i.e., accommodations and adaptations) rather than as different, and we emphasize that differentiation (e.g., a relative focus on code or language) must be driven by the particular strengths or weakness identified for an individual child or group of children and not by a sense that there is a generic approach that meets the needs of all deaf learners.

IMPLICATIONS FOR RESEARCH

We have already indicated in chapter 1 that in general, we need more research, more longitudinal research, and more intervention studies. In this chapter, we add briefly to this suggestion and argue for more research that pays attention to the language aspects of early literacy development, with respect to language growth, the efficacy of various approaches to making language accessible in the early years, the relationships between face-to-face language development and learning to read and write, and the efficacy of any interventions designed to improve language. Germane to this concern is the question of what "counts" as evidence in demonstrating language development, given the challenges in assessing and measuring language growth and given the fact that language interventions will not show the same kind of immediate "payoff" as those designed to improve code-related skills. As Neuman (2011) points out, even when we have measures to use, too often these measures are not subtle enough and are too distal from the intervention's goals to capture any change in overall language development. For example, it seems unlikely that direct teaching of a set of vocabulary items would have any marked impact on language development more globally. Therefore, in addition to giving more thought to how we measure language development in future research (e.g., a broader base of data sources including both quantitative and qualitative approaches such as retelling and discourse analysis), we must also design studies that track learners over time to truly capture whether interventions have had the desired impact.

REFERENCES

Akamatsu, C. T., Mayer, C., & Hardy-Braz, S. (2008). Why considerations of verbal aptitude are important in educating deaf and hard-of-hearing students. In M. Marschark & P. Hauser (Eds.), *Deaf cognition: Foundations and outcomes* (pp. 131–169). New York, NY: Oxford University Press.

Akhtar, N. (2005). The robustness of learning through overhearing. *Developmental Science, 8*, 199–209.

Archbold. S. (2010). *Deaf education: Changed by cochlear implantation?* Nijmegen, Netherlands: Thesis Radboud University Nijmegen Medical Centre.

Archbold, S., & Mayer, C. (2012). Deaf education: The impact of cochlear implantation? *Deafness Education International 14(1)*, 2–15.

Baker, A. E., & Woll, B. (2008*). Sign language acquisition.* Amsterdam, Netherlands: John Benjamin.

Belzner, K. A., & Seal, B. C. (2009). Children with cochlear implants: A review of demographic and communicative outcomes. *American Annals of the Deaf, 154*, 311–333. doi:10.1353/aad.0.0102

Bishop, D. V. M., & Snowling, M. J. (2004). Developmental dyslexia and specific language impairment: Same or different? *Psychological Bulletin, 130*, 858–888.

Catts, H. W. (1997). The early identification of language-based reading disabilities. *Language, Speech and Hearing Services in Schools, 28*, 86–89.

Catts H. W., & Kamhi, A. G. (2005). *The connections between language and reading disabilities.* Mahwah, NJ: Erlbaum.

Chall, J. S. (1996). *Stages of reading development* (2nd ed.). New York, NY: McGraw-Hill.

Chomsky, N. (1972). *Language and mind.* New York, NY: Harcourt Brace Jovanovich.

Chomsky, N. (1986). *Knowledge of language.* New York, NY: Praeger.

Chomsky, N. (1995). *The minimalist program.* Cambridge, MA: MIT Press.

Cummins, J. (1979). Cognitive academic language proficiency, linguistic interdependence, the optimum age question and some other matters. *Working Papers on Bilingualism 19*, 121–129.

Cummins, J. (1981). The role of primary language development in promoting educational success for language minority students. In California State Department of Education (Ed.), *Schooling and language minority students: A theoretical framework* (pp. 3–49). Los Angeles, CA: Evaluation, Dissemination and Assessment Center, California State University.

Cummins, J. (2000). *Language, power and pedagogy: Bilingual children in the crossfire.* Clevedon, United Kingdom: Multilingual Matters.

Dickinson, D., Golinkoff, R. M., & Hirsh-Pasek, K. (2010). Speaking out for language: Why language is central for learning development. *Educational Researcher, 29*, 305–310.

Dickinson, D. K., McCabe, A., Anastasopoulos, L., Peisner-Feinberg, E., & Poe, M. D. (2003). The comprehensive language approach to early literacy: The interrelationships among vocabulary, phonological sensitivity, and print knowledge among preschool-aged children. *Journal of Educational Psychology, 95*(3), 465–481.

Dickinson, D., McCabe, A., & Essex, M. (2006). A window of opportunity we must open to all: The case for preschool with high-quality support for language and literacy. In D. Dickinson & S. Neuman (Eds.), *Handbook of early literacy research* (Vol. 2, pp. 11–28). New York, NY: Guilford Press.

Dyson, A. (2001). Writing and children's symbolic repertoires: Development unhinged. In S. Neuman & D. Dickinson (Eds.), *Handbook of early literacy research* (Vol. 1, pp. 126–141). New York, NY: Guilford Press.

Ehri, L. (2009). Learning to read in English: Teaching phonics to beginning readers from diverse backgrounds. In L. M. Morrow, R. Rueda, & D. Lapp (Eds.), *Handbook of research on literacy and diversity* (pp. 292–319). New York, NY: Guilford Press.

Gee, J. P. (2001). A sociocultural perspective on early literacy development. In S. Neuman & D. Dickinson (Eds.), *Handbook of early literacy research* (Vol. 1, pp. 30–42). New York, NY: Guilford Press.

Geers, A. (2006). Spoken language in children with cochlear implants. In P. Spencer & M. Marschark (Eds.), *Advances in spoken language development of deaf and hard of hearing children* (pp. 244–270). New York, NY: Oxford University Press.

Geers, A., Nicholas, J. G., & Moog, A. (2007). Estimating the influence of cochlear implantation on language development in children. *Audiological Medicine, 5,* 262–273. doi:10.1080/16513860701659404

Grossi, E. (1990). Applying psychogenesis principles to literacy instruction of lower class children in Brazil. In Y. Goodman (Ed.), *How children construct literacy* (pp. 99–114). Newark, DE: International Reading Association.

Hall, M. L., & Bavelier, D. (2010). Working memory, deafness and sign language. In M. Marschark & P. Spencer (Eds.), *The Oxford handbook of deaf studies, Language, and Education* (Vol. 2, pp. 458–478). New York, NY: Oxford University Press.

Halliday, M. A. K. (1973). *Explorations in the functions of language.* London, United Kingdom: Arnold.

Halliday, M. A. K. (1975a). *Learning how to mean.* London, United Kingdom: Arnold.

Halliday, M. A. K. (1975b). Talking one's way in. In A. Davies (Ed.), *Problems of language and learning* (pp. 8–26). London, United Kingdom: Heinemann.

Halliday, M. A. K. (1989). *Spoken and written language.* Oxford, United Kingdom: Oxford University Press.

Halliday, M. A. K. (1993). Towards a language-based theory of learning. *Linguistics and Education, 5,* 93–116.

Harris, J., Golinkoff, R. M., & Hirsh-Pasek, K. (2011). Lessons from the crib for the classroom: How children really learn vocabulary. In S. Neuman & D. Dickinson (Eds.), *Handbook of early literacy research* (Vol. 3, pp. 49–65). New York, NY: Guilford Press.

Hart, B., & Risley, T. R. (1995). *Meaningful differences in the everyday experience of young American children.* Baltimore, MD: Brookes.

Hemphill, L., & Snow, C. (1996). Language and literacy development: Discontinuities and differences. In D. Olson & N. Torrance (Eds.),

Handbook of education and human development (pp. 173–201). Oxford, United Kingdom: Blackwell.

Hoff, E. (2003). How social contexts support and shape language development. *Developmental Review, 26*, 55–88.

Kaiser, A. P., Roberts, M. Y., & McLeod, R. H. (2011). Young children with language impairments: Challenges in transition to reading. In S. B. Neuman & D. K. Dickinson (Eds.), *Handbook of early literacy research* (Vol. 3, pp. 228–241). New York, NY: Guilford Press.

Kress, G. (1994). *Learning to write* (2nd ed.). London, United Kingdom: Routledge and Kegan Paul.

Marschark, M. (1993). *Psychological development of deaf children.* New York, NY: Oxford University Press.

Marschark, M., & Hauser, P. (2008). *Deaf cognition: Foundations and outcomes.* New York, NY: Oxford University Press.

Marschark, M., Lang, H., & Albertini, J. (2002). *Educating deaf students: From research to practice.* New York, NY: Oxford University Press.

Marschark, M., & Wauters, L. (2011). Cognitive functioning in deaf adults and children. In M. Marschark & P. Spencer (Eds.), *The Oxford handbook of deaf studies, language, and education,* (Vol. 1, 2nd ed., pp. 486–499). New York, NY: Oxford University Press.

Mayberry, R., del Giudice, A., & Lieberman, A. (2011). Reading achievement in relation to phonological coding and awareness in deaf readers: A meta-analysis. *Journal of Deaf Studies and Deaf Education, 16*, 164–188. doi:10.1093/deafed/enq049

Mayer, C. (2007). What matters in the early literacy development of deaf children. *Journal of Deaf Studies and Deaf Education, 12,* 411–431. doi:10.1093/deafed/enm020

Mayer, C. (2009). Issues in second language literacy education with learners who are deaf. *International Journal of Bilingual Education and Bilingualism 12(3),* 325–334.

Mayer, C., & Leigh, G. (2010). The changing context for sign bilingual education programs: Issues in language and the development of literacy. *International Journal of Bilingualism and Bilingual Education, 13(2),* 175–186.

Mayer, C., & Trezek, B. J. (2014). Is reading different for deaf individuals?: Reexamining the role of phonology. *American Annals of the Deaf, 159*(4), 359–371.

Mayer, C., & Trezek, B. J. (2011). New (?) answers to old questions: Literacy development in D/HH learners. In D. Moores (Ed.), *Partners in Education: Issues and Trends from the 21st International Congress on the Education of the Deaf* (pp. 62–74). Washington, DC: Gallaudet University Press.

Mayer, C., & Wells, G. (1996). Can the linguistic interdependence theory support a bilingual model of literacy education for deaf students? *Journal of Deaf Studies and Deaf Education, 1(2),* 93–107.

Mashie, S. (1995). *Educating deaf children bilingually.* Washington, DC: Gallaudet University Press.

Mitchell, R., & Karchmer, M. (2004). Chasing the mythical ten percent: Parental hearing status of deaf and hard of hearing students in the United States. *Sign Language Studies, 4(2),*138–163.

Moeller, M. P., Tomblin, J. B., Yoshinaga-Itano, C., Connor, C. M. & Jerger, S. (2007). Current state of knowledge: Language and literacy of children with hearing impairment. *Ear and Hearing, 28(6),* 740–753.

Muter, V., Hulme, C., Snowling, M. J., & Stevenson, J. (2004). Phonemes, rimes, vocabulary and grammatical skills as foundations of reading development: Evidence from a longitudinal study. *Developmental Psychology, 40(5),* 665–681.

National Early Literacy Panel. (2008). *Developing early literacy: Report of the National Early Literacy Panel.* Washington, DC: National Institute for Literacy. Available at http://lincs.ed.gov/publications/pdf/NELPReport09.pdf

Nelson, K. (1996). *Language in cognitive development: The emergence of the mediated mind.* New York, NY: Cambridge University Press.

Neuman, S. (2011). The challenge of teaching vocabulary in early education. In S. Neuman & D. Dickinson (Eds.), *Handbook of early literacy research* (Vol. 3, pp. 358–372). New York, NY: Guilford Press.

Neuman, S., & Dwyer, J. (2009). Missing in action: Vocabulary instruction in pre-K. *Reading Teacher, 62,* 384–392.

Olson, D. (1977). From utterance to text: The bias of language in speech and writing. *Harvard Educational Review, 47,* 257–281.

Olson, D. (1993). Thinking about thinking: Learning how to take statements and hold beliefs. *Educational Psychologist, 28,* 7–23.

Owens, R. E. (2012). *Language development: An introduction.* Upper Saddle River, NJ: Pearson Education.

Paatsch, L. E., Blaney, P. J., Sarant, J. Z., & Bow, C. P. (2006). The effects of speech production and vocabulary training on different components of spoken language performance. *Journal of Deaf Studies and Deaf Education, 11(1),* 39–55.

Paris, S. G. (2009). Constrained skills—so what? In K. M. Leander, D. K. Dickinson, M. K. Hundley, R. T. Jimenez, & V. J. Risko (Eds.), *59th yearbook of the National Reading Conference* (pp. 34–44). Oak Creek, WI: National Reading Conference.

Paris, S. G. (2011). Developmental differences in early reading skills. In S. Neuman & D. Dickinson (Eds.), *Handbook of early literacy research* (Vol. 3, pp. 228–241). New York, NY: Guilford Press.

Paul, P. (1998). *Literacy and deafness: The development of reading, writing, and literate thought.* Needham Heights, MA: Allyn & Bacon.

Paul, P. (2009). *Language and deafness* (4th ed.). Sudbury, MA: Jones & Bartlett.

Paul, P. (2011). Language and literacy issues. In D. Moores (Ed.), *Partners in education: Issues and trends from the 21st International Congress on the Education of the Deaf* (pp. 51–61). Washington, DC: Gallaudet University Press.

Paul, P., & Lee, C. (2010). Qualitative-similarity hypothesis. *American Annals of the Deaf, 154(5),* 456–462.

Perez, B. (2004). Writing across writing systems. In B. Perez (Ed.), *Sociocultural contexts of language and literacy* (2nd ed., pp. 57–75). Hillsdale, NJ: Erlbaum.

Perfetti, C. (1987). Language, speech, and print: Some asymmetries in the acquisition of literacy. In R. Horowitz & S. Samuels (Eds.), *Comprehending oral and written language* (pp. 355–369). San Diego, CA: Academic Press.

Perfetti, C. A., & Sandak, R. (2000). Reading optimally builds on spoken language. *Journal of Deaf Studies and Deaf Education, 5(1),* 32–50.

Pisoni, D. B., Conway, C. M., Kronenberger, W., Henning, S., & Anaya, S. (2010). Executive function, cognitive control, and sequence learning in deaf children with cochlear implants. In M. Marschark & P. Spencer (Eds.), *The Oxford handbook of deaf studies, language, and education* (2nd ed., Vol. 1, pp. 439–457). New York, NY: Oxford University Press.

Pugh, K. R., Sandak, R., Frost, S. J., Moore, D. L., & Mencl, W. E. (2006). Neurobiological investigations of skilled and impaired reading. In D. Dickinson & S. Neuman (Eds.), *Handbook of early literacy research* (Vol. 2, pp. 64–74). New York, NY: Guilford Press.

Ramsey, C. (1997). *Deaf children in public schools*. Washington, DC: Gallaudet University Press.

Rice, M. (1989). Children's language acquisition. *American Psychologist, 44(2),* 149–156.

Rönnberg, J. (2011). Working memory, neuroscience, and language evidence from deaf and hard-of-hearing individuals. In M. Marschark & P. Spencer (Eds.), *The Oxford handbook of deaf studies, language, and education* (Vol. 2, pp. 439–457). New York, NY: Oxford University Press.

Rottenberg, C., & Searfoss, L. (1992). Becoming literate in a pre-school class: Literacy development of hearing-impaired children. *Journal of Reading Behavior, 24,* 463–479.

Rowe, S. M., & Wertsch, J. (2002). Vygotsky's model of cognitive development. In U. Goswami (Ed.), *Blackwell handbook of childhood cognitive development* (pp. 538–554). Malden, MA: Blackwell.

Scarborough, H. (2001). Connecting early language and literacy to later reading (dis)abilities: Evidence, theory and practice. In S. Neuman & D. Dickinson (Eds.), *Handbook of early literacy research* (Vol. 1, pp. 97–110). New York, NY: Guilford Press.

Schick, B., Marschark, M., & Spencer, P. (2006). *Advances in the sign language development of deaf children*. New York, NY: Oxford University Press.

Small, A., & Mason, D. (2008). American Sign Language (ASL) bilingual bicultural education. In N. Hornberger (Ed.), *Encyclopedia of language and education* (Vol. 5, pp. 133–150). Boston, MA: Springer.

Spencer, P. (2010). Play and theory of mind: Indicators and engines of early cognitive growth. In M. Marschark & P. Spencer (Eds.), *The Oxford handbook of deaf Studies, language, and education* (Vol. 2, pp. 407–424). New York, NY: Oxford University Press.

Spencer, P., & Marschark, M. (2006). *Advances in spoken language development for deaf and hard-of-hearing children*. New York, NY: Oxford University Press.

Spencer, P., Marschark, M., & Spencer, L. (2011). Cochlear implants: Advances, issues and implications. In M. Marschark & P. Spencer (Eds.), *The Oxford Handbook of Deaf Studies, Language and Education* (2nd ed., Vol. 1, pp. 452–471). New York, NY: Oxford University Press.

Stanovich, K. (1986). Matthew effects in reading: Some consequences of individual differences in the acquisition of literacy. *Reading Research Quarterly, 21,* 360–407.

Storch, S., & Whitehurst, G. (2002). Oral language and code-related precursors to reading: Evidence from a longitudinal structural model. *Developmental Psychology, 38(6),* 934–947.

Stredler-Brown, A. (2010). Communication choices and outcomes during the early years: An assessment and evidence-based approach. In M. Marschark & P. Spencer (Eds.), *The Oxford handbook of deaf studies, language, and Education* (Vol. 2, pp. 292–315). New York, NY: Oxford University Press.

Sylva, K., Melhuish, E., Sammons, P., Siraj-Blatchford, I., & Taggart, B. (2011). Preschool quality and educational outcomes at age 11: Low quality has little benefit. *Journal of Early Childhood Research, 9(2),* 109–124.

Traxler, C. (2000). The Stanford Achievement Test, 9th edition: National norming and performance standards for deaf and hard of hearing students. *Journal of Deaf Studies and Deaf Education, 5,* 337–348. doi:10.1093/deafed/5.4.337

Trezek, B. J., Wang, Y., & Paul, P. V. (2010). *Reading and deafness: Theory, research and practice.* Clifton Park, NY: Cengage Learning.

Vasilyeva, M., & Waterfall, H. (2011). Variability in language development: Relation to socioeconomic status and environmental input. In S. Neuman & D. Dickinson (Eds.), *Handbook of early literacy research* (Vol. 3, pp. 36–48). New York, NY: Guilford Press.

Vygotsky, L. S. (1978). *Mind in society: The development of higher psychological processes.* Cambridge, MA: Harvard University Press.

Vygotsky, L. S. (1987). Thinking and speech (trans. N. Minnick). In R. W. Reiber & A. S. Carlton (Eds.), *The collected works of L. S. Vygotsky* (Vol. 1). New York, NY: Plenum Press.

Watson, R. (1996). Talk about text: Literate discourse and metaliterate knowledge. In K. Reeder, J. Shapiro, R. Watson, & H. Goelman (Eds.), *Literate apprenticeships: The emergence of language and literacy in the preschool years* (pp. 81–100). Norwood, NJ: Ablex.

Watson, R. (2001). Literacy and oral language: Implications for early literacy acquisition. In S. Neuman & D. Dickinson (Eds.), *Handbook of early literacy research* (Vol. 1, pp. 43–53). New York, NY: Guilford Press.

Wells, G. (1981). *Learning through interaction: The study of language development.* Cambridge, United Kingdom: Cambridge University Press.

Wells, G. (1994). The complementary contributions of Halliday and Vygotsky to a "language-based theory of learning." *Linguistics and Education, 6,* 41–90.

Wells, G. (2001). *Action, talk and text: Learning and teaching through inquiry.* New York, NY: Teachers College Press.

Wells, G. (2009). *The meaning makers: Learning to talk and talking to learn* (2nd ed.). Bristol, United Kingdom: Multilingual Matters.

Wertsch, J. (1985). *Vygotsky and the social formation of mind.* Cambridge, MA: Harvard University Press.

Whitehurst, G., & Lonigan, C. (1998). Child development and emergent literacy. *Child Development, 68,* 848–872.

Williams, C. (2004). Emergent literacy development of deaf children. *Journal of Deaf Studies and Deaf Education, 9,* 352–365.

3

Early Reading

Attention to the role of early literacy experiences in the development of later reading abilities has increased considerably over the past decade, as evidenced by the growing number of governmental reports and policy papers published on this topic in English-speaking countries such as Australia (Commonwealth of Australia, 2005), Canada (Canadian Language and Literacy Research Network, 2009), Ireland (Kennedy et al., 2012), New Zealand (Education Review Office, 2011), the United Kingdom (Rose, 2006), and the United States (National Reading Panel, 2000; National Early Literacy Panel, 2008). Many of these publications have focused on identifying how children learn to read, exploring how educators can foster the development of abilities and skills, and/or describing instructional practices associated with the early literacy learning years.

In terms of scientific research available on the development of early literacy in children, arguably the US National Early Literacy Panel (NELP) report (2008) represents the most comprehensive synthesis available to date. The need for a study of early literacy research followed closely after the publication of the National Reading Panel's findings (2000), as this original review panel did not specifically address the research findings related to practices employed with children from birth through age five or kindergarten. Therefore, the main goal of the NELP was to conduct an extensive review of available research and identify parenting activities along with educational interventions and instructional practices that foster the development of children's early literacy skills. The panel was primarily interested in identifying the skills and abilities in young children that predict later reading, writing, and spelling outcomes and in exploring what instructional, environmental, and child-based characteristics contribute to or inhibit gains in these areas.

Consistent with the theoretical framework described in chapter 2, we would suggest that the literacy requisites well documented for hearing children must also be mastered by deaf children in order for them to become proficient readers and writers (see also Mayer, 2007; Paul & Lee, 2010; Mayer & Trezek, 2011, 2014; Trezek, Wang, & Paul, 2010). Therefore, we will begin this chapter by providing a brief overview of the background and general findings of the NELP and then describe in greater detail the variables specifically related to the development of early reading. The abilities and skills explicated in this chapter align with phase 3 (linking language to print) within our theoretical model of literacy development outlined in chapter 2. Given the early literacy risk factors often associated with the presence of a hearing loss (e.g., language development), we will briefly explore the challenges to skill acquisition often documented for the population of children with language impairments and draw parallels from this literature to the population of deaf learners. We will also summarize the NELP's recommendations for efficacious programs, activities, and pedagogical approaches that foster the development and mastery of skills in young children. Finally, we will explore implications for practice by commenting on strategies that can be employed to supplement and support early reading experiences for those children requiring differentiation, in addition to recommending directions for future research in the area of early reading.

NATIONAL EARLY LITERACY PANEL (NELP)

The NELP was convened by the National Center for Family Literacy in the United States during 2002 to represent a multidisciplinary team of experts drawn from the areas of early literacy and language, early childhood education, reading, cognition, English as a second language, pediatrics, special education, and research methodology. The charge of the panel was to conduct a synthesis of scientific research related to early literacy skills and examine environmental influences on development. While approximately two thousand studies were originally identified for review, the criteria for inclusion in the meta-analysis (i.e., studies published in English in refereed journals representing empirical research examining English and other alphabetic languages with children between the ages of birth and five or kindergarten) narrowed the available pool of research articles that included both correlational and experimental studies and represented publications from various countries. As a result of its meta-analytic review, the NELP was able to determine the specific domains of early literacy skills and abilities that strongly predict later conventional literacy (e.g., decoding, comprehension, spelling, writing) and which programs and practices lead to the successful acquisition of skills and abilities within these domains.

Results of this review (National Early Literacy Panel, 2008) revealed six early/precursor literacy skills that are correlated with later measures of literacy development. These skills were identified as having medium to large predictive relations that maintained these associations, even after controlling for other variables (e.g., SES, IQ). The six early literacy skills included (1) phonological awareness, or the ability to recognize and manipulate the phonemes of the spoken language (e.g., words, syllables, phonemes) independent of meaning; (2) alphabet knowledge, or the understanding of the names and sounds associated with printed letters; (3) phonological memory, or the ability to remember spoken information for a short period of time; (4) rapid automatic naming of letters or digits presented in a random order; (5) rapid automatic naming of objects (represented by pictures) or colors that appear in a random order; and (6) writing, demonstrating the ability to write letters in isolation or write one's name upon request.

Five additional early literacy skills were also identified as promising correlates of later conventional literacy as a result of the NELP's meta-analysis. However, unlike the six aforementioned abilities, these five skills were only moderately correlated with one measure of later literacy achievement, and their predictive nature either did not persist or had not been directly evaluated by researchers. These five skills included (1) concepts of print, including knowledge of print conventions (e.g., directionality of text) and text features (e.g., title, author); (2) print knowledge, which includes elements of alphabet knowledge, concepts of print, and early decoding; (3) reading readiness, described as a combination of alphabet knowledge, concepts of print, vocabulary, memory, and phonological awareness; (4) visual processing, the ability to match and discriminate visually presented symbols; and (5) oral language,[1] or the ability to comprehend and produce spoken language including vocabulary and grammar.

According to the findings of the NELP, skills in the areas of phonological awareness and alphabet knowledge reflected considerable relations with later decoding and comprehension abilities. Other related studies exploring the influence of phonological awareness, letter knowledge, and oral language on early decoding skills (e.g., Lonigan, Burgess, & Anthony, 2000; Storch & Whitehurst, 2002) revealed that phonological awareness and letter knowledge contributed unique variance in developing and predicting later decoding skills. Therefore, in the following sections, we will focus on the areas of phonological awareness, letter knowledge, and alphabet knowledge and the reciprocal relations that exist among them (Burgess, 2006; Ehri & Roberts, 2006; Lonigan, 2006). We will also highlight the roles of the remaining skills identified by the NELP (e.g., rapid automatic naming, oral language) in the development of these three central abilities and their impact on early reading

---

[1] As we have stated earlier, when the term *oral language* is used, it reflects the terminology employed in the original source (e.g., NELP, a published study, etc.). This term is often used synonymously with *spoken language* in the broader literature in the field of literacy. It is only in the field of deafness that the distinction between oral and spoken language merits attention.

acquisition. Topics related to spelling and writing will be discussed in chapter 4.

PHONOLOGICAL AND PHONEMIC AWARENESS

Phonological awareness is defined as the ability to detect and manipulate the sound structures of oral language. It is often used as an umbrella term that includes a range of abilities such as recognizing and working with syllables, rhymes, and individual phonemes (i.e., sounds) of the language (Bryant, MacLean, Bradley, & Crossland, 1990; Burgess, 2006; National Early Literacy Panel, 2008; Wagner, Torgesen, & Rashotte, 1994). However, some researchers have suggested that phonological awareness refers specifically to the manipulation of language at the phoneme level (e.g., Morais, Cary, Alegria, & Bertelson, 1979), while others have used the term *phonemic awareness* to describe this skill (e.g., Phillips & Torgesen, 2006; National Reading Panel, 2000). Still others argue for a single conceptualization and a global definition of phonological awareness that includes several abilities regardless of their linguistic complexity (e.g., Anthony & Lonigan, 2004; Stahl & Murray, 1994). The term *phonological sensitivity* has also been recommended to refer to the broad array of abilities and skills associated with manipulating the sound structures of oral language (e.g., Stanovich, 1992).

Given the debate and confusion regarding definitions of phonological awareness, we recognize the importance of explicitly defining the terms we will use to refer to specific abilities and skills. We support the notion offered by Phillips and Torgesen (2006) that phonemic awareness is a conceptual understanding of language that also behaves like a skill. Using this two-pronged explanation, the conceptual understanding involves children's ability to recognize that words can be segmented into parts and that parts of language can be combined to form words. This knowledge then sets the stage for developing the specific skills (e.g., phoneme isolation, blending, segmenting) necessary to detect and manipulate increasingly complex linguistic elements.

Therefore, we will use the term *phonemic awareness* to describe the "explicit understanding that words are composed of segments of sound smaller than a syllable, as well as knowledge, or awareness, of the distinctive features of individual phonemes themselves" (Phillips & Torgesen, 2006, p. 102). The term *phonological awareness* will be used to refer to "supraphoneme awareness tasks that involve detection or manipulation of larger linguistic units" (Lonigan, 2006, p. 81), such as syllables, onsets, and rimes. Further recognizing the dual conceptualization of these phonological constructs (i.e., conceptual understanding and skill), we will make a distinction between the two by referring to phonological awareness *abilities* in contrast to phonemic awareness *skills*. The term *phonological sensitivity* will then be used when discussing the overarching category that includes both phonological and phonemic awareness.

Development

Regardless of terminology, the majority of researchers agree that the development of phonological sensitivity occurs in stages that parallel a hierarchical model (see Adams, 1990; Burgess, 2006). As they mature, children are able to acquire increasingly complex abilities that move from recognizing larger, more concrete aspects of language, such as words and syllables, to the smaller, more abstract linguistic units, such as phonemes. A review of studies conducted in several countries (e.g., Australia, New Zealand, United Kingdom, United States) revealed that phonological sensitivity is limited in two- and three-year-olds, rapidly develops between the ages of three and five, and is relatively secure by age six. This finding insinuates that there is a stable trajectory of phonological sensitivity development for the English language (see Gillon, 2004). While it has also been demonstrated that development tends to follow a particular order, moving from words to syllables, to onsets and rimes, to phoneme-level skills (see Burgess, 2006, for discussion), the acquisition process appears to be overlapping in nature, with some abilities and skills developing simultaneously (see Pufpaff, 2009, for review).

This specific developmental trajectory of phonological sensitivity may also be explained by the lexical restructuring model or hypothesis (see Fowler, 1991; Metsala & Walley, 1998; Walley, Metsala, & Garlock, 2003). This model suggests that young children initially acquire and store words as whole units and that lexical representations do not become "fine-grained and segmented" (Lonigan, 2006, p. 84) until the preschool and early elementary years, when the ability to remember words becomes increasingly demanding. Evidence indicates that growth in vocabulary contributes to the lexical restructuring process, as it becomes necessary for children to recall words in terms of their phonological components and similarities in order for word learning, storage, and retrieval to become more efficient. The application of the lexical restructuring model also explains why children with smaller vocabularies may experience challenges and/or delays in developing phonological awareness abilities, since the need to move from holistic to more specified word representations for these children has yet to be realized (Lonigan, 2006).

The lexical restructuring model also supports the importance of two related abilities identified by the NELP: phonological memory and phonological access to lexical store. As previously indicated, phonological memory is the ability to remember spoken information for a short period of time. Temporary storage of oral language in working (short-term) memory requires information to be coded and retrieved using phonological components, and access to lexical store refers to the efficiency with which these phonological codes are retrieved from permanent memory. Lexical access is typically measured by rapid automatic naming of pictures, colors, letters, and/or digits, so abilities in this domain are often referred to simply as rapid automatic naming, or RAN. The speed and efficiency of retrieving phonological information from short- and long-term memory become increasingly important as children begin to decode printed words (see discussion later in this chapter), since during this process cognitive energy needs to shift to identifying and comprehending words (Chall, 1996; Lonigan, 2006).

Importance

The importance of phonological sensitivity to the development of conventional literacy is supported by studies documenting the causal role between these abilities and skills and the development of literacy in alphabetic languages such as English (e.g., Ball & Blachman, 1988; National Early Literacy Panel, 2008; Wagner et al., 1994). Along with phonological memory and phonological access to lexical store, phonological sensitivity abilities have been strongly associated with subsequent word decoding skills and with stable individual differences demonstrated beginning in preschool (e.g., Burgess & Lonigan, 1998; Lonigan et al., 2000; Wagner, Torgesen, Laughton, Simmons, & Roshotte, 1993; Wagner et al., 1994; Wagner et al., 1997). Even after controlling for variance because of age, letter knowledge, and oral language abilities, measures of phonological sensitivity administered in preschool reliably predict children's later word decoding skills (Burgess, 2002, 2006) and subsequent phonological sensitivity abilities (Bryant et al., 1990; Burgess, 2006; Burgess & Lonigan, 1998).

Support for the role of phonological sensitivity in the development of early and later conventional reading skills can also be drawn from studies of struggling readers, as deficits in core phonological sensitivity abilities have been consistently documented for the majority of children identified as poor readers (e.g., Stanovich, 1988; Wagner et al., 1994; Wagner et al., 1997). Additionally, the notion of a "double deficit," or delays in both phonological sensitivity and vocabulary/lexical knowledge, has been documented for many poor readers (e.g., Stanovich & Siegel, 1994). The relationship between vocabulary acquisition and the development of phonological sensitivity illustrated by the lexical restructuring hypothesis provides further theoretical support to substantiate this phenomenon.

There is some debate about the predictive reliability and importance of various types of phonological sensitivity abilities. For example, some researchers argue that phonemic awareness skills, such as phoneme blending and segmenting, are more highly associated with later reading achievement (Hatcher & Hulme, 1999; Hulme, 2002; Hulme et al.,

2002; Hulme, Muter, & Snowling, 1998; Muter, Hulme, Snowling, & Taylor, 1997; Nation & Hulme, 1997) than are other phonological sensitivity abilities, such as rhyming. Others indicate that rhyming may simply contribute differently to the developmental process (e.g., Bryant, 1998; Goswami & Bryant, 1990). However, there is a growing body of research evidence to support the position that phonological sensitivity should be considered a "unitary construct" (Burgess, 2006, p. 91) and that all phonological tasks, regardless of linguistic complexity (e.g., onset and rime, phoneme level), reflect the same underlying abilities (e.g., Anthony et al., 2002; Schatschneider, Francis, Foorman, Fletcher, & Mehta, 1999; Wagner et al., 1997).

While phonological sensitivity abilities clearly appear to be necessary to facilitate the acquisition of early reading, this knowledge alone is not sufficient for the development of early reading abilities such as word identification skills (Phillips & Torgesen, 2006). Results of recent investigations indicate that phonological sensitivity was predictive of both letter and alphabet knowledge and that the relationship among these abilities appears to be bidirectional in nature (Burgess, 2002; Burgess & Lonigan, 1998; Lonigan et al., 2000). Therefore, the roles that letter and alphabet knowledge play in development of early word reading abilities and reciprocity with phonological sensitivity abilities will be explored in the following section.

LETTER AND ALPHABET KNOWLEDGE

As with the term *phonological awareness, alphabet knowledge* is often used as an umbrella term that encompasses both letter knowledge (ability to name individual letters of the alphabet) and knowledge of the alphabetic principle (understanding the link between letters of the alphabet and sounds). We distinguish these abilities and recognize the difference between naming letters (graphemes) and developing the alphabetic principle, or the ability to associate graphemes with specific phonemes of the language. While we will make the distinction between the two, we also acknowledge that letter and alphabetic knowledge are closely intertwined.

The majority of researchers agree that there is a reciprocal relationship between phonological sensitivity abilities and letter knowledge (Burgess & Lonigan, 1998; de Jong & Olson, 2004; Murray, Stahl, & Ivey, 1996). While knowledge of letter names may not be necessary for children to develop phonological awareness abilities (e.g., recognizing rhyme), the development of phonemic awareness skills appears to be enhanced by letter knowledge (Burgess & Lonigan, 1998). One explanation is that letter knowledge draws children's attention to the notion that words are constructed of smaller units (Burgess, 2006) and further illustrates how spoken language is represented in print (Phillips &

Torgesen, 2006). Studies have also demonstrated that letter knowledge facilitates the ability to manipulate language at the level of the phoneme and that higher levels of letter knowledge are associated with improved phonemic awareness skills (e.g., Bowey, 1994; Stahl & Murray, 1994; Wagner et al., 1994, 1997).

The phonological information embedded within the letter names themselves also contributes to understanding the relationship between the development of letter knowledge and phonological sensitivity. Work conducted by Treiman and colleagues (e.g., Treiman, 1992; Treiman, Tincoff, & Richmond-Welty, 1997; Treiman, Tincoff, Rodriguez, Mouzaki, & Francis, 1998) suggests that interacting with the phonological aspects of letter names enhances children's early print experiences because there is phonological information included in all letters except the consonant w and the short vowel sounds (see Ehri & Roberts, 2006). For example, when saying the letter name d in English (/d/ /e/), the phoneme /d/ is produced by the initial sound. Similarly, when saying the letter name m (/e/ /m/), the phoneme /m/ is produced by the final sound. This connection between letter names and the phonemes they represent can be exploited when developing the alphabetic principle, as many children already know letter names prior to receiving instruction in linking graphemes to the phonemes they represent. Investigations have also revealed that children learn grapheme-phoneme relations more readily when letter names contain relevant phonological information and that this effect is even more pronounced when the phonological source appears at the beginning (d) as compared with the end (m) of the letter name (see Treiman et al., 1998; Burgess, 2006, for discussions).

These descriptions and research findings also help illuminate the differences between letter and alphabet knowledge skills and fingerspelling. In both the one- and two-handed manual alphabets, hand configurations and movements are used to represent graphemes of the written language. As discussed above, the development of letter knowledge involves not only recognizing graphemes but also naming them (e.g., /e/ /m/ for m), which inherently involves a phonological component. Fingerspelling, on the other hand, maps onto a graphic (not a phonologic) representation of the letter and, unless accompanied simultaneously by spoken language, does not include phonological information about the grapheme's name. Therefore, it is important to acknowledge that fingerspelling and letter knowledge should not be considered synonymous.

A study conducted by Harris and Beech (1998) further supports this position and highlights the differential contribution of fingerspelling to early literacy development as compared with the role of letter knowledge discussed in this chapter. In this investigation, the researchers found that while deaf children's knowledge of British Sign Language (BSL) and fingerspelling were positively correlated with each other and associated with language comprehension, they were not found to correlate with gains in reading. Additionally, both BSL and fingerspelling skills were negatively correlated with oral language abilities, and signing skills were negatively correlated with implicit phonological awareness (see chapter 1 for review). Based on the descriptions and findings described here, it is important to keep the distinction between fingerspelling and letter knowledge in mind when teaching and assessing abilities among deaf children, to ensure that these skills are recognized as different and not conflated.

An additional aspect to consider in terms of developing letter knowledge for all young literacy learners relates to the graphemes themselves and the need for children to identify and name both upper- and lower-case letters. In English, there are only twelve pairs of upper- and lower-case letters that share similar written configurations (e.g., *S* and *s*, *W* and *w*); therefore, children must learn forty distinctive graphemes and the phonemes associated with them. While upper-case letters tend to be learned more readily, since their shapes are generally more distinct (see Ehri & Roberts, 2006, for discussion), it also needs to be recognized that lower-case letters appear more frequently in texts and therefore may need to be prioritized during instruction.

While children often evidence their greatest growth in letter knowledge between the ages of four and five (e.g., Warden & Boettcher, 1990), it has been suggested that children as young as two years old could recognize phonological information within letter names; however, the understanding of the alphabetic principle appears to develop at a much slower rate (see Burgess, 2006, for discussion). For example, in a study of approximately two hundred kindergarteners, nearly half knew fewer than seven grapheme-phoneme relationships (Wagner et al., 1994). These findings have led researchers to question whether this reflects the developmental trajectory of phonological processing abilities or a lack of direct, skill-based instruction focused on teaching letter names and grapheme-phoneme relations (Burgess, 2006; Wagner et al., 1997). Contributing to this situation, it has also been observed that letter knowledge instruction is often delayed until after age three because of an underestimation of preschool children's abilities in this area (Burgess, 2002, 2006). Because reading is considered a learned behavior, direct teaching is essential to develop letter and alphabetic knowledge and apply this information to early reading activities through the development of phonemic decoding abilities (Adams, 1990; Braze, McRoberts, & McDonough, 2011; Burgess, 2006; Chall, 1996).

PHONEMIC DECODING

Phonemic decoding, or using knowledge of the alphabetic principle to relate phonemes of the language to a sequence of written graphemes, is necessary for children to read words they have not previously encountered in print (Phillips & Torgesen, 2006). Children use this same combination of skills to segment words by phonemes and relate them to graphemes in the process of phonemic encoding or spelling (see chapter 4 for further discussion). Phonemic awareness also plays an essential role in the phonemic decoding process in two ways. First, the conceptual understanding that phonemes of the language can be combined to form words makes the decoding or "sounding out" process understandable to young children. Second, specific phonemic awareness skills such as phoneme identification and blending are necessary to facilitate the decoding process (Phillips & Torgesen, 2006).

While it has been demonstrated that children use a variety of strategies in early reading, including the use of phonological analogies and prediction (Ehri & Roberts, 2006), understanding the systematic relationship between graphemes and phonemes has been identified as the single most reliable strategy for identifying unknown words in print (Share, 1995, 1999; Share & Stanovich, 1995). Because of the nature of the English language, the words young children first encounter in print typically have a consonant-vowel-consonant pattern and often differ by only one grapheme. Therefore, a "global or gestalt image of a word is not sufficient" (Phillips & Torgesen, 2006, p. 106) to reliably and consistently recognize it. Children must learn to read through words, connecting specific phonemes to each individual grapheme, in order to facilitate the development of dependable phonemic decoding skills (Share & Stanovich, 1995).

Development

The process of developing phonemic decoding skills appears to occur in stages that become increasingly specified in each subsequent phase (see Ehri, 2005; Ehri & Roberts, 2006). For example, children who lack phonological sensitivity abilities and letter knowledge fall into the *pre-alphabetic* phase of development. During this period, children employ a variety of strategies, including relying on visual configurations of words, pictures, and context cues, and general memorization of stories that have been previously read to them (see also Chall, 1996). Children are not actually reading in the conventional sense at this stage, because they lack the connection between the words they recite and those that appear in print. This is evidenced by their inability to point directly to individual words as they "read" (see Morris, 1993).

As children begin to learn names of graphemes and the phonemes associated with them and have developed the conceptual understanding of phonemic awareness, they enter the *partial alphabetic* stage. Using their basic knowledge of grapheme-phoneme relationships, such as initial and final phoneme identification, children employ this knowledge, along with contextual and picture cues, to begin to make connections with words in print. Children at this stage confuse similarly spelled words, because they have not mastered the full alphabetic system, most notably vowels. This lack of knowledge is further reflected in young children's spelling, which often excludes medial vowel sounds (Ehri, 2005; Ehri & Roberts, 2006).

Once phonemic awareness skills such as blending and segmenting are taught, children move into the *full alphabetic* phase of development and use this knowledge to decode and encode words both in isolation and within connected text. The final stage of development, *consolidated alphabetic*, develops during the elementary years and involves decoding and encoding multisyllabic words, understanding syllable types, and applying morphemic analysis (Ehri, 2005; Ehri & Roberts, 2006; see also Chall, 1996; National Reading Panel, 2000). Phonemic decoding and its prerequisite abilities (e.g., letter and alphabet knowledge, concepts of print) have been described as constrained skills, ones that tend to be learned early and entirely. In other words, most children acquire these skills by the age of eight, and that simply rate of mastery, rather than level of final knowledge, appears to be what differs among subgroups of children (Paris, 2011).

Research has documented that phonemic awareness skills are causally related to the development of phonemic decoding of single-word reading and text reading accuracy (see Phillips & Torgesen, 2006; Burns, 2003; National Reading Panel, 2000). The development of word reading accuracy at multiple levels (single words, phrases, sentences, passages) requires children to process text effortlessly, effectively, and rapidly (Chall, 1996; National Reading Panel, 2000), and the development of these abilities requires children to read words "by sight" or at a single glance (Ehri, 2005; Ehri & Roberts, 2006; Phillips & Torgesen, 2006).

While the phrase *by sight* or *sight word reading* may suggest that children are recognizing words holistically and employing a visual strategy, these terms are actually a bit misleading. Sight word reading involves automatically applying the alphabetic principle to recognize words and immediately associating meaning with the resulting word. Multiple exposures and formulating consistent and accurate grapheme-phoneme connections are required for children to develop what some researchers have described as orthographic representations that are fully specified (Share & Stanovich, 1995; Share, 1995, 1999).

Research for decades has explored how children acquire the vast number of these specified orthographic representations during the "learning to read" (Chall, 1996) stage of development, which typically begins in kindergarten (National Early Literacy Panel, 2008; National Reading Panel, 2000). It appears that phonemic decoding skills provide the requisites for these representations to develop, and without them, it would be nearly impossible to acquire the necessary number of representations (Share, 1995, 1999; Share & Stanovich, 1995) to transition to the "reading to learn" phase of development, which occurs in second or third grade (Chall 1996; National Reading Panel, 2000). The self-teaching theory of early reading acquisition (Share, 1995, 1999; Share & Stanovich, 1995) also helps explain the acquisition of representations and how phonemic decoding skills facilitate the process of adding words to children's orthographic reading vocabulary.

Self-Teaching Theory

According to the self-teaching theory, the order of graphemes in words will not make sense to young children and may actually appear arbitrary unless they are linked to the specific phonemes they represent (Share, 1999). Share (2011) indicated that children must possess "some algorithm ... for *independently* identifying words encountered for the first time" (p. 49) and that knowledge of the alphabetic principle provides readers with a powerful algorithm or mnemonic device to make consistent connections between graphemes, phonemes, and meanings of words present in their lexicon. Therefore, children require phonemic decoding skills in order to progress in their independent word reading abilities and to move from a slow, deliberate, phoneme-by-phoneme decoding process to one that is automatic and fluent and allows them to identify words by sight. Further support for the self-teaching theory can be drawn from the evidence suggesting that older struggling readers are unable to fully compensate for poor phonemic decoding skills, even if they possess and exploit superior orthographic skills (see Share, 2011, for discussion).

It is important to clarify what is meant by identifying words encountered for the first time (Share, 2011). As children learn the alphabetic principle and apply it to reading words, they are making connections between their face-to-face language and print. Words that young children come across in early reading experiences are typically well established in their face-to-face vocabulary. In other words, words encountered for the first time are those that have never been seen in print or read before, although the meanings of the words are usually known.

For example, when a child comes across the printed word *man* for the first time, he or she must make the connection between the grapheme *m* and the phoneme /m/, the grapheme *a* and the phoneme /a/, and the grapheme *n* and the phoneme /n/ in order to decode the word. Once the phonemes are blended to form the word *man*, meaning can immediately be associated, because the word *man* is likely in the child's lexicon. This example further underscores that even the most basic beginning reading skills are dependent on having a foundation in the language to be read. Therefore, the role of language-related abilities in the development of early reading and implications for children who may be considered at risk in these areas (e.g., deaf children, children with language impairments, English language learners) will be examined.

LANGUAGE-RELATED ABILITIES

While the results of several multivariate studies have not illustrated the direct role of oral language abilities in the development of early reading skills, links between phonological processing skills, print knowledge, and oral language have been demonstrated (see National Early Literacy Panel, 2008). Findings suggest that code-related abilities (e.g., phonological awareness, phonemic awareness, and word reading skills) and language-related abilities (e.g., semantic and syntactic) play their most significant roles at different stages within the developmental process. For example, code-related abilities appear to have a stronger influence in the early phases, when the focus of reading is on developing phonemic decoding skills. On the other hand, the relationship between language-related abilities and reading performance is greater once phonemic decoding skills are solidified and attention shifts to comprehending text (see Chall, 1996; Storch & Whitehurst, 2002, for discussions).

In a seminal investigation exploring the influence of code- and language-related abilities in developing reading, a longitudinal study was conducted (Storch & Whitehurst, 2002). Participants of this study were more than six hundred children who were served through Head Start[2] programs and attended public schools in subsequent years. Children were assessed over a six-year period beginning in preschool and continuing through fourth grade. Structural equation modeling was used to evaluate the effects of multiple skills and abilities on reading comprehension outcomes and to explore the changing nature of reading over time.

Results of this investigation revealed significant correlations between the language-related (vocabulary) and code-related (phonological awareness) domains during the preschool years. However, as children began receiving formal reading instruction during kindergarten, the association between the two lessened. The model developed by Storch and Whitehurst (2002) illustrates that the relationship between language-related abilities and early reading skills during this time period are mediated by code-related skills such as phonological awareness and print concepts. Because phonological awareness activities typically involve manipulating language without the support of print, oral language abilities are obviously also implicated in this process. Therefore, it is clear that oral language plays an essential, although indirect, role in the early reading acquisition process. These findings also provide further support for a dual conceptualization of phonemic

---

[2] Head Start is a federally funded preschool program in the United States that promotes school readiness for children from birth to age five from low-income families.

awareness as both a language-related ability (conceptual understanding) and a code-related skill.

The results of this study also established the link between word reading accuracy and reading comprehension in the early stages of development and provided additional evidence to support previous conclusions that deficiencies in understanding and applying the alphabetic principle to word reading (i.e., phonemic decoding) served as the primary barrier to comprehension during this phase (e.g., Shankweiler et al., 1999). Given that the participants in the Storch and Whitehurst (2002) investigation were also found to be consistently scoring below the national average on standardized measures within both the code- and language-related domains, parallels can be made between these children and children who experience language delays and deficits.

IMPACT OF LANGUAGE DELAYS AND DEFICITS

In their discussion of young children with language impairments, Kaiser, Roberts, and McLeod (2011) identified the following aspects of language associated with the development of early reading abilities: (1) basic phonological processing, (2) vocabulary, (3) semantic relations, and (4) syntax. In relation to reading, these areas of language are often discussed using the two broad categories of phonological awareness and general language abilities. Given the importance of these precursor abilities, outlined throughout this chapter and also discussed in chapter 2, children who exhibit language delays and/or deficits will most likely experience challenges in early reading skill acquisition.

Our earlier discussion of the lexical restructuring hypothesis illustrates the relationship between delays in vocabulary acquisition and their subsequent impact on the development of phonological sensitivity, which in turn affects the development of phonemic decoding skills. In the area of semantics, children with language impairments characteristically struggle to acquire new vocabulary, produce fewer words, and know and use pronouns and verbs less frequently (see Moyle, Weismer, Evans, & Lindstrom, 2007, for discussion). Syntactically, these children tend to omit morphological markers for plurals and for indicating tense (e.g., past, present progressive), confuse word order, and experience difficulty following directions (see Leonard, 2000, for further discussion).

Deficiencies in the areas of phonological sensitivity and vocabulary have also been documented in recent studies involving young deaf learners (e.g., Easterbrooks, Lederberg, Miller, Bergeron, & Conner, 2008; Harris & Beech, 1998; Kyle & Harris, 2011), and it has been well documented that these abilities, along with syntactic abilities, have historically posed challenges for this population of children (see Mayer, 2007; Mayer & Trezek, 2011; Paul, 2009; Trezek et al., 2010, for reviews). Therefore, briefly exploring the research related to skill acquisition in these areas among other groups of children might serve to inform practice for deaf learners.

Research conducted with young English language learners indicates that phonological sensitivity abilities and letter/alphabet knowledge serve the same role in developing later reading abilities as they do with monolingual children. While research findings suggest that it is optimal for English language learners to achieve some competence in English prior to receiving early reading instruction, recent investigations suggest that children can learn about the alphabetic principle even when sufficient oral language proficiency in English is lacking (see Ehri & Roberts, 2006, for discussion). For example, after receiving sixteen weeks of instruction in rhyming and letter names, three- and four-year-old children at the early stages of English language learning demonstrated abilities commensurate with those typically exhibited by middle-class children entering kindergarten (Roberts & Neal, 2004).

Studies have also shown that learning the letters of the alphabet and the phonemes they represent can enhance children's capability to build vocabulary. In one such investigation, the ability of children to learn the meanings of low-frequency vocabulary under two conditions was compared. In the first condition, children were simply asked to repeat pronunciations for words that were displayed in pictures and defined using a sentence. In the second condition, spellings were paired with the pictures, definitional sentences, and pronunciations. Findings revealed that children exposed to the spellings were better able to recall the newly acquired vocabulary than those who relied solely on the pronunciations. These results led the researchers to conclude that learning the alphabetic system served as a mnemonic device to support children's ability to secure both the pronunciations and the definitions of new vocabulary in memory (see discussion in Ehri, 2005).

Beyond associating meaning with individual words, the in-depth and precise knowledge of word meanings, along with understanding the relationships among words, plays a critical role in developing later reading abilities, most notably comprehension. The NELP explored the role of oral language in the development of early and later literacy skills. While the panel found that global oral language abilities were only moderately correlated with conventional literacy skills, some language components were more predictive of later abilities. For example, measures of definitional vocabulary, listening comprehension, and grammar yielded stronger relations with later conventional literacy achievement than did assessments of receptive and expressive vocabulary. These results do not imply that vocabulary skills are inconsequential but rather highlight the significance of both semantic and syntactical abilities in developing overall reading proficiency (see also National Early Literacy Panel, 2008). Furthermore, it has been suggested that the relationship between vocabulary and syntactic development is reciprocal in nature, with growth in one supporting the development of the other (see also Moyle et al., 2007).

Early intervention and remediation are clearly essential to minimize the impact of language delays and deficits on beginning reading skills acquisition. Research findings indicate that when language delays are resolved by approximately five years of age, children tend to evidence typical reading development during the early elementary years (e.g., Bishop & Adams, 1990). However, if language deficits persist beyond this period, children are more likely to be identified as having reading disabilities (e.g., Catts, 2002), to experience struggles with reading comprehension during elementary school, and to exhibit issues with word reading, spelling, and comprehension well into high school (e.g., Stothard, Snowling, Bishop, Chipchase, & Kaplan, 1998). It has also been demonstrated that children who do not master the forty-one grapheme-phoneme relations by the age of nine are often diagnosed with dyslexia or some form of language impairment (Gillon, 2004; see also Paris, 2011, for discussion).

In addition to providing the necessary interventions to reduce the effects of language impairments on the development of early reading abilities, it is also crucial to understand the activities and pedagogical approaches to foster the development of skills and the recommended strategies for differentiating instruction for those children requiring supplementary supports. Therefore, the findings of the NELP regarding programs, interventions, and instructional practices that enhance early literacy skill development will be summarized in the next section.

FOSTERING EARLY READING DEVELOPMENT

In its pursuit of determining the effectiveness of early literacy instructional practices, programs, and strategies, the NELP reviewed nearly two hundred studies in the following five categories of interventions: (1) code-focused (e.g., phonological sensitivity, alphabet knowledge, early decoding) interventions, (2) shared reading interventions, (3) parent and home programs, (4) preschool and kindergarten programs, and (5) language enhancement interventions. The panel was interested in determining the impact of these interventions and programs on children's abilities and skills, including oral language, general cognition, reading readiness, spelling, and conventional literacy. Findings revealed statistically significant effects for all categories examined; however, the influence of interventions on specific types of abilities and skills and the degree of effect did vary to some extent.

The NELP was also interested in determining the influence of child-based characteristics on the overall effectiveness reported for interventions and programs. While the panel acknowledged some restrictions in addressing this question caused by reporting limitations within the original studies, in general, they identified relatively few demographic differences in learning patterns. For example, variables such as SES, race, and children's language status (e.g., English language learners, language impairments) did not appear to influence the overall effectiveness of the interventions and programs studied. In regard to age specifically, the majority of interventions evidenced similar results with both preschool and kindergarten children, with the exception of language enhancements, which exhibited greater efficacy with younger children. However, the panel did note that there have been relatively few studies exploring the differential effects of interventions implemented in preschool as compared with kindergarten; therefore, future investigations examining these differences were recommended. Given that the various types of interventions reviewed by the NELP yielded slightly different findings in terms of abilities and skills addressed and in overall effect sizes, findings in each category will be discussed separately.

Code-Focused Interventions

Code-focused interventions represented the largest category of studies (eighty-three) identified by the NELP and focused on various aspects of developing the alphabetic principle, including phonological sensitivity, alphabet knowledge, and early decoding skills (phonemic decoding). The majority of children receiving these interventions were enrolled in a preschool or kindergarten program, with the code-focused instruction being implemented with treatment students to augment the activities already in place before the investigation. Comparison group participants, on the other hand, continued to receive the typical instructional activities and at times received an alternative intervention developed to contrast with the code-focused teaching.

Because nearly all of the studies reviewed by the NELP included some type of phonological sensitivity instruction (e.g., phoneme identification, blending, segmenting), two subcategories of code-focused interventions were identified. The first combined phonological sensitivity activities and instruction in alphabet knowledge (letter names and sounds), and the second coupled phonological sensitivity training with specific phonemic decoding strategy instruction. The panel was interested in determining the overall effectiveness of these interventions on children's early and conventional literacy skills and in identifying instructional and child-based variables that moderated the effects. The outcome measures employed in the majority of these interventions included assessments of phonological sensitivity, alphabet knowledge, reading, spelling, and oral language. Measures of cognitive ability, memory, print knowledge, RAN, reading readiness, and writing were also utilized in some studies but to a much lesser degree. Interestingly, none of the reviewed studies examined the impact of code-focused interventions on visual or perceptual processing.

Findings of the NELP revealed that code-focused interventions resulted in moderate to large effects on both precursor and conventional literacy skills, with the largest impact being demonstrated on measures of phonological sensitivity. Furthermore, the type of study (randomized control trial, quasi-experimental design), level of linguistic complexity and/or cognitive operation targeted through activities (e.g., phonological analysis or synthesis task), participants' age (preschool versus kindergarten), and/or developmental level (e.g., nonreader versus reader) did not appear to have a significant impact on the overall effectiveness of these interventions. Because the code-focused interventions reviewed by the NELP were generally implemented in individual or small-group instructional arrangements, results obtained for children receiving whole-class instruction have yet to be substantiated.

Regarding demographic variables, the NELP reported that effect size estimates for code-focused interventions did not vary significantly in terms of SES on some outcome measures (alphabet knowledge, oral language, reading) but did influence differences in others (phonological sensitivity, spelling). However, the panel cautioned that the small number of studies may have influenced these results; therefore, these findings should "not be given substantial interpretive credence" (National Early Literacy Panel, 2008, p. 116). The panel also indicated that because many studies included in its meta-analysis did not report ethnicity of study participants or the population density where studies were conducted (rural, urban, suburban, mixed), it was impossible to definitively determine the impact of these demographic characteristics. Nevertheless, based on the available evidence, the panel suggested that these variables should not be considered a factor affecting children's performance on code-focused interventions.

Shared Reading Interventions

Shared reading interventions involve having parents and/or teachers read books to preschoolers. This practice has often been recognized as the single most important task adults can undertake to promote emergent literacy skill development among young children. A total of nineteen studies of shared reading interventions evaluating the effectiveness of this approach using various measures of precursor and conventional literacy abilities were included in the meta-analysis conducted by the NELP. Because of the widely accepted benefits of the shared reading process, the majority of investigations included in the panel's review explored a variety of levels of intensity, frequency of implementation, and manner of activities (e.g., active engagement in retelling, implementation of dialogic reading techniques) employed in these interventions.

In terms of outcome measures, the vast majority of studies examined the impact of shared reading on oral language skills, although a few studies included measures of phonological sensitivity, general cognitive ability, alphabet knowledge, print knowledge, reading readiness, and writing. Based on the studies reviewed, the NELP determined that shared reading interventions had a moderate effect on measures of oral language, print knowledge, and writing. While shared reading did not appear to have an impact on children's phonological sensitivity or alphabet knowledge, the NELP acknowledged that the limited number of studies employing measures of these constructs might have contributed to this finding. In a related finding, other researchers have suggested that exposure to alphabet books might be more effective in developing skills in the areas of phonological sensitivity and alphabet knowledge as compared with picture books (e.g., Murray et al., 1996).

Given the limited number of studies and types of outcome assessments utilized, the NELP could only conduct additional analyses on studies that explored the impact of shared reading interventions on the development of oral language abilities. As indicated earlier in this chapter, the NELP determined that measures of complex language abilities (e.g., definitional vocabulary, listening comprehension, grammar) were stronger predictors of conventional literacy skills than were measures of receptive and expressive vocabulary. Therefore, the panel was interested in determining the impact of shared reading interventions at various levels of language complexity. While the results of this analysis revealed greater effect size estimates for vocabulary than composite oral language measures (0.60 and 0.35, respectively), the panel indicated that these differences could not be considered statistically reliable.

As with the code-focused interventions, ethnicity of study participants and population density did not appear to moderate the impact of shared reading interventions on children's outcomes. In regard to other demographic variables, such as age, the NELP found that shared reading interventions were equally effective for children before entering kindergarten as they were for kindergarteners. The panel also investigated the impact of shared reading interventions for children based on their risk status. Even though larger effects were reported in studies of children not considered at risk as compared with those who were (0.82 and 0.47, respectively), the panel again questioned the statistical reliability of these findings. Additional variables, such as type of shared reading experience (e.g., degree of interaction), agent of the intervention (e.g., parent, teacher, computer-based program), and whether books were provided as part of the intervention, also yielded statistically unstable results. Amount of shared reading training provided and total time children were exposed to the shared reading intervention were also examined, with no statistically significant relationships reported.

Parent and Home Programs

Parent and home programs were the subjects of thirty-two of the studies included in the NELP review of existing research. Previous research findings have suggested that children who engage in vocabulary-rich conversations and literacy-related activities in the home have more well-established language and literacy skills upon school entry (see Hart & Risley, 1995; Snow, Burns, & Griffin, 1998). Therefore, the primary focus of these investigations was to determine the connection between active and supportive parental involvement and children's early literacy skill development. As with the shared reading interventions, the panel found that the majority of studies examining the effects of parent and home programs explored oral language abilities as an outcome measure, although some studies did employ measures of other literacy-related skills, such as alphabet knowledge, phonological sensitivity, reading, reading readiness, spelling, and writing, along with the domains of cognition and memory.

Generally speaking, parent and home programs evidenced small effects on oral language and moderate to large effects on cognitive abilities. While statistically significant effects were also reported in the areas of memory and writing, each of these findings was based on only one study; therefore, results need to be interpreted accordingly. The panel was also interested in determining specific program features that affect children's outcomes; however, because of the limited number of studies in this category, only those that used oral language as an outcome measure could be included in these analyses. Even though findings suggested that studies employing nonrandomized study design tended to produce larger effects than quasi-experimental studies, the panel cautioned against the statistical reliability of this claim.

As with the shared reading interventions, the NELP also considered the differential impact of parent and home programs on measures of basic versus complex language abilities. Even though effect size estimates for vocabulary were larger than for composite measures of language (0.41 and 0.27, respectively), these differences were not considered statistically reliable. In terms of demographic characteristics, children's age (from birth to three years old or from three to five years old) did not appear to be a factor moderating children's outcomes. Because of the limited number of studies reporting other variables such as SES, ethnicity, and/or population density, a more in-depth analysis of these characteristics was not feasible. However, the available evidence suggested that these factors did not appear to have an impact on the effectiveness of parent and home programs.

Preschool and Kindergarten Programs

Beginning in the early 1960s, organized early childhood programs emerged in the educational landscape. Many of these programs received governmental funding and were designed to enhance the educational and social outcomes for children living in poverty or those considered at risk prior to school entry (e.g., Head Start). Additional services such as health and nutrition, social services, and parental support were often included to augment the direct interventions the children were receiving. A longitudinal approach that followed children through elementary school and beyond was a common characteristic of many of these preschool and kindergarten programs. As with the previous categories of interventions, the NELP was interested in determining the overall effectiveness of these programs in children's early and conventional literacy skills.

A total of thirty-three studies of preschool and kindergarten programs met the NELP's criteria for review. A large portion of the investigations tracked study participants longitudinally and measured outcomes using assessments of oral language and reading. Fewer studies examined the impact of programming on alphabet knowledge, cognitive abilities, spelling, phonological sensitivity, memory, print awareness, and writing. Interestingly, nearly one-third of the identified studies (ten) examined the effectiveness of one specific program, the Abecedarian project.[3]

Overall findings of the panel's meta-analysis of preschool and kindergarten programs revealed large and statistically significant outcomes on measures of readiness and small to moderate effects on spelling. While other analyses indicated a positive impact of programming on outcomes such as alphabet knowledge, reading, and writing, the findings were not considered statistically significant. The panel noted that the limited number of studies employing outcome measures in these areas, particularly alphabet knowledge (four) and writing (two), may have contributed to this finding. Surprisingly, the overall findings for studies using oral language assessments to measure outcomes resulted in statistically insignificant outcomes.

Because of incomplete information reported in several of the original studies, the NELP was unable to analyze the moderating effects of characteristics such as SES, ethnicity, age, population density, and parental involvement. However, in considering studies that utilized an oral language and/or reading outcome measure separately, analyses of some variables were possible. For example, when oral language assessments were employed, the panel reported that

---

[3] The Abecedarian project involved four cohorts of children born between 1972 and 1977 from low-income families in the United States. As infants, children were randomly assigned to either an intervention or a control group. Treatment children received full-time educational programming through age five. Follow-up studies were conducted at ages twelve, fifteen, and twenty-one.

there was no evidence that children's age or type of study design affected outcomes. As with the previous two categories of studies, the NELP also examined the differential impact of preschool and kindergarten programs on measures of basic versus complex language abilities. Even though effect size estimates for composite language measures were larger than those reported for vocabulary (0.40 and 0.13, respectively), these differences were not considered statistically reliable.

Several studies investigating the efficacy of literacy-focused curricula specifically were also included in the NELP review. For the investigations that used oral language as an outcome measure, the effects were considered large and statistically significant. However, when comparing the findings for curricula with those for other interventions in this category that also used an oral language measure, no statistically significant differences were noted. On the other hand, when reading outcome measures were employed, literacy-focused curricula produced significantly better results than those that utilized other interventions, with findings indicating effect sizes approximately three and a half to four times larger. The impact of professional development on children's outcomes was also of interest to the NELP; however, because of the overlap between this subcategory and literacy-focused curricula, the very strong effects for professional development on the reading outcome may have been conflated.

Language Enhancement Interventions

The final category investigated by the NELP examined the efficacy of language enhancement interventions. While the panel acknowledged that many of the studies in the previous four categories examined language learning to some degree, the instructional practices, programs, and strategies employed examined incidental learning, whereas the studies described in this category explored interventions designed to explicitly address language skills such as vocabulary development, syntactic sophistication, and listening comprehension.

A total of nineteen studies of language enhancement programs were reviewed. The majority of these investigations involved preschool and kindergarten children, although some included infants and toddlers as study participants. Children with and without language deficits/delays also served as study participants in the studies reviewed. The NELP reported great variability in the characteristics of the interventions in terms of amount of structure provided, delivery method, and specific language ability targeted. All of the studies in this category included a measure of language, most often vocabulary, and in some instances, other early literacy-related abilities and skills, such as cognitive ability, memory, RAN, readiness, phonemic awareness, decoding, print knowledge, and reading.

As with the preceding categories, the diversity in measures used and the limited number of studies did not allow the panel to evaluate the impact of language enhancements on multiple literacy-related outcomes. However, because all nineteen of the studies used some measure of language, the panel was able to investigate the impact of the language enhancement interventions on general oral language abilities, which revealed moderate effects. The demographic variables of ethnicity, SES, and population density did not appear to moderate the effects of language enhancement interventions. In regard to age, the panel viewed two categories of children separately. Preschoolers and kindergarteners made up one group, and children younger than three years old were in the other. While language enhancement interventions were found to be equally effective for preschool- and kindergarten-age children, greater effects for these programs were reported for studies that involved children younger than three.

The panel was also interested in examining whether play-based activities resulted in greater outcomes when compared with other types of language enhancement interventions; however, results of this analysis did not reveal significantly different outcomes. Differences were also not found based on the language status of the children (e.g., language impaired versus typically developing), the individual administering the intervention (e.g., teacher versus parent), amount of feedback provided to children, or whether children were required to provide specific responses to prompts provided by interventionists. The findings of the NELP's meta-analysis evaluating the effectiveness of instructional interventions for early literacy provide a wealth of research data and information that can be used to inform pedagogical approaches employed with young deaf children; therefore, implications for both practice and research will be explored.

IMPLICATIONS FOR PRACTICE

As indicated in the introduction to this chapter, we strongly advocate the implementation of instructional strategies and approaches recognized as effective for hearing children to develop the same early literacy requisite abilities and skills among deaf learners. These include those addressing phonological sensitivity and letter and alphabet knowledge and application of these abilities to the development of phonemic decoding skills. While these requisite abilities and skills fall primarily in the code-related domain, as illustrated in this chapter, language-related abilities are also implicated throughout the early reading developmental process.

As discussed extensively in chapter 2, while differences may rest with the learner engaging in the process of literacy learning, the process itself remains constant. In other words, deaf children may require *differentiated* instruction to compensate for deficits in English language abilities and/or challenges in acquiring phonological sensitivity abilities, but the requisite abilities and skills and associated instructional strategies themselves are not *different*. Therefore, considering the information presented in chapter 2 and throughout this chapter, we offer the following recommendations for differentiating effective early reading instructional practices to meet the needs of deaf learners.

1. Language enhancement interventions should be implemented before the age of three and focus on developing both English vocabulary and syntax, with the ultimate goal of resolving children's language deficits prior to the introduction of formal reading instruction in kindergarten.

Because challenges in language acquisition are often documented for many children with hearing loss (see Paul, 2009, for review), we recognize that delays and deficits in this domain must be addressed through early intervention in order to minimize the impact on both early and later literacy learning. This situation is not dissimilar to the one that exists for other populations of children who exhibit challenges in language development, such as those identified with language impairments and some English language learners. As illustrated by the findings of the NELP, language enhancement interventions that systematically and explicitly target phonological, semantic, and syntactic abilities using a variety of approaches, including direct instruction, incidental teaching, and play experiences, evidenced their greatest impact on children younger than three and were found to be equally effective for all children regardless of language status. These findings, coupled with those indicating the importance of resolving language deficits before the age of five to reduce the negative impact on the development of reading skills (e.g., Bishop & Adams, 1990), provide ongoing support for the implementation of early intervention and preschool programs for deaf children.

Results of studies reporting delays in language-related abilities among deaf early literacy learners and the impact of these deficits on early reading skill acquisition (e.g., Easterbrooks et al., 2008; Kyle & Harris, 2011; Harris & Beech, 1998) further corroborate these findings. Of particular relevance to meeting the needs of deaf children who experience language deficits, the results of the NELP's meta-analysis revealed that measures of complex language abilities were stronger predictors of conventional literacy skills as compared with results of vocabulary assessments. These findings were also echoed in a review of early writing for deaf learners conducted by Williams and Mayer (in press), who recommended an increased focus on addressing and evaluating the syntactic abilities of deaf children (see chapter 1).

Therefore, it is highly recommended that the type of language enhancement interventions documented as efficacious in meeting the needs of other struggling populations of early literacy learners be implemented with young deaf children. As discussed in chapter 2, the primary method of differentiating this instruction for deaf learners involves making the language of instruction (e.g., English) accessible. This includes exploiting auditory access, employing visual access, or some combination of the two. While limited in number and scope, studies reporting the positive impact of early exposure to Cued Speech (Colin, Leybaert, Ecalle, & Magnan, 2013) and a signed form of English (Nielsen & Luetke-Stahlman, 2002) provide further support for the importance of developing English language abilities and their role in early and later literacy learning.

2. **With advancements in hearing technologies, many deaf children are able to develop phonological sensitivity abilities primarily through audition alone. However, for children for whom this is not the case, multisensory instructional tools and/or communication systems can be used to provide supplemental access to code-related interventions.**

The findings of several recent studies have demonstrated the efficacy of using Visual Phonics to support developing phonemic awareness skills, the alphabetic principle, and the phonemic decoding abilities of young deaf children (see Beal-Alvarez, Lederberg, & Easterbrooks, 2012; Smith & Wang, 2010; Trezek & Wang, 2006; Trezek, Wang, Woods, Gampp, & Paul, 2007; Wang, Spychala, Harris, & Oetting, 2013). As discussed briefly in chapter 1, See-the-Sound Visual Phonics (more commonly known as Visual Phonics) is an instructional tool designed to supplement speech and/or speechreading and provide the learner with information regarding the articulatory features of phonemes. In contrast with the communication system Cued Speech (see LaSasso, Crain, & Leybaert, 2010), which uses eight distinct handshapes to represent consonant sounds and four placements near the mouth to signify the vowels of the English language (see http://www.cuedspeech.org for cue charts), Visual Phonics is a system of forty-four hand gestures and written symbols designed to represent the individual phonemes of the English language (see http://seethesound.org/ for examples).

For example, when using Visual Phonics to represent the phoneme /m/, a flat hand is held horizontally next to the mouth, and as the hand is moved forward, the fingers are waved slightly to indicate the vibration that occurs when producing this continuous phoneme. Similarly, the Visual Phonics hand cues for stop phonemes were designed to provide the learner with information about manner of production. For instance, the hand cue for the /d/ sound is produced by holding a crooked index finger at the corner of the mouth and quickly "dotting" the finger downward and then returning it to the original position (see Morrison, Trezek, & Paul, 2008; Trezek et al., 2010, for further discussions).

Because Visual Phonics and other similar multisensory tools such as Cued Articulation (http://cuedarticulation.com) and Visual Phonics by Hand (http://visualphonicsbyhand.co.uk) provide phonological representations at the sublexical and lexical levels only, these systems are effective tools for developing skills that require children to manipulate individual phonemes and/or short strings of phonemes within words. Therefore, these tools provide an appropriate supplement to develop a variety of phonological sensitivity abilities among deaf learners, including (1) phonological awareness abilities, such as identifying and producing rhyming words; (2) phonemic awareness skills, including phoneme identification, substitution, and deletion tasks; and (3) phonemic decoding skills, such as blending and segmenting. The differences between the names of letters (/e/ /m/) and the sounds they produce (/m/) can also be easily communicated using these multisensory tools.

Despite the multiple benefits of these instructional tools in making the aspects of English phonology accessible to deaf learners, the constraints of these systems must also be acknowledged. Because they utilize phoneme-by-phoneme representations only, these multisensory tools are inherently too cumbersome to convey the stream of language. Consequently, these tools alone do not provide an effective means of addressing children's deficits in English syntax. While it is possible to represent individual words and short phrases using these tools, an alternative representation (e.g., spoken and/or signed communication) must be used to fully represent the grammatical and syntactic structures of the language.

Unlike the multisensory instructional tools that use phoneme-by-phoneme representations, Cued Speech uses consonant-vowel pairings to create basic cued syllables. For example, the word *man* would be produced in two steps. The first involves using the handshape signifying the consonant sound /m/ (handshape 5) placed at the throat to indicate the short vowel /a/. Moving the handshape for the final phoneme /n/ (handshape 4) to the neutral position near the side of the face indicates that this consonant is not immediately followed by a vowel. When producing these cues, the articulatory gestures of the phonemes would be simultaneously produced on the mouth (/ma/ and /n/), either with or without accompanying vocalizations (see Shull & Crain, 2010). Using these basic cued syllables allows the user of Cued Speech to visually represent language at the rate of typical conversation and also to convey additional features of the language such as coarticulation of phonemes and features of prosody such as intonation and stress (see also LaSasso et al., 2010).

Placing a consonant handshape in the neutral position near the side of the face or using the "null handshape" (Shull & Crain, 2010, p. 39) (handshape 5) at one of the four vowel placements also allows Cued Speech to be used as an effective instructional tool to provide children with access to phonemic awareness and phonemic decoding activities such as segmenting the word *man* into three distinct phonemes (/m/, /a/, and /n/). The consonant-vowel dyads described above are then used to illustrate the blending of phonemes (/ma/ /n/) to form a word. As illustrated by these examples, Cued Speech can be utilized to develop both language-related abilities (e.g., vocabulary, syntax) and code-related abilities (e.g., phonological sensitivity abilities, early reading skills) among deaf children.

In addition to multisensory tools and communication systems, alternative strategies employed to differentiate phonological sensitivity instruction for struggling hearing learners may also be used to support the early reading development of deaf learners. Because spoken phonemes are ephemeral and disappear as soon as they are spoken, the use of markers (e.g., blocks, chips) have helped other children make sense of the abstract nature of phoneme manipulation tasks such as segmentation, deletion, and addition (see Ehri & Roberts, 2006). Pictures of the mouth that make children consciously aware of the articulatory characteristics of individual phonemes (e.g., tongue placement, mouth movement, etc.) have also proven to be effective in developing phonological sensitivity abilities and alphabetic knowledge (see Castiglioni-Spalten & Ehri, 2003; Lindamood & Lindamood, 2011). First sound mnemonic picture cards and/or actions can also be used to support the development of both letter and alphabet knowledge. Pictures and/or actions that mimic the shape of the target grapheme, such as a snake forming the shape of the letter *s* or the hand moving in an *s* configuration, have been found to be particularly beneficial (see Ehri & Roberts, 2006). It is important to note that the alternative instructional strategies discussed here and Visual Phonics and Cued Speech are not mutually exclusive; rather, they can be effectively used in concert to support early reading skill acquisition among the population of deaf children.

3. Developmentally appropriate practices with previously demonstrated efficacy should be employed to meet the early reading needs of young deaf learners.

As indicated earlier in this chapter, direct teaching of the alphabetic principle and phonemic decoding abilities typically occurs at the onset of formal reading instruction in kindergarten. While presumably implementing direct instruction before kindergarten would give at-risk readers an advantage by providing them with earlier instruction in conventional literacy skills, the NELP found very few interventions implemented with preschoolers that directly targeted these skills. The panel also indicated that not only were these types of interventions rare, but it was unlikely that they would be considered developmentally appropriate for preschool-age children (younger than five). It has also been suggested that phonemic awareness instructional activities may be too difficult for preschool children and that those centered on manipulating larger linguistic units (e.g., syllables, rhymes) are more appropriate for this age group (see Lonigan, 2006). Before kindergarten, it is recommended that the emphasis be placed on developing requisite language-related abilities (e.g., vocabulary, syntax), phonological awareness, and letter knowledge skills rather than on explicit instruction in the alphabetic principle.

Recent studies examining the literacy development in young deaf children have revealed deficits in phonological awareness abilities, such as recognizing rhyme, alliteration, and phoneme similarities and blending and segmenting syllables and words (Easterbrooks et al., 2008; Kyle & Harris, 2011; Harris & Beech, 1998; see also chapter 1). Earlier in this chapter, we stated that phonological sensitivity abilities appear to develop in a specific order, moving from concrete linguistic units (e.g., words, syllables) to those that are more abstract (e.g., phoneme-level skills) (see Burgess, 2006, for discussion). The acquisition of these abilities subsequently forms the foundation for instruction focused on directly teaching grapheme-phoneme relationships.

All of the intervention studies to date that have examined the implementation of phonologically based curricula with preschool-age deaf children have focused on developing the alphabetic principle and phonemic decoding abilities (Beal-Alvarez et al., 2012; Bergeron, Lederberg, Easterbrooks, Miller, & Connor, 2009; Smith & Wang, 2010; Wang et al., 2013). In reviewing these studies (see chapter 1), we wondered whether participants had acquired the more abstract phonological sensitivity abilities prior to receiving instruction in the alphabetic principle and its application to phonemic decoding. This may also be the case in the intervention studies conducted with deaf children at the onset of formal reading instruction in kindergarten and first grade (Trezek & Wang, 2006; Trezek et al., 2007).

In viewing phonemic awareness as a conceptual understanding of language that also behaves like a skill, it may be that the conceptualization of phonemes typically developed through phonological awareness tasks (e.g., rhyming, onsets, rimes) and presented "through the air" presents a more abstract learning condition for young deaf children in comparison with the skill-based teaching of grapheme-phoneme relations that are inherently more concrete because they involve printed letters. In other words, it may be that the more abstract phases of phonological sensitivity development are not being addressed in favor of teaching more discrete skills that are easier for deaf children to grasp. A similar conclusion was reached in the review of early writing discussed in chapter 1 in relation to the number of spelling intervention studies conducted over those concentrated on more complex writing abilities (Williams & Mayer, in press).

Because none of the intervention studies included measures of phonological awareness abilities (e.g., alliteration, rhyme, syllables), it is difficult to draw conclusions about whether the deaf children in these investigations had acquired what research findings suggest are important prerequisite phonological awareness abilities. It is also unclear whether it is necessary to develop these broader phonological sensitivity abilities before instruction in the alphabetic principle is provided. Nevertheless, we would recommend that future instructional attention be given to developing a wide range of phonological sensitivity abilities among preschool-age deaf children before, or in conjunction with, implementing instruction in the alphabetic principle.

Parents and educators can also engage children in activities that implicitly teach phonological awareness abilities and letter knowledge skills, such as reciting nursery rhymes and reading both alphabet books and those that include rhyme and alliteration. Resources for early reading activities are readily available on many early reading websites; however, we find those included on the Florida Center for Reading Research (www.fcrr.org) and Reading Rockets (www.readingrockets.org) sites particularly beneficial, as these websites are not only free of charge but are also updated regularly to provide both research and practical resources for a wide range of consumers.

In general, children at risk for developing early reading and conventional literacy skills will benefit greatly from receiving both implicit and explicit instruction to master these critical prerequisite abilities in both the code-related and language-related domains. For example, the NELP found that shared reading interventions had positive impact on children's language outcomes. Given that parent and home programs also demonstrated moderate to large effects on children's oral language and cognitive abilities, it would be important for both educators and parents working with young deaf children to implement shared reading interventions that employ specific strategies for directly addressing language abilities and early reading skills such as dialogic reading (see What Works Clearinghouse, 2007).

IMPLICATIONS FOR RESEARCH

Reflecting on the literature presented in chapter 1, the findings of the NELP (2008), and the information related to early reading discussed throughout this chapter, we offer our impressions regarding current research in the field of deaf education and discuss recommendations for future investigations. As previously indicated, the NELP found that language enhancement interventions had their greatest impact when implemented with children before the age of three, regardless of their language status. In the section on implications for practice above, we suggested that implementations of various language enhancement instructional approaches, such as direct instruction, incidental teaching, and play experiences, also warrant consideration for deaf learners. Therefore, it is recommended that future research studies explore the impact of these various language enhancement interventions on the outcomes evidenced by deaf children and that investigations include multiple assessments of early literacy outcomes, most notably composite language measures, to measure their effectiveness.

Finding of the NELP meta-analysis of effective interventions (National Early Literacy Panel, 2008) also revealed that storybook reading evidenced positive outcomes on measures of children's language, particularly in the area of vocabulary. While there have been many publications reporting storybook reading and storytelling practices employed with deaf children and their parents and/or teachers (see Williams, 2004, and chapter 1 for reviews), the vast majority of these studies have focused on describing and analyzing the strategies utilized and the level of interaction displayed, with relatively few investigations exploring the impact of these approaches on early and conventional literacy outcomes. Therefore, it is highly recommended that future studies of shared reading interventions not only describe the strategies and techniques employed but also report the results of these practices with regard to the specific literacy outcomes (e.g., vocabulary, syntax, phonological sensitivity, letter and alphabet knowledge, writing) of deaf learners.

According to the NELP, parent and home programs implemented with young literacy learners have also had positive outcomes for children's language, specifically in the area of vocabulary. Although quite limited, the studies of parental involvement conducted with young deaf learners have indicated that parental communication skills are associated with the outcomes documented for their children (Bailes, Erting, Erting, & Thumann-Prezioso, 2009; Calderon, 2000; see also chapter 1). Given the importance of early literacy experiences and their link with later achievement, this area merits additional investigation. As with shared reading interventions, increased attention to evaluating the impact of parent and home programs on specific early literacy outcomes in both the code-related and language-related domains is recommended.

The effects of preschool and kindergarten programs were also examined and resulted in moderate to large effects on spelling and reading readiness. Available studies in the field of deaf education have focused on investigating either the type of educational program (e.g., inclusive, self-contained) that children attend (Most, Aram, & Andorn, 2006) or the literacy environment created by teachers (Easterbrooks, Lederberg, & Connor, 2010). While these researchers should be commended for including measures of both code- and language-related abilities in these studies, the extremely limited number of investigations in this area makes it difficult to draw overall conclusions regarding the efficacy of instructional programs. Therefore, we advocate additional studies that not only describe the practices employed in preschool and kindergarten programs but also evaluate the effectiveness of these approaches in relation to children's early and conventional literacy outcomes.

Code-based interventions focusing on the development of phonological sensitivity, alphabet knowledge, and early decoding have reportedly resulted in moderate to large effects across early literacy outcomes. Several recent studies exploring the implementation of code-focused interventions with deaf children have focused primarily on the development of alphabet knowledge and its application to phonemic decoding skills (Beal-Alvarez et al., 2012; Bergeron, et al., 2009; Smith & Wang, 2010; Trezek & Wang, 2006; Trezek et al., 2007; Wang et al., 2013). All of these studies have employed supplemental instructional supports (e.g., semantic association strategies, language experience approach, Visual Phonics) to address the perceived language and phonological challenges encountered by deaf learners during early reading instruction.

While the findings of these studies have been encouraging and have demonstrated that instruction in alphabet knowledge and phonemic decoding can be differentiated to meet the needs of young deaf learners, further research is certainly needed. Specifically, the examination of prerequisite phonological sensitivity abilities and the longitudinal impact of these interventions on the conventional literacy outcomes of children, particularly measures of reading comprehension, would be of particular interest to both researchers and educators. Furthermore, the relationship between assessments of code-related and language-related abilities in the development of both early and conventional reading skills and also the reciprocity between the development of reading and writing abilities would also be areas of interest for future investigations of code-related interventions.

REFERENCES

Adams, M. (1990). *Beginning to read: Thinking and learning about print.* Cambridge, MA: MIT Press.

Anthony, J. L., & Lonigan, C. J. (2004). The nature of phonological sensitivity: Converging evidence from four studies of preschool and early-grade school children. *Journal of Educational Psychology, 96,* 43–55.

Anthony, J. L., Lonigan, C. J., Burgess, S. R., Driscoll, K., Phillips, B. M., & Cantor, B. G. (2002). Structure of preschool phonological sensitivity: Overlapping sensitivity to rhyme, words, syllables, and phonemes. *Journal of Experimental Child Psychology, 82,* 65–92.

Bailes, C. N., Erting, C. J., Erting, L. C., & Thumann-Prezioso, C. (2009). Language and literacy acquisition through parental mediation in American Sign Language. *Sign Language Studies, 9(4)*, 417–456.

Ball, E., & Blachman, B. (1988). Phonological segmentation training: Effects of reading readiness. *Annals of Dyslexia, 38*, 208–225.

Beal-Alvarez, J., Lederberg, A. R., & Easterbrooks, S. R. (2012). Grapheme-phoneme acquisition of deaf preschoolers. *Journal of Deaf Studies and Deaf Education, 17*, 39–60. doi:10.1093/deafed/enr030

Bergeron, J., Lederberg, A. R., Easterbrooks, S. R., Miller, E. M., & Connor, C. (2009). Building the alphabetic principle in young children who are deaf or hard of hearing. *Volta Review, 109*, 87–119.

Bishop, D., & Adams, C. (1990). A prospective study of the relationship between specific language impairment, phonological disorders and reading retardation. *Journal of Child Psychology and Psychiatry and Allied Disciplines, 31*, 1027–1050.

Bowey, J. A. (1994). Phonological sensitivity in novice readers and nonreaders. *Journal of Experimental Child Psychology, 58*, 134–159.

Braze, D., McRoberts, G. W., & McDonough, C. (2011). Early precursors of reading-relevant phonological skills. In S. A. Brady, D. Braze, & C. A. Fowler (Eds.), *Explaining individual differences in reading: Theory and evidence* (pp. 23–43). New York, NY: Taylor & Francis.

Bryant, P. (1998). Sensitivity to onset and rhyme does predict young children's reading: A comment on Muter, Hulme, Snowling, and Taylor (1997). *Journal of Experimental Child Psychology, 71*, 29–37. doi:10.1006/jecp.1998.2455

Bryant, P. E., MacLean, M., Bradley, L. L., & Crossland, J. (1990). Rhyme and alliteration, phoneme detection, and learning to read. *Developmental Psychology, 26*, 429–438.

Burns, M. K. (2003). Reexamining data form the National Reading Panel's meta-analysis: Implications for school psychology. *Psychology in the Schools, 40*, 605–612.

Burgess, S. R. (2002). The influence of speech perception, oral language ability, the home literacy environment, and pre-reading knowledge on the growth of phonological sensitivity: A one-year longitudinal investigation. *Reading and Writing: An Interdisciplinary Journal, 15*, 709–737.

Burgess, S. R. (2006). The development of phonological sensitivity. In D. K. Dickinson & S. B. Neuman (Eds.), *Handbook of early literacy research* (Vol. 2, pp. 90–100). New York, NY: Guilford Press.

Burgess, S. R., & Lonigan, C. J. (1998). Bidirectional relations of phonological sensitivity prereading abilities: Evidence from a preschool sample. *Journal of Experimental Child Psychology, 70*, 117–141.

Calderon, R. (2000). Parental involvement in deaf children's education programs as a predictor of child's language, early reading, and social emotional development. *Journal of Deaf Studies and Deaf Education, 5(2)*, 140–155.

Canadian Language and Literacy Research Network (2009). *Foundations for literacy: An evidence-based toolkit for the effective reading and writing teacher.* Available at http://foundationsforliteracy.cllrnet.ca/pdf/ReadWriteKit08.pdf

Castiglioni-Spalten, M., & Ehri, L. (2003). Contribution of articulatory segmentation to novice beginners' reading and spelling. *Scientific Studies of Reading, 7*, 25–52.

Catts, H. W. (1997). The early identification of language-based reading disabilities. *Language, Speech, and Hearing Services in Schools, 28*, 86–89.

Catts, H. W., Fey, M. E., Zhang, X., & Tomblin, J. B. (2002). A longitudinal investigation of reading outcomes in children with language impairments. *Journal of Speech, Language, and Hearing Research, 45*(6), 1142–1157.

Chall, J. S. (1996). *Stages of reading development* (2nd ed.). New York, NY: McGraw-Hill.

Colin, S., Leybaert, J., Ecalle, J., & Magnan, A. (2013). The development of word recognition, sentence comprehension, word spelling, and vocabulary in children with deafness: A longitudinal study. *Research in Developmental Disabilities, 34(5)*, 1781–1793. doi:10.1016/j.ridd.2013.02.001

Commonwealth of Australia (2005). *Teaching reading.* Australian Government Department of Education, Science and Training, Canberra.

De Jong, P. F., & Olson, R. K. (2004). Early prediction of letter knowledge. *Journal of Experimental Child Psychology, 88*, 254–273.

Easterbrooks, S. R., Lederberg, A. R., & Connor, C. M. (2010). Contributions of the emergent literacy environment to literacy outcomes for young children who are deaf. *American Annals of the Deaf, 155(4)*, 467–480.

Easterbrooks, S. R., Lederberg, A. R., Miller, E. M., Bergeron, J. P., & Conner, C. M. (2008). Emergent literacy skills during early childhood in children with hearing loss: Strengths and weaknesses. *Volta Review, 108*, 91–114.

Education Review Office (2011). *Literacy in early childhood services: Teaching and learning.* Available at http://www.ero.govt.nz/National-Reports/Literacy-in-Early-Childhood-Services-Teaching-and-Learning-February-2011

Ehri, L. C. (2005). Learning to read words: Theory, findings, and issues. *Scientific Studies of Reading, 9*, 167–188.

Ehri, L. C., & Roberts, T. (2006). The roots of learning to read and write: Acquisition of letters and phonemic awareness. In D. K. Dickinson & S. B. Neuman (Eds.), *Handbook of early literacy research* (Vol. 2, pp. 113–131). New York, NY: Guilford Press.

Fowler, A. E. (1991). How early phonological development might set the stage for phoneme awareness. In S. A. Brady & D. P. Shankweiler (Eds.), *Phonological processes in literacy* (pp. 97–117). Hillsdale, NJ: Erlbaum.

Gillon, G. T. (2004). *Phonological awareness: From research to practice.* New York, NY: Guilford Press.

Goswami, U., & Bryant, P. E. (1990). *Phonological skills and learning to read.* Hillsdale, NJ: Erlbaum.

Harris, M., & Beech, J. R. (1998). Implicit phonological awareness and early reading development in prelingually deaf children. *Journal of Deaf Studies and Deaf Education, 3*, 205–216.

Hart, B., & Risley, T. R. (1995). *Meaningful differences in the everyday experiences of young American children.* Baltimore, MD: Brookes.

Hatcher, P. J., & Hulme, C. (1999). Phonemes, rhymes and intelligence as predictors of children's responsiveness to remedial reading instruction: Evidence from a longitudinal intervention study. *Journal of Experimental Child Psychology, 72*, 130–153. doi:10.1006/jecp.1998.2480

Hulme, C. (2002). Phonemes, rimes and the mechanisms of early reading development. *Journal of Experimental Child Psychology, 82*, 58–64. doi:10.1006/jecp.2002.2674

Hulme, C., Hatcher, P. J., Nation, K., Brown, A., Adams, J., & Stuart, G. (2002). Segmentation does predict early progress in learning to read better than rhyme: A reply to Bryant. *Journal of Experimental Child Psychology, 82*, 2–28.

Hulme, C., Muter, V., & Snowling, M. J. (1998). Segmentation does predict early progress in learning to read better than rhyme: A reply to Bryant. *Journal of Experimental Child Psychology, 71*, 39–44. doi:10.1006/jecp.1998.2456

Kaiser, A. P., Roberts, M. Y., & McLeod, R. H. (2011). Young children with language impairments: Challenges in transition to reading. In S. B. Neuman & D. K. Dickinson (Eds.), *Handbook of early literacy research* (Vol. 3, pp. 228–241). New York, NY: Guilford Press.

Kennedy, E., Dunphy, E., Dwyer, B., Hayes, G., McPhillips, T., Marsh, J.... Shiel, G. (2012). *Literacy in early childhood and primary education (3–8 years).* National Council for Curriculum and Assessment, Dublin, Ireland.

Kyle, F. E., & Harris, M. (2011). Longitudinal patterns of emerging literacy in beginning deaf and hearing readers. *Journal of Deaf Studies and Deaf Education, 16*, 289–304.

LaSasso, C. J., Crain, K. L., & Leybaert, J. (Eds.). (2010). *Cued Speech and Cued Language for deaf and hard of hearing children.* San Diego, CA: Plural

Leonard, L. (2000). *Children with specific language impairment.* Cambridge, MA: MIT Press.

Lindamood, C., & Lindamood, P. (2011). *The Lindamood phoneme sequencing program for reading, spelling, and speech: The LiPS program* (4th ed.) Avila Beach, CA: Gander.

Lonigan, C. J. (2006). Conceptualizing phonological processing skills in prereaders. In D. K. Dickinson & S. B. Neuman (Eds.), *Handbook of early literacy research* (Vol. 2, pp. 77–89). New York, NY: Guilford Press.

Lonigan, C. J., Burgess, S. R., & Anthony, J. L. (2000). Development of emergent literacy and early reading skills in preschool children: Evidence from a latent-variable longitudinal study. *Developmental Psychology, 36*, 596–613.

Mayer, C. (2007). What matters in the early literacy development of deaf children. *Journal of Deaf Studies and Deaf Education, 12*, 411–431. doi:10.1093/deafed/enm020.

Mayer, C., & Trezek, B. J. (2011). New (?) answers to old questions: Literacy development in D/HH learners. In *Partners in education: Issues and trends from the 21st International Congress on the Education of the Deaf* (pp. 62–74). Washington, DC: Gallaudet University Press.

Mayer, C., & Trezek, B. J. (2014). Is reading different for deaf individuals?: Reexamining the role of phonology. *American Annals of the Deaf, 159*(4), 359–371.

Metsala, J. L., & Walley, A. C. (1998). Spoken vocabulary growth and the segmental restructuring of lexical representations: Precursors to phonemic awareness and early reading ability. In J. L. Metsala & L. C. Ehri (Eds.), *Word recognition in beginning literacy* (pp. 89–120). Mahwah, NJ: Erlbaum.

Morais, J., Cary, L., Alegria, J., & Bertelson, P. (1979). Does awareness of speech as a sequence of phones arise spontaneously? *Cognition, 7*, 323–331.

Morris, D. (1993). The relationship between children's concept of word in text and phoneme awareness in learning to read: A longitudinal study. *Research in the Teaching of English, 27*, 133–154.

Morrison, D., Trezek, B., & Paul, P. (2008). Can you see that sound? A rationale for a multisensory intervention tool for struggling readers. *Journal of Balanced Reading Instruction, 15,* 11–26.

Most, T., Aram, D., & Andorn, T. (2006). Early literacy in children with hearing loss: A comparison between two educational systems. *Volta Review, 106(1),* 5–28.

Moyle, M. J., Weismer, S. E., Evans, J. L., & Lindstrom, M. J. (2007). Longitudinal relationships between lexical and grammatical development in typical and late-talking children. *Journal of Speech, Language, and Hearing Research, 50,* 508–528.

Murray, B. A., Stahl, S. A., & Ivey, M. G. (1996). Developing phoneme awareness through alphabet books. *Reading and Writing, 8,* 307–322.

Muter, V., Hulme, C., Snowling, M., & Taylor, S. (1997). Segmentation, not rhyming, predicts early progress in learning to read. *Journal of Experimental Child Psychology, 65,* 370–396. doi:10.1006/jecp.1996.2365

Nation, K., & Hulme, C. (1997). Phonemic segmentation, not onset-rime segmentation, predicts early reading and spelling skills. *Reading Research Quarterly, 32,* 154–167. doi:10.1598/RRQ.32.2.2

National Early Literacy Panel. (2008). *Developing early literacy: Report of the National Early Literacy Panel.* Washington, DC: National Institute for Literacy. Available at http://lincs.ed.gov/publications/pdf/NELPReport09.pdf

National Reading Panel. (2000). *Report of the National Reading Panel: Teaching children to read–An evidence-based assessment of the scientific research literature on reading and its implications for reading instruction.* Jessup, MD: National Institute for Literacy at EDPubs.

Nielsen, D. C., & Luetke-Stahlman, B. (2002). The benefit of assessment-based language and reading instruction: Perspectives from a case study. *Journal of Deaf Studies and Deaf Education, 7(2),* 149–186.

Paris, S. G. (2011). Developmental differences in early reading skills. In S. B. Neuman & D. K. Dickinson (Eds.), *Handbook of early literacy research* (Vol. 3, pp. 228–241). New York, NY: Guilford Press.

Paul, P. V. (2009). *Language and deafness* (4th ed.). Sudbury, MA: Jones and Bartlett.

Paul, P., & Lee, C. (2010). Qualitative-similarity hypothesis. *American Annals of the Deaf, 154,* 456–462.

Phillips, B. M., & Torgesen, J. K. (2006). Phonemic awareness and reading: Beyond the growth of initial reading accuracy. In D. K. Dickinson & S. B. Neuman (Eds.), *Handbook of early literacy research* (Vol. 2, pp. 101–112). New York, NY: Guilford Press.

Pufpaff, L. A. (2009). A developmental continuum of phonological sensitivity skills. *Psychology in the Schools, 00,* 1–13. doi:10.1002/pits.20407

Roberts, T., & Neal, H. (2004). Relationships among preschool English language learners' oral proficiency in English, instructional experience and literacy development. *Contemporary Educational Psychology, 29,* 283–311.

Rose, J. (2006). *Independent review of the teaching of early reading.* Department for Education and Skills, Nottingham, United Kingdom. Available at www.standards.dfes.gov.uk/rosereview

Schatschneider, C., Francis, D. J., Foorman, B. R., Fletcher, J. M., & Mehta, P. (1999). The dimensionality of phonological awareness: An application of item response theory. *Journal of Educational Psychology, 91,* 439–449.

Shankweiler, D., Lundquist, E., Katz, L., Stuebing, K. K., Fletcher, J. M., Brady...Shaywitz, B. A. (1999). Comprehension and decoding patterns of association in children with reading difficulties. *Scientific Studies of Reading, 3,* 69–94.

Share, D. L. (1995). Phonological recoding and self-teaching: *Sine qua non* of reading acquisition. *Cognition, 55,* 151–218.

Share, D. L. (1999). Phonological recoding and orthographic learning: A direct test of the self-teaching hypothesis. *Journal of Experimental Child Psychology, 72,* 95–129.

Share, D. L. (2011). On the role of phonology in reading acquisition: The self-teaching hypothesis. In S. A. Brady, D. Braze, & C. A. Fowler (Eds.), *Explaining individual differences in reading: Theory and evidence* (pp. 45–68). New York, NY: Taylor & Francis.

Share, D. L., & Stanovich, K. E. (1995). Cognitive processes in early reading development: A model of acquisition and individual differences. *Issues in Education: Contributions from Educational Psychology, 1,* 1–57.

Shull, T. F., & Crain, K. L. (2010). Fundamental principles of Cued Speech and Cued Language. In C. J. LaSasso, K. L. Crain, & J. Leybaert (Eds.), *Cued Speech and Cued Language for deaf and hard of hearing children* (pp. 27–51). San Diego, CA: Plural.

Smith, A., & Wang, Y. (2010). The impact of Visual Phonics on the phonological awareness and speech production of a student who is deaf: A case study. *American Annals of the Deaf, 155(2),* 124–130.

Snow, C., Burns, S., & Griffin, P. (Eds.). (1998). *Preventing reading difficulties in young children.* Washington, DC: National Academy Press.

Stahl, S. A., & Murray, B. A. (1994). Defining phonological awareness and its relationship to early reading. *Journal of Educational Psychology, 86,* 221–234.

Stanovich, K. E. (1988). The right and wrong places to look for the cognitive locus of reading disability. *Annals of Dyslexia, 38,* 154–157. doi:10.1007/BF02648254

Stanovich, K. E. (1992). Speculations on the causes and consequences of individual differences in reading acquisition. In P. B. Gough, L. C. Ehri, & R. Treiman (Eds.), *Reading acquisition* (pp. 307–342). Hillsdale, NJ: Erlbaum.

Stanovich, K. E., & Siegel, L. S. (1994). Phenotypic performance profile of children with reading disabilities: A regression-based test of the phonological-core variable-difference model. *Journal of Educational Psychology, 38,* 934–947.

Storch, S., & Whitehurst, G. (2002). Oral language and code-related precursors to reading: Evidence from a longitudinal structural model. *Developmental Psychology, 38(6),* 934–947.

Stothard, S., Snowling, M., Bishop, D., Chipchase, B., & Kaplan, C. (1998). Language impaired preschoolers: A follow-up into adolescence. *Journal of Speech, Language, and Hearing Research, 41,* 407–418.

Treiman, R. (1992). The role of intrasyllabic units in learning to read and spell. In P. D. Gough, L. C. Ehri, & R. Treiman (Eds.), *Reading acquisition* (pp. 307–342). Hillsdale, NJ: Erlbaum.

Treiman, R., Tincoff, R., & Richmond-Welty, E. D. (1997) Beyond zebra: Preschoolers' knowledge about letters. *Applied Psycholinguistics, 18,* 391–409.

Treiman, R., Tincoff, R., Rodriguez, K., Mouzaki, A., & Francis, D. (1998). The foundations of literacy: Learning the sounds of letters. *Child Development, 69,* 1524–1540.

Trezek, B. J., & Wang, Y. (2006). Implications of utilizing a phonics-based reading curriculum with children who are deaf or hard of hearing. *Journal of Deaf Studies and Deaf Education, 10,* 202–213. doi:10.1093/deafed/enj031

Trezek, B. J., Wang, Y., & Paul, P. V. (2010). *Reading and deafness: Theory, research and practice.* Clifton Park, NY: Cengage Learning.

Trezek, B. J., Wang, Y., Woods, D. G., Gampp, T. L., & Paul, P. (2007). Using Visual Phonics to supplement beginning reading instruction for students who are deaf or hard of hearing. *Journal of Deaf Studies and Deaf Education, 12* (3), 373–384. doi:10.1093/deafed/enm014

Wagner, R. K., Torgesen, J. K., Laughton, P., Simmons, K., & Roshotte, C. A. (1993). The development of young readers' phonological processing abilities. *Journal of Educational Psychology, 85,* 1–20.

Wagner, R. K., Torgesen, J. K., & Rashotte, C. A. (1994). Development of reading-related phonological processing abilities: New evidence of bidirectional causality from a latent variable longitudinal study. *Developmental Psychology, 30,* 73–87.

Wagner, R. K., Torgesen, J. K., Rashotte, C. A., Hecht, S. A., Barker, T. A., Burgess, S. R....Garen, T. (1997). Changing relations between phonological processing abilities and word-level reading as children develop from beginning to skilled readers: A 5-year longitudinal study. *Developmental Psychology, 33,* 468–479.

Walley, A. C., Metsala, J. L., & Garlock, V. M. (2003). Spoken vocabulary growth: Its role in the development of phoneme awareness and early reading ability. *Reading and Writing: An Interdisciplinary Journal, 16,* 5–10.

Wang, Y., Spychala, H., Harris, R. S., & Oetting, T. L. (2013). The effectiveness of a phonics-based early intervention for deaf and hard of hearing preschool children and its possible impact on reading skills in elementary school: A case study. *American Annals of the Deaf, 158*(2), 107–120.

Warden, P. E., & Boettcher, W. (1990). Young children's acquisition of alphabet knowledge. *Journal of Reading Behavior, 22,* 277–295.

What Works Clearinghouse (2007). *Dialogic reading.* U.S. Department of Education, Institute of Educational Sciences. Available at http://ies.ed.gov/ncee/wwc/pdf/intervention_reports/WWC_Dialogic_Reading_020807.pdf

Williams, C., & Mayer, C. (in press). Writing in young deaf children. *Review of Educational Research.*

4

Early Writing

Well before they can form letters or have much knowledge of the alphabet, children show an interest in writing—in making meaning by putting marks on a page. Children's early interest in writing has been a focus of attention since the start of the twentieth century, and in foreshadowing the early literacy work to come, Iredell (1898) suggested that "scribbling is to writing what babbling is to talking, preceding it, holding the same office of forming the organ, giving practice in shaping the elements. As a babbling child thinks he talks, so the scribbling child thinks he writes.. . . We are told, 'He must learn to read and write.' As if he had not already taken the first steps, and of his own volition, his efforts unrecognised for what they are" (p. 235). Taking a similar perspective, several decades later, Hildreth (1936) identified three levels of scribbling in name writing that were recognized in children from three to four and a half years of age. At about the same time, Luria (1929/1978) and Vygotsky investigated whether three-, four-, and five-year-old children could use writing as a means for recalling sentences to serve a mnemonic function. They found that the indiscriminate scrawls the children produced did not function as an aid to memory, prompting them to label this sort of early written production as undifferentiated-noninstrumental.

Yet it remains the case that historically, there has been relatively less research attention paid to learning to write, in contrast with the massive amount of work done on learning to read (Kress, 1994). Kress suggests that this may be a consequence of the differences in the ways in which the relationship between code and making meaning in the processes of learning to read and write are often viewed. That is, in the process of learning to read, a child must learn to decode the encoded form of the language to glean the intended meaning of an absent writer. In contrast, the young child writer is in control of the meaning he or she intends to make and must only learn how to encode it. In such a conceptualization, learning to read seems to present a greater challenge than learning to write and would therefore warrant more research attention.

However, such a take is ironic when one considers that for most individuals, reading is seen as more pleasurable and easier than writing, and it would be a fair assumption to suggest that while the majority of the population would call themselves readers, far fewer would refer to themselves as writers. This is not surprising, given that writing is often regarded as the most demanding, complex cognitive activity that most individuals undertake (Singer & Bashir, 2004). And as Kress (1994) remarks with respect to the early years, "Considering how painlessly children learn to talk, the difficulties they face in learning to write are quite pronounced. Indeed some children never learn to write at all, and many fall far short of proficiency in the task" (p. ix). For deaf children, the situation is no different, and we would suggest that these children face challenges in learning to write that are as great as, or arguably even greater than, those they face in learning to read (Moores, 1987; Mayer, 2010). As one of our deaf students so aptly remarked, "When I read, the English is already there. When I write, I have to put the English on the page." Yet in the early years, it could be argued that children are naturally motivated to explore writing, with the first urges being to write rather than to read, and that we have not taken advantage of this fact in either research or practice (Clay, 1983; Graves, 1978).

We would suggest that it is possible to reconcile these apparent contradictions and tensions if one considers the process of learning to write as an evolving process, through the lens of the relative roles played by code-related and language-related skills in the move from first scribbles to the composition of extended text. This is the conceptualization that we will explore in this chapter. This line of thinking is consistent with and informed by current views of young children learning to write in which the process is viewed from a developmental perspective, one in which children are first sensitive to the presence and use of writing in their worlds and then develop understandings of how the writing system works (Tolchinsky, 2006). Since the seminal work of Ferreiro and her colleagues (Ferreiro, 1986, 1990; Ferreiro & Teberosky, 1982), who examined early writing development in Spanish-speaking children, this process has been investigated in numerous other languages and contexts (e.g., Bissex, 1980; Chan, 1998; Clay, 1983; Dyson, 1984; Harste, Woodward & Burke, 1984; Levin & Bus, 2003; Pontecorvo & Zuccchermaglio, 1988; Sulzby, 1989; Tolchinsky & Landsmann, 1986). In all of these investigations, children are characterized as being dynamic constructors of knowledge about written language and the ways in which print can be used to make meaning. In this developmental process, children must sort out the arbitrariness of the ways written symbols come to stand in for the words and ideas they can speak or think, learning to establish the relationships between the symbols and the units of language they represent along the way, and seeming to progress through a similar process irrespective of language or writing system (Perez, 2004).

Following from this and consistent with our view that deaf children must master the same set of knowledge and skills as hearing children in the early years if they are to become proficient readers and writers, we will appeal to the framework for learning to write that has been well documented for hearing children. More specifically, we will adopt the three levels suggested by Ferreiro (1990) as the basis for discussing what is essential in the early writing development of deaf children. Ferreiro's levels are particularly expedient, as they concentrate on the ways in which the relationships between face-to-face language and text are realized in the course of development (see Mayer, 2007, for an additional discussion). The focus is on how children come to understand three different representation systems for making meaning—spoken language, drawing, and writing—and how the emergence of writing moves from a general understanding that writing is distinct from drawing to an understanding of phoneme-grapheme correspondence (Perez, 2004). In adopting this perspective, we take the view that children are active theory builders who make sense of the writing system as they engage in text-based activities mediated through their interactions with parents, caregivers, other adults, and peers.

In the following sections, we will use these levels to describe the processes that are the focus of phase 3 in early literacy development, the stage at which children must sort out the relationships between their face-to-face language and print (see description in chapter 2). To illustrate the nature of development during this phase, we will present writing samples from both hearing and deaf children, drawing attention to the similarities and differences in order to inform our understandings of what is critical at each step of the process and to identify what is (or should be) happening at each stage. Any divergence from the typical, expected pattern of development is worthy of attention, as it could indicate potential difficulties with future literacy learning (Clay, 2002; Cramer, 2006) and shed light on how code-related and language-related abilities are implicated in the process.

STAGES OF WRITTEN LANGUAGE DEVELOPMENT IN PHASE 3

Before presenting a description of the stages of early writing development, we would caution that these levels should not be understood as a series of discrete, linear steps. Given the intricacy of written language as a complex web of interconnecting syntactic, semantic, and discourse systems (Nelson, 1996), it is reasonable to assume that children will not make sense of this system in a neat, tidy, and sequential order. Rather, we propose, as do others (Chang-Wells & Wells, 1996; Edelsky, 1986; Kress, 1994), that this process is more malleable and involves organizing and reorganizing along the way, as children learn to simultaneously balance the competing demands of the orthographic, semantic, syntactic, and pragmatic systems that are part and parcel of learning to write. That being said, using these levels as the basis for this discussion does provide a platform for considering children's meaning construction over the course of the early years of development, providing evidence of what they know and have gained control of and, more specifically for our purposes, how early reading and writing are related and how code-related and language-related abilities and skills come into play at different stages in the process.[1]

Level 1: Distinguishing Drawing from Writing

This first level is concerned with learning to make the distinction between writing and other systems for representing meaning (i.e., speaking, signing, and drawing) but in particular between the visual representations of drawing and writing. In the very young child, early scribbling or drawing functions as writing, and from the ages of twelve months to eighteen months, as soon as young children are able to hold a crayon, they make undifferentiated scribbles on a page (Sulzby, 1989). (See figure 4.1.) In these very early attempts, writing and drawing are undifferentiated as systems for making meaning, and it is not until about two to three years of age that children begin to differentiate between the two (Sulzby, 1991).

At this point, Harste et al. (1984) argue that children, "regardless of race, or socioeconomic status, differentiated writing from drawing.... Generally the children's art was characterized as being global, centralized and connected.... Their writing on the other hand was typically linear, spaced, and located off-center" (pp. 127–128). The ability to make this differentiation rests on the child's growing awareness that as systems for representing meaning, drawing and writing function differently in terms of what they are meant to signify, even though the same kinds of lines or marks are used in both activities. Drawings look like the objects they are meant to represent, whereas written words do not (e.g., drawing a picture of a tree versus writing the word *tree*), and in this sense, writing exists outside the iconic domain (Ferreiro, 1990). In other words, children must come to see that the lines used in writing have nothing to do with the form of the object being referred to. Unlike drawing, the written word, unless it is mediated through the spoken form of the language it represents, bears no relationship to the referent directly; that is, it constitutes a second-order representation and, as such, is a more complex system to master (see also the discussion in chapter 2).

As children come to understand this difference and recognize the arbitrary nature of the written system, they attempt to capture this in their efforts. Their writing begins to display the features common to script in almost any language: linearity, presence of distinguishable

---

[1] This discussion expands on the description of these levels as presented in Mayer (2007).

Figure 4.1 Scribble writing, twenty-month-old hearing child.

units, regularity of blanks, and directionality (Tolchinsky, 2006). As a consequence of exposure to print and given active opportunities to engage with text (e.g., being read to), writing begins to assume this text-like form (e.g., scribbles that move from left to right, parallel rows of scribbles, spaces between scribbles), and children may also begin to incorporate standard letters into their writing in a random fashion. In doing so, we would argue that they essentially draw a picture of the texts they have seen, creating a graphic representation of the written language they have encountered in their environment.

Ferreiro (1990) labeled this stage "undifferentiated writing," as neither the composer of the text (the child) nor the reader (the adult) can interpret what is meant from the written display alone (Ferreiro & Teberosky, 1982). At this level, children understand that written language is a form of communication and assign meaning to the text, but as the graphic representations are not standard, the meaning cannot be reconstructed from the text without the assistance of the author. As the text itself does not drive the rereading, the interpretation of the text may change from one iteration to the next, the meaning being driven by the intent of the writer or the context, but not by the text in which this meaning is represented.

Overall, this first level in children's writing produces two major accomplishments: "[1] to consider strings of letters as substitute objects, and [2] to make a clear distinction between two modes of representation—the iconic mode (to draw) and the noniconic mode (to write)" (Ferreiro, 1990, p. 16). At this stage, the reading-writing connection is tenuous, as children have not yet made sense of written language as a second-order representation system, as standing for the spoken language and not the object. While language-related skills come into play at this level, as children understand that it is the meaning of their face-to-face language that is captured in the text, there is no control of the code-related skills that allow the child to make the links between talk and text.

A consideration of texts at this level reveals very little difference between the writing of hearing children and that of deaf children (see figures 4.2 and 4.3), and we would suggest from our own experience and from the available research literature that deaf children readily produce this kind of writing, perhaps accounting for the observation that development in the earliest years is similar between the two groups (Williams, 2004). In both examples, it is possible to identify the difference between the drawing and the writing, with the writing featuring scribbles or marks in spaced, linear rows. Both hearing and deaf children are able to attach a meaning to these texts and to recount the meaning of the text in spoken and/or signed face-to-face language. They have a clear sense of what they want to write about,

Figure 4.2 Level 1, drawing versus writing, four-year-old hearing child.

Figure 4.3 Level 1, drawing versus writing, six-year-old deaf child.

and they recognize that the text can carry this meaning. As is consistent with development at this stage, they are using text-like features in producing this written message, but there is no relationship between the graphic representation and the face-to-face language. Any recounting of the message is not bound by the constraints of the text, and the "reading" may change from one instance to the next.

We would suggest that the similarity in development that is evidenced at this stage is a result of the fact that the written language is nonrepresentational of the spoken language. While language underpins literacy development at this stage, any potential mismatch between language and the arbitrary symbol system in which the language is encoded will not yet be apparent. All children at this age are operating on the hypothesis that written language represents the object or the meaning directly, and this understanding relies primarily on what can be gleaned via the visual, not the auditory channel, an avenue that is not inherently problematic for young deaf children.

Level 2: Incorporating Properties of Written Text

Development at the second level is typified by an increasing understanding of the arbitrariness of writing and a greater influence of the texts that the child has encountered in his or her environment. It also marks the phase when children are exploring features of writing and, in the process, discovering that some elements are distinctive to the particular writing system they are engaged with. For example, children arrange their written productions with an eye to properties of text that include linearly distinctive units, with spacing that is consistent with the writing systems of the language to which they have been exposed. Children also become aware of quantitative and qualitative principles for creating words (Ferreiro, 1990; Perez, 2004), developing the sense that in any given language, there are a minimum or a maximum number of letters in a word and that certain arrangements of letters within a word are improbable (e.g., repeating the same letter three times in consecutive position in Spanish). These "rules that children impose on number and variety are not mere inventions, they represent the actual distribution of word length and intraword variation found in real text" (Tolchinsky, 2006, p. 89).

At this level, children do not invent graphics for letters but utilize the standard letters of the script provided by their environment, coming to see that identical letter strings represent the same object. One of the well-documented avenues into text for young writers at this stage is through learning to write their own names. It is often the first time children learn to use conventional letters to correctly represent written language, and even children as young as three or four will remember and recognize their names in print, something that is not usually the case for other words (see Bloodgood, 1999: Puranik & Lonigan, 2011; Tolchinsky, Landsmann, & Levin, 1985, for discussions). Coming to these understandings is a consequence of continued exposure and interaction with text, as children's writing evidences the features of the writing system they have experienced. For example, in the case of English, this means the use of the standard alphabet and the incorporation of some memorized patterns (e.g., child's name, high-frequency vocabulary).

One of the additional features of this stage is that younger children will conflate the physical properties of the object with the linguistic representation. In this sense, they continue to see the text as representing the thing directly, a first-order representation. For example, children will use longer words to denote bigger objects (e.g., *train* must be a long word because a train is a long vehicle) (Papandropoulou & Sinclair, 1974). When asked to write *three ducks*, children will make three marks, which they will then read individually as *duck, duck, duck*. However, when asked to read it "all together," they will say *three ducks* (Ferreiro & Teberosky, 1982). Writing phrases such as *There aren't any birds* proves especially confusing for young children, as they cannot reconcile making a mark on the page with a representation of negation, or "nothingness." At this stage, the presence of marks or letters seems incompatible with the absence of the object (Ferreiro, 1986, as cited in Kamawar & Homer, 2000). Homer and Olson (1999) drew similar conclusions in a study of English-speaking children between three and six years of age. As a group, the younger children, when asked to write expressions including a quantity (e.g., *two dogs*) and a negation (e.g., *no dog*), responded in similar fashion to the Spanish-speaking children in Ferreiro's studies. Olson (1994) gives the example of preschool children who, when asked to write *cat*, will write a short string of letters and then, if asked to write *three cats*, will repeat the same string three times. Just as in the previous examples, the text produced is emblematic of the objects themselves, the cats, rather than of the words, *three cats*.

What marks this stage is that, just as in the previous level, it precedes any knowledge of the second-order relationship that exists between the face-to-face language and the written representation. Although there is a growing awareness that the written language is in some way related to the face-to-face form, the young writer at this level is continuing to make a first-order, direct relationship between the object and the text. Even though the child understands that the text conveys the meaning of the spoken and/or signed utterance, there is no explicit understanding of how one representation is captured in the other. The child is using the text as a form of iconic representation of the object itself, rather than as a representation of the word or sign for that object. A similar manifestation of this understanding is when young children "read" logos such as *McDonald's* and *Coke*, interpreting these items as standing directly for the things themselves, not for the words they represent (Olson, 1994).

Just as in level 1, there is little to differentiate the texts of deaf and hearing writers. In fact, deaf children will often use a greater number of standard letters and overlearned words in their writing, as, by virtue of more opportunities for structured early language teaching, they have had more systematic instruction in these areas than the typical hearing child. The samples in figure 4.4 (created by a five-year-old hearing child) and figure 4.5 (created by a six-year-old deaf child) exhibit the features that are typical of development at this stage. Both writers use standard alphabet letters in combinations of vowels and consonants to create words, applying principles of quantity and quality, with words of reasonable length (at least three letters and no more than nine), and using a different set of letter combinations to represent different meanings. The writing is organized in a text-like fashion, and both children are readily able to provide an oral and/or signed interpretation for what they have written.

It remains the case for both groups of children that although they are learning more about the visual aspects of text (i.e., code-related, print-based concepts such as directionality, letter formation, spacing), they are not yet making any explicit auditory link between the graphic

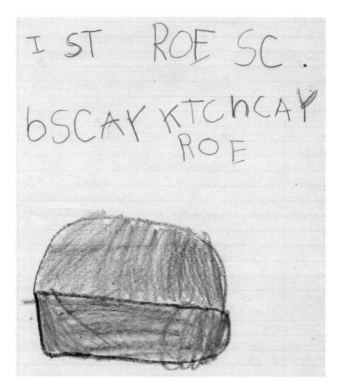

Figure 4.4 Level 2, properties of text, five-year-old hearing child.

representation and the spoken language. Their writing is still nonphonetic. This being the case, any challenges deaf children may have in developing the phonological aspects of encoding would not be evident at this level.

Level 3: Connecting Spoken/Signed Language to Written Language

At this third level, young children make the most critical move from emergent to conventional literacy. An in-depth examination of what occurs at this stage is particularly crucial to our discussion, as this is when the writing of many deaf children begins to look markedly different from that of their hearing peers. Teale (2003) suggests that "understanding this transition is especially critical [for all young literacy learners] because a significant number of children get hung up in their learning during this time, and because what happens during this period seems to have significant influence on children's progress in literacy achievement across later grade levels" (p. 26). We would argue that this observation is definitely applicable to the situation of the young deaf writer.

Figure 4.5 Level 2, properties of text, six-year-old deaf child.

Children must begin to understand that sounds correspond to letters, discovering in the process that every word and utterance has a phonic aspect. Ferreiro calls this the "phonetization of the written representation" (1990, p. 20) and describes this all-important shift as one in which children "learn that letters serve the function of representing that fundamental property of objects that drawing is not able to achieve, that is, their names" (1986, p. 28). In other words, this is the stage at which children come to see that there is not a direct relationship between object and written language. Rather, there is an intermediary link, that is, the words and/or signs of the face-to-face language that mediate the creation of the text.

The challenge for children in learning to write at this juncture is to bring together two sets of understandings: their knowledge of the face-to-face language and what they have come to know about how print works. They must find or detect aspects of their own implicit linguistic structure that can be mapped onto or be represented by the script (Olson, 1994). For this to be accomplished, children must have familiarity with both the spoken and written forms of the *same* language. They will rely on their implicit knowledge and control of the structures of this face-to-face language (i.e., its semantic, syntactic, and phonological aspects) to provide the data for reflecting on the language and being able to capture it in print. They must also have access to a set of conventional print categories (e.g., letters, written words) into which this language knowledge can be organized (Homer & Olson, 1999). In the normal course of events, these two sets of understandings converge, as there is a culturally predetermined way in which any language is represented in its script. Young writers face the task of uncovering this relationship.

Regardless of language or writing system, children must sort out the systematic relationships between their face-to-face language and the text. In the process, they reassess their language in terms of this relationship, and they begin to understand their spoken and/or signed language in new ways (Ferreiro and Teberosky, 1982; Olson, 1994). Watson (2001) contends that "any orthography necessarily creates conceptual categories for thinking about language in that it requires the user to segment the stream of speech into units that can be described by that orthography. Orthographies can be thought of as the theories of language they are created or adapted to represent" (p. 44).

All beginning writers must unravel this symbiotic relationship between face-to-face language and text and learn how each form makes sense in terms of the other (Homer & Olson, 1999; Olson, 1994). Children do this by using the structures of their spoken language as the platform for making sense of text, and in turn, the text provides a model for rethinking the nature of the spoken language. Concepts and categories such as letter, word, and sentence only become evident through the process of committing language to paper, but as they are made explicit, the child is able to use them as a way to reflect on the spoken or signed language. In this way, learning to write drives metalinguistic awareness.

For example, in the course of speaking, people do not generally pause between words; words are typically grouped into units that often do not coincide with a grammatical notion of *word* (e.g., saying versus writing "I don't know") (see Tolchinsky, 2006, for a discussion). At the level of letter, consider the English example of *elemeno*. As a consequence of numerous recitations of the alphabet and singing of the alphabet song, children say the letters *l, m, n, o* as a single unit (i.e., *elemeno*). It is only after exposure to the alphabet in its printed form that they come to realize that these are separate letters and not a word. These are instructive examples of the ways in which print brings spoken language into consciousness, thus helping the young writer make the connections between the two.

In making these connections between face-to-face language and text, children employ a range of strategies arising from two interdependent sets of processes and skills: *outside-in* and *inside-out* (Whitehurst & Lonigan, 1998, 2001). Outside-in components develop through informal social processes in the preschool years and stand outside the printed word. These include general language competencies such as knowledge of concepts, words, syntax, story structure, and the conventions of print. Inside-out components are more specific to text and are derived from sources of information inside the printed word. These are the skills that allow for the rendering of sounds into letters and include knowing letter names, letter-sound associations, and phonological awareness (Pressley, 2006). Whereas outside-in skills support general comprehension and are more important somewhat later in the literacy learning process, inside-out skills are particularly important in the early sequence of learning to write when the emphasis is on making sense of the linguistic code itself (Lonigan, 2006).

The focus of much debate, especially in the field of deaf education, has been on these inside-out, code-related skills, specifically the notion of phonological awareness (see Mayer & Trezek, 2014; also the discussion in chapter 3). For the purposes of this discussion, we will refer to phonological awareness as "the ability to detect or manipulate the sound structure of oral language"[1] (Lonigan, 2006, p. 78). It is the chief means by which young writers make the systematic connection between talk and text and the only variable that has shown a causal, rather than a correlational, relationship in the development of literacy (Phillips & Torgensen, 2006; Pressley, 2006; Scarborough, 2001). The centrality of its role for young hearing literacy learners is considerable, making it a better predictor of early literacy success than any other variable including IQ (Stanovich, 2000). "Although phonological recoding may play a minor role in skilled adult reading [and writing], it plays a critical role in helping the child become a skilled reader [and writer]" (Form & Share, 1983, p. 105). As discussed in chapter 2, these code-related abilities assume relatively different importance at various stages of the literacy learning process, and we would suggest that at this stage of learning to write, these code-related, phonological skills are central and necessary in learning how to encode spoken language in written text. In the majority of cases where young children encounter difficulties in learning to read and write, these are attributable to deficits in phonological awareness (Scarborough, 2001; Stanovich, 2000). This suggests that it may be a question not of whether, but of how phonological processing abilities play a role in early literacy development.

With respect to deaf children, arguments have been made about whether phonological awareness plays a role in the process of reading

---

[1] When the term *oral language* is used, it reflects the terminology employed in the original source (e.g., NELP, a published study, etc.). This term is often used synonymously with *spoken language* in the broader literature in the field of literacy. It is only in the field of deafness that the distinction between oral and spoken language merits attention.

and learning to read (e.g., Allen et al., 2009; Burden & Campbell, 1994; Hanson, 1986, 1989, 1991; Hanson & Fowler, 1987; Kelly, 1993, 1995; Leybaert, 1993; Miller 2002, 2006; Paul, Wang, Trezek, & Luckner, 2009; Wang, Trezek, Luckner, & Paul, 2008; Waters & Doehring, 1990; see also the review in chapter 1). It has even been suggested that "the 43 or 44 phonemes of spoken American English present a barrier to reading [and writing], when our print system has only 26 symbols and that there is a closer relation between print and the manual alphabet, thus enabling us [deaf learners] to bypass phonology" (Moores, 2001, p. 3). The implication is that young deaf children can learn to write by engaging with print in the absence of any code-related, phonological mediation, the strategy that for hearing children is the hallmark of this stage of development.

What phonological awareness affords, and what makes it so crucial in the development of early literacy, is that it is the primary means by which young readers and writers make the systematic connections between spoken language and text. Even though there may not always be a one-to-one match between sound and symbol, it is the strategy that is most effective in allowing writers to think about their language in terms of the text, holding true in every language studied to date, even Chinese (Ashby & Rayner, 2006). It is the means by which young writers encode their language in the written form. While learning to write rests on more than encoding every word, children cannot capture their meaning and intent in the text if they are not first able to capture their talk (at the level of word) in the written code. As children move on to composing more syntactically and semantically complex texts, a level of automaticity in encoding must be achieved so that cognitive attention can be shifted to these semantic and syntactic aspects of making meaning with written language.

In alphabetic languages (e.g., English, Spanish, French), children come to learn that letters represent individual sounds (i.e., the alphabetic principle), and as they make sense of this in their early writing, they tend to ignore any irregularities in the orthography of the target language. This poses more challenges in languages with deep orthographies in which the correspondence between phoneme and grapheme is irregular (e.g., English) than in languages with a shallow orthography where one grapheme always represents one phoneme (e.g., Finnish).

At this level in the process of learning to write, spelling provides a unique window into how children are coming to terms with making the connection between talk and text, at least at the sublexical and lexical levels. It provides insights into how code and language come together in the process of encoding words that are already in the young writer's spoken or signed vocabulary. It could even be argued that a child's potential grasp of the alphabetic principle can be underestimated if one only considers decoding, as "spelling [encoding] is the primary early indicator of this potential and can form the basis of later expression of the alphabetic principles in decoding" (Rayner, Foorman, Perfetti, Pesetsky, & Seidenberg, 2001, p. 41). In some sense, spelling (encoding) is writing at this early stage, as the major challenge facing children is how to represent their spoken and/or signed language in print. Children themselves do not disambiguate between the two, and as Kress (2000) notes, children will typically say "How do you write Charlie?" rather than "How do you spell Charlie?"

Invented spellings, characteristic of children's work at this stage, provide a particularly informative insight into how young writers deal with the challenge of representing spoken language in a written form. In the process, children exploit what they know about phoneme-grapheme correspondences in order to commit spoken language to paper (Kress, 1997). Individuals fluent in the language are able to read these texts using their decoding strategies, their knowledge of that particular language's sound-symbol correspondences. Moreover, the use of invented spelling, which is phonologically rather than orthographically driven, strongly predicts later progress in decoding and understanding the alphabetic principle (see Whitehurst & Lonigan, 2001, for discussion). In inventing these spellings, children use the point of articulation as a reference for making sound-symbol decisions, and they can often be seen to exaggerate articulations in an attempt to get a feel for the sounds they are attempting to write (Juel, 2006). It is in this process that hearing children draw on their knowledge of letter names as they write, to aid in making sense of grapheme-phoneme associations. With the exception of *W*, letter names in English contain some of the relevant phonemes that are symbolized by that letter (e.g., *T* contains /t/, and *F* contains /f/) (Ehri & Roberts, 2006; see also chapter 3), and therefore, it is reasonable that young writers would make use of this relationship as they encode. Consider the examples in figures 4.6 and 4.7, and note the spellings of *Ferankkenstyn* for *Frankenstein* (figure 4.6) and *siyens* for *science* and *kownt* for *count* (figure 4.7) in the texts of two young hearing writers.

Deaf students who use predominantly oral (Johnson, Padak & Barton, 1994) and signed (Mayer, 1994, 1998; Schleper, 1992) modes of communication have also been shown to use invented spellings. Like hearing children, they are analytical and logical in the process, understanding that there is a relationship to be made between spoken or signed communication and text. Although both groups of deaf students used invented spellings, only the oral group made use of phoneme-grapheme relationships similar to those of hearing children. Children with cochlear implants, whose primary mode of communication is spoken language, evidence the use of invented spellings that are indistinguishable from that seen in hearing writers. In the example in figure 4.8, a six-year-old deaf child (implanted at 1.10 years) writes *Brz h s* for *Bryar's house.* In figure 4.9, a seven-year-old deaf child (implanted

Figure 4.6 Level 3, spoken to written language, six-year-old hearing child.

Figure 4.7 Level 3, spoken to written language, six-year-old hearing child.

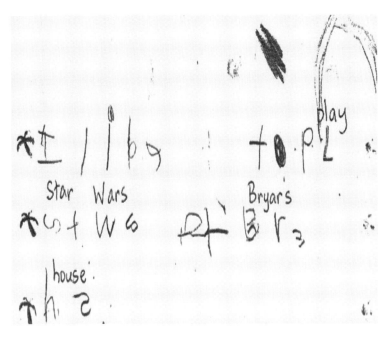

Figure 4.8 Level 3, spoken to written language, six-year-old deaf child with a cochlear implant (implanted at 1.10 years old).

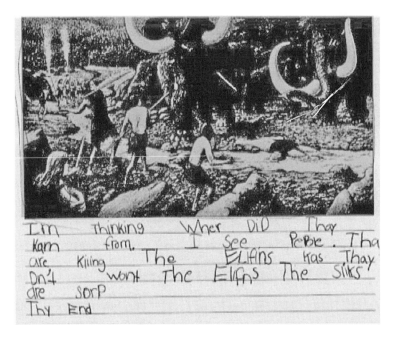

Figure 4.9 Level 3, spoken to written language, seven-year-old deaf child with a cochlear implant (implanted at 1.3 years).

at 1.3 years) uses a number of invented spellings in writing the sentence *Tha are kiling The ELifins kas Thay dn't wont The ELifns* (*They are killing the elephants because they don't want the elephants*).

In contrast, the signing children made connections that were distinctive to making this relationship between a signed utterance and the written form. They employed strategies such as mapping handshapes onto English words and linking fingerspelling to text (e.g., spelling the word *apple* with *x* as the first letter, because in ASL, the sign for *apple* is made with an *x* handshape). Figure 4.10 provides an example from a seven-year-old-deaf writer. Unlike the previous examples in figures 4.6, it is not possible to read the text, with the exception of a few isolated words and phrases (e.g., *I LoVe Vailentine*). Note also how *drink* is spelled as *cies*. The writer has based this spelling

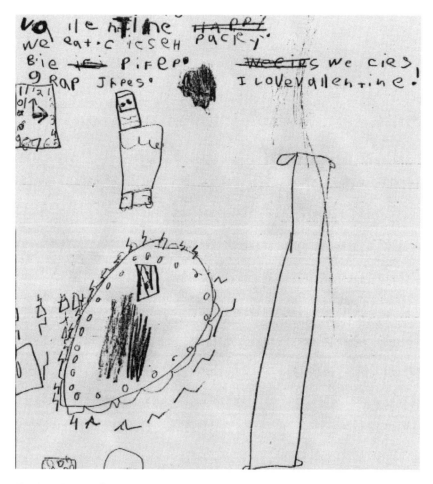

Figure 4.10 Level 3, sign to written language, seven-year-old deaf child.

Figure 4.11 Level 3, sign to written language, six-year-old deaf child.

on the ASL sign for the word *drink* that is made with a *c* handshape. In figure 4.11, notice how in the second line of her text, a six-year-old deaf writer uses *kiss* for the word *punk*, as the ASL sign for the word is produced with a *k* handshape, and in the next line, she relies on the *c* handshape (the ASL classifier used to make the sign) when writing *crases* to mean *long hair.*

To sum up, the child's major accomplishment at the third level of early literacy development is learning that writing represents spoken language, and not meaning directly, and that writing is mediated by the spoken form of the language, including its phonology. In coming to terms with the alphabetic principle, or whatever systematic strategy applies given the nature of the language (see Juel, 2006, for a discussion), children find a stable frame for representing any language in text, and in this transition, children rely primarily on auditory and not visual strategies. At this stage, learning to write depends more on ear than on eye.

In examining written language samples from young hearing and deaf writers at this stage, it becomes apparent that the writing of some deaf children does not parallel that of their hearing peers (e.g., figures 4.10 and 4.11). We would suggest that, in contrast with the other young writers, these children did not have the necessary control of either the language-related or code-related requisites to sort out the relationships at this stage. Although these children do understand what writing is and actively try to map their spoken and/or signed language to written text, they lack both the linguistic competence that allows them to orally compose in the language of the text and the related ability in the phonological, code-related skills that allow for the encoding of this language. It is not surprising that differences become apparent at this stage, as this is the point in the process of learning to write when children rely more on audition than on vision. This is borne out by the fact that the deaf children who have more potential to use these auditory strategies (e.g., those with cochlear implants) do not evidence the same kinds of deficits.

We would argue that it is these interrelated challenges of language and code that lie at the heart of the early literacy challenges facing these deaf writers and are at the core of why they do not go on to develop the conventional early literacy skills that are necessary for more advanced reading and writing development at phase 4, the use of academic, school-based texts. Unless we can provide ways to give all deaf writers access to the auditory aspects of the language of the text, including hearing technologies and those visual strategies that allow the eye to stand in for the ear, they will continue to struggle to develop the early literacy foundation that is essential for becoming a proficient writer.

IMPLICATIONS FOR PRACTICE

1. **Given the central role language plays in learning to write, it is critical to ensure that deaf children have the requisite foundation in place, in the face-to-face form of the language of the text, and that there is a continued emphasis on the development of this language.**

There is no getting around the fact that learning to write depends on having a foundation in a face-to-face form of the language of the text (e.g., communicative competence in spoken English); as in all languages, written systems are derived from their spoken form. It is this linguistic facility that allows the child to orally compose, to first generate the language "through the air" so that it can then be written down. In this way, writing can be characterized as a process of transcription. A critical feature of this transcription process involves learning how to capture or encode this spoken language in a print form. Language knowledge is necessary to sort this out, as children must uncover the systematic yet arbitrary relationships between language and text that are unique to each language (e.g., sound-symbol relationships that differ across alphabetic languages, grapheme-to-syllable relationships in syllabic-based writing systems). For deaf children, as we emphasized in chapter 2, this language competence is the prerequisite for learning to write, and children who attempt to do so without this foundation are destined to struggle.

2. **Early writing programs for young deaf children should be designed to reflect what is known to be best practice for other young literacy learners.**

The motivation for using language in any form is to make meaning, and writing is no exception in this regard. Early writing programs should be designed to reflect this principle, ensuring that the interactions with text are relevant, purposeful, and functional for the learner. All children should be given daily opportunities to experiment with reading and writing, linking the use of text with real-life experiences and the active use of language (Teale & Sulzby, 1989). Well-designed programs should reflect a balance between a focus on meaning (writing in use) and skills instruction, taking advantage of the strengths of both (Pressley, 2006; Stanovich, 2000). For at-risk learners, including those who are deaf, the balance in an integrated literacy program may need to be adjusted to provide extra support in areas of weakness (Xue & Meisels, 2004), but this should not be taken as an endorsement for reducing early writing programs to the teaching of a discrete set of skills. Rather, we would argue for a pedagogical approach in which areas of relative need are identified via assessment, and interventions designed to address any gaps (e.g., direct teaching of sound-symbol relationships).

With respect to a model for early writing instruction, we would argue for the efficacy of a process writing approach (Graves, 1978), and such programs have been implemented with young deaf children (e.g., Conway, 1985; Ewoldt, 1985; Mayer, 1994; Williams, 1993, 2011). Overall, children in these programs have demonstrated positive benefits, such as more meaningful engagement with text, a more positive attitude toward writing, and the incorporation of richer content and ideas. However, many children continue to face challenges with respect to developing the encoding abilities that are necessary to achieve conventional literacy (see Mayer, 2010, for a discussion). This is not to say that we abandon a process writing model, as it has demonstrated efficacy with hearing learners, but that we should be mindful of designing learning environments that also afford opportunities for the attainment of the linguistic, phonologic, and orthographic understandings and skills that are necessary to engage meaningfully in the process.

3. **Recognize the importance of developing the code-related strategies (particularly phonological awareness) that are necessary for encoding spoken and/or signed language in written text.**

We recognize that there continues to be debate on this point in the field, and in their review of the issue, Schirmer and McGough (2005) note that it is not yet known whether explicit training in phonological awareness is effective for deaf children. They speculate about whether it is possible that making visual connections between language and text (e.g., fingerspelling and signing) can work in ways that are comparable to what phonological processing affords for hearing children. Padden (2006) takes the view that fingerspelling should be a part of preschool children's language development, as they can use it to make a link to words and the development of literacy, describing this as pushing toward "a convergence of skills where the skill of fingerspelling is aligned to the skill of reading and written spelling" (p. 197).

While there may be some benefits in making links in these ways, we would contend that these visual connections are not commensurate with those that hearing children make via phonological processing, and do not build the same insights about what is captured in the written mode for young writers as they talk their way into text. As was described in chapter 3 with respect to learning to read, fingerspelling represents the grapheme directly (i.e., the handshape for the letter *a* stands for the written letter and gives no clue to the letter name). While fingerspelling can be used to highlight some aspects of spoken language as children attempt to capture their language on paper (e.g., using the manual alphabet to mark word endings such as "*s*" that can be difficult to hear, almost as a form of manual highlighting), this is fundamentally not the same process and therefore is not an adequate substitute for the range of phonological processing strategies that hearing children employ as they learn to write.

Therefore, we would argue that in like fashion to their hearing peers, deaf children must be able to make use of the strategies that have been shown to be most effective and necessary in making the link between face-to-face and written language. As we suggested above, for hearing children, the inside-out strategies related to phonological processing (i.e., making phoneme-grapheme, spelling-sound correspondences) have been shown to be pivotal in linking talk and text, allowing them to write any words that are in their face-to-face language by sounding them out.

This emphasis on the centrality of phonological processing to the activity of learning to write should not be taken as an argument against the use of visual strategies. As we have argued elsewhere (Mayer, 1999; Mayer 1998; Trezek, Wang, & Paul, 2010; Wang et al., 2008), there are ways in which the substance of phonological processing can be realized via alternative routes in which the eye can stand in for what is typically accomplished by ear alone. While all young writers make use of more than audition alone as they "sound out" words (e.g., tactile-kinesthetic feedback), some of these strategies are unique to deaf learners and are a consequence of the idiosyncratic ways in which signed and spoken modes can be combined. Although the focus for the use of these alternative strategies in the literature is usually discussed in terms of learning to read, we would suggest that they apply equally to learning to write. For example, if the phonological code can be derived receptively through speechreading (e.g., Harris and Moreno, 2006; Kyle & Harris, 2011; Marschark, Siple, Lillo-Martin, Campbell, & Everhart, 1997), its expressive counterpart (mouthing) can play a role in making sense of the phonological stream in the process of encoding (Mayer, 1999).

Similar arguments have been made for the use of Cued Speech (Leybaert, Colin, & LaSasso, 2010) and Visual Phonics (Trezek & Wang, 2006; Trezek, Wang, Woods, Gampp, & Paul, 2007; see also chapter 3), especially as they can be used to develop phonological, code-related abilities in the process of learning to read. While they have not yet been investigated to the same extent, these avenues could provide visual support for developing the phonological abilities that are equally critical for learning to write. It has also been proposed that it is through the multimodal integration of numerous input sources (audition, articulation, speechreading, fingerspelling, cueing, visual phonics, and writing) that phonological abilities can be accessed and developed (Leybaert, 1993; Mayer, 1998; Mayer, 2007; Trezek et al., 2010; Wang et al., 2008). We would argue that taking advantage of the viability of any or all of these routes (or others that may yet be identified) can afford the possibility for all young deaf writers to develop the phonologically based, code-related skills that are necessary to encode spoken language. Such an approach is particularly relevant in the current context of improvements in hearing technologies that allow the overwhelming majority of deaf children meaningful access to spoken language input, including its phonological aspects. Supplementing this auditory information with visual input where necessary allows children access to the phonological stream of the language when ears alone are not enough (Mayer, 2012; in press). In sum, for us, the issue is not how we develop these code-related abilities but rather that we do.

Before leaving this topic, it is important to briefly address the issue of those code-related skills that are print-related. As described above with respect to the first two levels of development in phase 3, deaf children's writing demonstrates the same print-related understandings as that of their hearing counterparts. They seem to face few challenges in coming to understand that writing is different from drawing and that text conveys meaning, readily acquiring concepts of print such as directionality, spacing, and the incorporation of standard graphemes. While this set of skills is important in learning to write, we would argue that it is generally not necessary to focus an inordinate amount of attention on them, as the evidence suggests that this is not a particularly challenging aspect of learning to write for deaf children.

IMPLICATIONS FOR RESEARCH

As already indicated in our review of the literature in chapter 1, there is an overall paucity of research evidence available with respect to the early literacy development of deaf children, in marked contrast with the overwhelming body of research on the early literacy development of hearing children. But even with regard to this research on hearing learners, more attention is paid to reading than to writing. This is particularly evident in our field, where there are few studies of early writing in deaf children (Williams & Mayer, in press). Clearly, this is an area that needs to be addressed, first from the perspective of the need for more research of any description.

But beyond the need for more research, we would suggest focusing more deliberately on those questions most germane to the process of learning to write. To this end, it would be instructive to bring the body of research evidence from hearing learners to bear on a consideration of which issues are worth investigating in the context of the deaf writer. We make this suggestion based on the fact that all available evidence suggests that there is little difference among subgroups of hearing learners (e.g., children with disabilities, second-language [L2] learners) regarding the sets of skills and abilities necessary to develop conventional literacy (e.g., face-to-face competence in the language to be written, phonological processing skills). While there are differences with regard to the relative strengths (e.g, an established first-language literacy base in L2 learners) or weaknesses (e.g., learning disabilities related to auditory processing) they bring to the activity, the fundamental issues of what counts in early literacy development do not change as a consequence of the nature of the learner. We would not see deaf children as unique in this respect, and to date, there is no research evidence to convincingly support the claim that deaf children bypass or do not need to acquire the same understandings as all other young literacy learners.

That said and given our view that a foundation in the language of the text is a fundamental requisite, and that phonologically based, encoding strategies are necessary to develop conventional writing, we would argue for more systematic investigations of the nature of development as it is realized at level 3, when children are making the explicit links between spoken/signed language and text. Studies at this level are critical, as this is when the writing development of deaf children often deviates from that of their hearing peers in ways that have a negative impact on outcomes. It would be important to better understand the interplay between language-related and code-related abilities at this level, and we would advocate including measures of both language and phonological awareness in studies of early writing, with a particular emphasis on examining the encoding strategies that deaf children are using (e.g., the nature of their invented spelling). In this way, research has the potential to meaningfully inform practice.

As researchers of early literacy, we must be more accountable for including outcome data, as only in this way can we determine whether children are performing at age-appropriate levels. In studies of early writing, this should include examples of the texts that children produce, given that in the absence of many standardized measures of writing for this age group, they provide the clearest evidence of current levels of functioning. There is also a need to carry out longitudinal investigations of writing development that track children from first scribbles to the use of conventional text. As we have discussed, it may appear as though deaf children are evidencing development parallel to that of their hearing peers in the earliest stages of learning to write, but this is not always an indication that development will continue in this fashion or that it will result in age-appropriate outcomes. With respect to practice, in the absence of tracking children over time, it is impossible to know whether any particular early intervention or approach has been successful, and we lose sight of the overarching goal: that deaf children learn to write.

REFERENCES

Allen, T., Clark, M. D., del Giudice, A., Koo, D., Lieberman, A., Mayberry, R., & Miller, P. (2009). Phonology and reading: A response to Wang, Trezek, Luckner, and Paul. *American Annals of the Deaf, 154,* 338–345.

Ashby, J., & Rayner, K. (2006). Literacy development: Insights from research on skilled reading. In D. Dickinson & S. Neuman (Eds.), *Handbook of early literacy research* (Vol. 2, pp. 52–63). New York, NY: Guilford Press.

Bissex, G. L. (1980). *GNYS AT WORK: A child learns to read and write.* Cambridge, MA: Harvard University Press.

Bloodgood, J. (1999). What's in a name? Children's name writing and literacy acquisition. *Reading Research Quarterly, 34,* 342–367.

Burden, V., & Campbell, R. (1994). The development of word coding skills in the born-deaf. *British Journal of Developmental Psychology, 12,* 331–349.

Chan, L. (1998). Children's understandings of the formal and functional characteristics of written Chinese. *Applied Psycholinguistics, 19,* 115–131.

Chang-Wells, G. L., & Wells, G. (1996). Dynamics of discourse: Literacy and the construction of knowledge. In E. A. Forman, N. Minnick, & C. A. Stone (Eds.), *Contexts for learning: Sociocultural dynamics in children's development* (pp. 58–90). New York, NY: Oxford University Press.

Clay, M. (1983). Getting a theory of writing. In B. Kroll & G. Wells (Eds.), *Explorations in the development of writing* (pp. 259–284). London, United Kingdom: Wiley.

Clay, M. (2002). *An observation survey of early literacy achievement.* Portsmouth, NH: Heinemann.

Conway, D. (1985). Children (re)creating writing: A preliminary look at the purpose of free choice writing of hearing impaired kindergarteners. *Volta Review, 87*(5), 91–107.

Cramer, E. (2006). In the beginning: Phonological awareness. In J. Shay Schumm (Ed.), *Reading assessment and instruction for all learners* (pp. 89–117). New York, NY: Guilford Press.

Dyson, A. H. (1984). Learning to write/learning to do school. *Research in the Teaching of English, 6*, 233–264.

Edelsky, C. (1986). *Writing in a bilingual program: Había una vez.* Norwood, NJ: Ablex.

Ehri, L., & Roberts, T. (2006). The roots of learning to read and write: Acquisition of letters and phonemic awareness. In D. Dickinson & S. Neuman (Eds.), *Handbook of early literacy research* (Vol. 2, pp. 113–131). New York, NY: Guilford Press.

Ewoldt, C. (1985). A descriptive study of the developing literacy of young hearing-impaired children. *Volta Review, 87*, 109–126.

Ferreiro, E. (1986). The interplay between information and assimilation in beginning literacy. In W. Teale & E. Sulzby (Eds.), *Emergent literacy: Reading and writing* (pp. 15–49). Norwood, NJ: Ablex.

Ferreiro, E. (1990). Literacy development: Psychogenesis. In Y. Goodman (Ed.), *How children construct literacy* (pp. 12–25). Newark, DE: International Reading Association.

Ferreiro, E., & Teberosky, A. (1982). *Literacy before schooling.* Exeter, NH: Heinemann.

Form, A., & Share, D. (1983). Phonological recoding and reading acquisition. *Applied Psycholinguistics, 4*, 103–147.

Graves, D. H. (1978). *Writing: Teachers and children at work.* Portsmouth, NH: Heinemann.

Hanson, V. (1986). Access to spoken language and the acquisition of orthographic structure: Evidence from deaf readers. *Quarterly Journal of Experimental Psychology, 38A*, 193–212.

Hanson, V. (1989). Deaf readers and phonology. In D. Shankweiler & I. Lieberman (Eds.), *Phonology and reading disability: Solving the reading puzzle.* Ann Arbor, MI: University of Michigan Press.

Hanson, V. (1991). Phonological processing without sound. In S. Brady & D. Shankweiler (Eds.), *Phonological processes in literacy: A tribute to Isabelle Y. Liberman* (pp. 153–161). Hillsdale, NJ: Erlbaum.

Hanson, V., & Fowler, C. (1987). Phonological coding in word reading: Evidence from hearing and deaf readers. *Memory and Cognition, 15*, 199–207.

Harris, M., & Moreno, C. (2006). Speech reading and learning to read: A comparison of 8-year-old profoundly deaf children with good and poor reading ability. *Journal of Deaf Studies and Deaf Education, 11*, 189–201.

Harste, J., Woodward, V., & Burke, C. (1984). *Language stories and literacy lessons.* Portsmouth, NH: Heinemann.

Hildreth, G. (1936). Developmental sequence in name writing. *Child Development, 7*, 291–303.

Homer, B., & Olson, B. (1999). Literacy and children's conceptions of words. *Written Language and Literacy, 2(1),* 113–140.

Iredell, H. (1898). Eleanor learns to read. *Education, 19,* 233–238.

Johnson, H. A., Padak, N. D., & Barton, L. E. (1994). Developmental strategies of hearing impaired children. *Reading and Writing Quarterly, 10,* 359–367.

Juel, C. (2006). The impact of early school experiences on initial reading. In D. Dickinson & S. Neuman (Eds.), *Handbook of early literacy research* (Vol. 2, pp. 410–416). New York, NY: Guilford Press.

Kamawar, D., & Homer, D. (2000). Internal and external notions of metarepresentation: A developmental perspective. In J. W. Astington (Ed.), *Minds in the making: Essays in honor of David Olson* (pp. 197–211). Oxford, United Kingdom: Blackwell.

Kelly, L. (1993). Recall of English function words and inflections by skilled and average deaf readers. *American Annals of the Deaf, 138,* 288–296.

Kelly, L. (1995). Processing of bottom-up and top-down information by skilled and average deaf readers and implications for whole language instruction. *Exceptional Children, 61,* 318–334.

Kress, G. (1994). *Learning to write* (2nd ed.). New York: Routledge.

Kress, G. (1997). *Before writing: Rethinking the paths to literacy.* New York, NY: Routledge.

Kress, G. (2000). *Early spelling: Between convention and creativity.* New York, NY: Routledge.

Kyle, F. E., & Harris, M. (2011). Longitudinal patterns of emergent literacy in beginning deaf and hearing readers. *Journal of Deaf Studies and Deaf Education, 16(3),* 289–304.

Levin, I., & Bus, A. G. (2003). How is emergent writing based on drawing? Analyses of children's products and their sorting by children and mothers. *Developmental Psychology, 39,* 891–905.

Leybaert, J. (1993). Reading in the deaf: The role of phonological codes. In M. Marschark & D. Clark (Eds.), *Psychological perspectives on deafness* (pp. 269–309). Hillsdale, NJ: Erlbaum.

Leybaert, J., Colin, S., & LaSasso, C. (2010). Cued speech for the deaf students' mastery of the alphabetic principle. In C. LaSasso, K. L. Crain, & J. Leybaert (Eds.), *Cued speech and cued language for deaf and hard of hearing children* (pp. 245–283). San Diego, CA: Plural.

Lonigan, C. (2006). Conceptualizing phonological processing skills in prereaders. In D. Dickinson & S. Neuman (Eds.), *Handbook of early literacy research* (Vol. 2, pp. 77–89). New York, NY: Guilford Press.

Luria, A. R. (1929/1978). The development of writing in the child. In M. Cole (Ed.), *The selected writings of A. R. Luria.* New York, NY: Sharpe.

Marschark, M., Siple, P., Lillo-Martin, D., Campbell, R., & Everhart, V. (1997). *Relations of language and thought: The view from sign language and deaf children.* New York, NY: Oxford University Press.

Mayer, C. (1994). Action research: The story of a partnership. In G. Wells (Ed.), *Changing schools from within: Creating communities of inquiry* (pp. 151–170). Portsmouth, NH: Heinemann.

Mayer, C. (1998). Deaf children learning to spell. *Research in the Teaching of English, 33,* 158–180.

Mayer, C. (1999). Shaping at the point of utterance: An investigation of the composing processes of the deaf student writer. *Journal of Deaf Studies and Deaf Education, 4*, 37–49.

Mayer, C. (2007). What matters in the early literacy development of deaf children. *Journal of Deaf Studies and Deaf Education, 12*, 411–431. doi:10.1093/deafed/enm020

Mayer, C. (2010). The demands of writing and the deaf writer. In M. Marschark & P. Spencer (Eds.), *The Oxford handbook of deaf studies, language, and education* (Vol. 2, pp. 144–155). New York, NY: Oxford University Press.

Mayer, C. (2012). A role for Total Communication in 2012? *British Association of Teachers of the Deaf Magazine (March 2012)*, 12–13.

Mayer, C. (in press). Rethinking total communication: Looking back, moving forward. In M.Marschark & P. Spencer (Eds.), The Oxford handbook of deaf studies in language: Research, policy, and practice. New York, NY: Oxford University Press.

Mayer, C., & Trezek, B. J. (2014). Is reading different for deaf individuals?: Reexamining the role of phonology. *American Annals of the Deaf, 159*(4), 359–371.

Miller, P. (2002). Communication mode and the processing of printed words: Evidence from readers with prelingually acquired deafness. *Journal of Deaf Studies and Deaf Education, 7*, 312–329.

Miller, P. (2006). What the processing of real words and pseudo-words tell about the development of orthographic knowledge in prelingually deafened individuals. *Journal of Deaf Studies and Deaf Education, 11*, 21–38.

Moores, D. (1987). *Educating the deaf: Psychology, principles and practices*. Boston, MA: Houghton Mifflin.

Moores, D. (2001). Sign and phonology. *American Annals of the Deaf, 146*, 3–4.

Nelson, K. (1996). *Language in cognitive development: The emergence of the mediated mind*. New York, NY: Cambridge University Press.

Olson, D. (1994). *The world on paper*. Cambridge, United Kingdom: Cambridge University Press.

Padden, C. (2006). Learning to fingerspell twice: Young children's acquisition of fingerspelling. In B. Schick, M. Marschark, & P. Spencer (Eds.), *Advances in the sign language development of deaf children* (pp. 189–201). New York, NY: Oxford University Press.

Papandropoulou, I., & Sinclair, H. (1974). What is a word? Experimental studies of children's ideas on grammar. *Human Development, 17*, 241–258.

Paul, P. V., Wang, Y., Trezek, B. J., & Luckner, J. L. (2009). Phonology is necessary, but not sufficient: A rejoinder. *American Annals of the Deaf, 154*, 346–356.

Perez, B. (2004). Writing across writing systems. In B. Perez (Ed.), *Sociocultural contexts of language and literacy* (2nd ed., pp. 57–75). Hillsdale, NJ: Erlbaum.

Phillips, B., & Torgensen, J. (2006). Phonemic awareness and reading: Beyond the growth of initial reading accuracy. In D. Dickinson & S. Neuman (Eds.), *Handbook of early literacy research* (Vol. 2, pp. 101–112). New York, NY: Guilford Press.

Pontecorvo, C., & Zuchermaglio, C. (1988). Modes of differentiation in children's writing construction. *European Journal of the Psychology of Education, 3*(4), 371–384.

Pressley, M. (2006). *Reading instruction that works: The case for balanced teaching* (3rd ed.). New York, NY: Guilford Press.

Puranik, C. S., & Lonigan, C. J. (2011). From scribbles to scrabble: Preschool children's developing knowledge of written language. *Reading and Writing, 24*, 567–589. doi10.1007/s11145-009-9220-8

Rayner, K., Foorman, B., Perfetti, C., Pesetsky, D., & Seidenberg, M. (2001). How psychological science informs the teaching of reading. *Psychological Science in the Public Interest, 2*, 31–74.

Scarborough, H. (2001). Connecting early language and literacy to later reading (dis)abilities: Evidence, theory and practice. In S. Neuman & D. Dickinson (Eds.), *Handbook of early literacy research* (Vol. 1, pp. 97–110). New York, NY: Guilford Press.

Schirmer, B., & McGough, S. (2005). Teaching reading to children who are deaf: Do the conclusions of the National Reading Panel apply? *Review of Educational Research, 75*, 83–117.

Schleper, D. (1992). When "F" spells "Cat": Spelling in a whole language program. *Perspectives in Deaf Education, 11*, 11–14.

Singer, B. D., & Bashir, A. S. (2004). Developmental variation in writing composition skills. In C. Stone, E. Silliman, B. J. Ehren, & K. Apel (Eds.), *Handbook of language and literacy: Development and disorders* (pp. 559–582). New York, NY: Guilford Press.

Stanovich, K. (2000). *Progress in understanding reading: Scientific foundations and new frontiers.* New York, NY: Guilford Press.

Sulzby, E. (1989). Forms of writing and rereading from writing: A preliminary report. In J. Mason (Ed.), *Reading and writing connections* (pp. 51–63). Boston, MA: Allyn & Bacon.

Sulzby, E. (1991). The development of the young child and the emergence of literacy. In J. Flood, J. M. Jensen, D. Lapp, & J. R. Squire (Eds.), *Handbook of research on teaching the English language arts* (pp. 273–285). New York, NY: Macmillan.

Teale, W. (2003). Questions about early literacy learning that need asking—and some that don't. In D. Barone & L. Mandel Morrow (Eds.), *Literacy and young children: Research-based practices* (pp. 23–44). New York: Guilford Press.

Teale, W., & Sulzby, E. (1989). Emergent literacy: New perspectives. In D. Strickland & L. Morrow (Eds.), *Emerging literacy: Young children learn to read and write* (pp. 1–15). Newark, DE: International Reading Association.

Tolchinsky, L. (2006). The emergence of writing. In C. A. MacArthur, S. Graham, & J. Fitzgerald (Eds.), *Handbook of writing research* (pp. 83–95). New York, NY: Guilford Press.

Tolchinsky, L., & Landsmann, L. (1986). Literacy development and pedagogical implications: Evidence from the Hebrew system of writing. In Y. M. Goodman (Ed.), *How children construct literacy* (pp. 26–44). Newark, DE: International Reading Association.

Tolchinsky, L., Landsmann, L., & Levin, I. (1985). Writing in preschoolers: An age related analysis. *Applied Psycholinguistics, 6*, 319–339.

Trezek, B. J., & Wang, Y. (2006). Implications of utilizing a phonics-based reading curriculum with children who are deaf or hard of hearing. *Journal of Deaf Studies and Deaf Education, 10*(2), 202–213. doi:10.1093/deafed/enj031

Trezek, B. J., Wang, Y., & Paul, P. V. (2010). *Reading and deafness: Theory, research and practice*. Clifton Park, NY: Cengage Learning.

Trezek, B. J., Wang, Y., Woods, D. G., Gampp, T. L., & Paul, P. (2007). Using Visual Phonics to supplement beginning reading instruction for students who are deaf or hard of hearing. *Journal of Deaf Studies and Deaf Education, 12(3)*, 373–384. doi:10.1093/deafed/enm014

Wang, Y., Trezek, B. J., Luckner, J. L., & Paul, P. V. (2008). The role of phonology and phonological-related skills in reading instruction for students who are deaf or hard of hearing. *American Annals of the Deaf, 153*, 396–407.

Waters, G., & Doehring, D. (1990). The nature and role of phonological information in reading acquisition: Insights from congenitally deaf children who communicate orally. In T. Carr & B. Levy (Eds.), *Reading and its development: Component skills approaches* (pp. 323–373). New York, NY: Academic Press.

Watson, R. (2001). Literacy and oral language: Implications for early literacy acquisition. In S. Neuman & D. Dickinson (Eds.), *Handbook of early literacy research* (Vol. 1, pp. 43–53). New York, NY: Guilford Press.

Whitehurst, G., & Lonigan, C. (1998). Child development and emergent literacy. *Child Development, 68*, 848–872.

Whitehurst, G., & Lonigan, C. (2001). Emergent literacy: Development from prereaders to readers. In S. Neuman & D. Dickinson (Eds.), *Handbook of early literacy research* (Vol. 1, pp. 11–29). New York, NY: Guilford Press.

Williams, C. (1993). Learning to write: Social interaction among preschool auditory/oral and total communication children. *Sign Language Studies, 80*, 267–284.

Williams, C. (2004). Emergent literacy of deaf children. *Journal of Deaf Studies and Deaf Education, 9*, 352–365.

Williams, C. (2011). Adapted interactive writing instruction with kindergarten children who are deaf or hard of hearing. *American Annals of the Deaf, 156*, 23–34. doi:10.1353/aad.2011.0011

Williams, C., & Mayer, C. (in press). Writing in young deaf children. *Review of Educational Research.*.

Xue, Y., & Meisels, S. (2004). Early literacy instruction and learning in kindergarten: Evidence from the early childhood longitudinal study—kindergarten class of 1998–1999. *American Educational Research Journal, 41*, 191–229.

5

Bilingualism and Early Literacy Development

Before beginning a discussion of bilingualism and biliteracy, it is important to clarify what is meant when we say that a deaf child is bilingual, as this can have implications for the subsequent development of literacy. The characterization of a deaf child as bilingual is not straightforward, and even with respect to hearing children, we cannot assume that what has been learned about one group of bilingual learners, with regard to skill development and cognitive competencies, applies in the same way to the other (Bialystok, 2011). Some children grow up exposed to two languages in the home from birth, in an environment that meets the criterion for both languages to be acquired through meaningful interaction with others (see Meisel, 2004, for a discussion). Given that these two languages develop simultaneously, it could be suggested that there is no discernible first language (L1) or second language (L2), although it is usually the case that one language will come to be more dominant (e.g., if one of the languages is the majority language of the community). Some children acquire one language in the home and encounter a second language on school entry. It may be the case that the home L1 is the minority language in the community and the L2 is the majority language of school (e.g., English language learners in the United Kingdom). Or it may be the situation that in a bilingual context (e.g., French and English in Canada), one of the languages is naturally acquired in the home and the other is learned at school (e.g., French immersion programs).

In principle, deaf children can fall into any of these categories. Reflecting the shifts in the broader population, there are increasing numbers of deaf children who come from homes in which a minority language is spoken, putting these deaf children in the same situation as many hearing children who need to learn a second, majority language when they begin schooling. Some deaf children, although we would suspect that this is a relatively small number, grow up bilingually, simultaneously acquiring two spoken and/or signed languages (e.g., Spanish and English, BSL and English). Deaf children may also learn a second language at school in bilingual educational settings (e.g., French as a second language in the Canadian context).

What differentiates the situation of the deaf child from that of other bilingual learners rests on the issues of language acquisition that were addressed in chapter 2. To recap, the argument was made that in order for any language to be acquired, four conditions need to be in place in the child's environment: (1) quantity and quality of exposure (2) to an accessible language (3) used in meaningful interactions (4) with others who are already capable users of the language (Mayer, 2007). As discussed, the fact that these conditions are often not met in the child's environment (especially with regard to linguistic access) accounts for the language delays and deficits often seen in young deaf learners. Spoken languages by definition are not fully accessible to deaf children unless appropriate interventions (e.g., hearing technologies) are put into place, and when this does not happen or is not successful, language is not acquired. The challenge is somewhat different in the case of acquiring a natural signed language (e.g., ASL, BSL, Sign Language of the Netherlands [SLN]). These visual-gestural languages are fully accessible, but by virtue of the fact that the vast majority of deaf children have hearing parents who are not capable users of the language, there is little possibility for rich meaningful interaction to occur. It would not be overstating the case to suggest that as a consequence, significant numbers of deaf children do not have any firmly established L1 (Mayer, 2009; Mayer & Leigh, 2010).

With simultaneous bilingualism, it is not a case of having developed L1 before L2 but, rather, that the four conditions described are in place with respect to acquiring both languages. Given that the same challenges apply in regard to access to the languages or to capable users in the environment, deaf children in this situation may not develop competence in either or both of the languages to which they have been exposed (e.g., deaf children of hearing parents acquiring ASL and English). In all of these situations, it seems premature to talk about bilingualism and/or the development of biliteracy when it is not clear that any L1 has been fully established. Therefore, we would caution that interpreting the remaining discussion in this chapter is predicated on the understanding that children must have a threshold level of L1 in place before it makes any sense to talk about an L2.

LEARNING TO READ AND WRITE IN TWO LANGUAGES

Vygotsky (1962) was one of the first theorists to suggest that bilingualism could affect the course of development in positive ways. In the process of learning two language systems, he observed, "the child can transfer to the new language the system of meanings he already has in own.... [He] learns to see his language as one particular system among many, to view phenomena under more general categories, and this leads to the awareness of his linguistics operations" (p. 110).

In their seminal work, Peal and Lambert (1962) demonstrated that bilingualism could accrue positive benefits for the learner with regard to the development of cognition (concept formation, mental flexibility), outperforming monolinguals in this regard. In the ensuing years, in addition to investigating cognitive benefits, researchers have focused on social development advantages (e.g., socioeconomic, cultural awareness, identity) (see Garcia, 2009, for a discussion) and on the ways in which bilingualism affects various aspects of both language (e.g., word and syntactic awareness) and literacy development. While acknowledging the broader range of potential benefits, in this chapter, we will be focusing on the relationship between bilingualism and literacy development and how it applies in the case of young deaf children.

One of the central theoretical frameworks that has been used in the field of deaf education to make the case for how bilingualism can support early literacy development is the linguistic interdependence model (Cummins, 1989, 1991), which posits the existence of a common proficiency underlying all languages. On this theoretical basis, it is argued that young literacy learners can transfer the cognitive/academic or literacy skills acquired in their L1 to the learning of related skills in L2. In theory, there would be no reason to expect that this notion of interdependence would not be relevant in the case of deaf learners. Therefore, the suggestion has been made that with respect to literacy development, deaf children will use their L1 to advantage in learning to read and write in L2. However, we would argue that in applying the linguistic interdependence theory to the context of the young deaf literacy learner, assumptions have been made on the basis of an incomplete reading of the theory and a failure to take into account the relevant research evidence from the context of hearing bilingual children (see Mayer & Wells, 1996; Mayer, 2009; Mayer & Leigh, 2010, for discussions).

Interestingly, even with respect to hearing learners, a research gap has been identified in the area of biliteracy development, particularly in the emergent stages (Bialystok, 2001; see Zecker, 2004, for a discussion). In one of the earliest studies to investigate this issue, Edelsky (1986) conducted a yearlong investigation of Spanish-speaking first to third graders, comparing their writing development in English and Spanish, to discover the relationships between the two languages. Her conclusion was that writing in L1 did not interfere with writing in L2; rather, Spanish helped the children "fill in" when writing in English when needed (Allen, 1991). Although more work has been done in this area of late (e.g., Kenner, 2000, 2004a, 2004b, in the United Kingdom; LeSaux & Siegel, 2003, in the United States), in its executive summary, the National Literacy Panel on Language-Minority Children and Youth (August & Shanahan, 2006) reported that the research on acquiring literacy in a second language remains limited, and the research on some topics is scant.

The research evidence in the context of deaf learners is even more limited, with the bulk of the attention being focused on those learners in sign bilingual programs (see Mayer & Akamatsu, 2011, for a review of the literature). However, we would suggest that an equally important and growing group to consider would be those deaf children with two spoken languages (see Klossner & Crain, 2010, for a study of this cohort). Overall, the studies that explicitly focus on the early literacy learning years tend to be descriptions of programs or case studies and do not typically include any standardized measures of language and/or literacy (see the review in chapter 1), particularly in regard to assessing proficiency in a natural signed language where very few measures are available. What we do know is that there are no data to suggest that, as a group, students in bilingual programs are achieving at the age-appropriate language and literacy levels that were predicted when bilingual models were first implemented (Small & Mason, 2008; Wilbur, 2000). Given this lack of compelling empirical evidence, it would seem instructive to revisit the model and consider some of the concerns that were raised about its particular implementation with deaf learners as a way to think about why outcomes have been less than anticipated.

In considering the sum of the available evidence from hearing learners, Bialystok (2011) reminds us that if any one thing is clear, it is that there is a complex set of relationships between bilingualism and early literacy development, in which there are "sometimes benefits for bilingual children, sometimes deficits, and sometimes no consequences at all" (p. 121). Given that the effects of transfer can be positive, negative, or neutral, it would be an oversimplification to suggest that simply knowing one language ensures effortless development of literacy in the second, particularly in the singular context of a signed L1 (e.g., ASL) and a spoken L2 (e.g., English) in which the L1 has no written form and in which we have such a thin research evidence base. We would argue that what is required is a careful examination of the available evidence and a consideration of the effects for young deaf children. With respect to the question of how bilingualism is implicated in the development of early literacy skills and in the nature of any transfer, the following issues warrant particular attention: (1) the level of proficiency in spoken and/or signed L1 and L2, (2) development of print concepts, and (3) awareness of metalinguistic concepts required for literacy learning (Bialystok, 2006).

PROFICIENCY IN L1 AND L2

In the previous chapters, we emphasized that any discussion of early literacy development in a monolingual context is contingent on children having mastered a face-to-face form of the language of the text as a prerequisite for learning to read and write. This same condition holds true in a bilingual context, and we would caution against framing development in terms of bilingualism or biliteracy when there is no established, identifiable L1. As noted above, this can be the unfortunate situation for some deaf children who, by dint of not having the conditions in place for language acquisition to occur, have not developed a full L1. It seems intemperate to characterize these children as bilingual learners when they have limited or little proficiency in any L1, signed or spoken (Mayer & Leigh, 2010), and therefore are not in a position to realize the demonstrated benefits of bilingualism in learning to read and write.

Cummins (1979) addressed the issue of language proficiency as it pertains to hearing learners, even though there would be very few (if any) of these children who demonstrate the same kind of L1 developmental lag or deficit as their deaf counterparts. He proposed a threshold hypothesis in which he mooted three types of bilingualism (limited, partial, and full) to account for the effect of varying levels of language proficiency on learning in a bilingual situation, including literacy development. Limited bilingualism refers to a situation in which a child lacks age-appropriate development in both L1 and L2. In partial bilingualism, age-appropriate proficiency has been achieved in at least one of the two languages. Full or proficient bilingualism denotes age-appropriate proficiency in both languages.

Cummins made the argument that there would be no negative repercussions in the case of either partial or full bilingualism, and research evidence supports his claim that, even for unbalanced (i.e., partial) bilinguals, benefits accrue, and children can reap cognitive and linguistic gains (see Bialystok, 2001, 2006, for discussions). Put simply, a minimal level of bilingualism is required to avoid deficits, and higher levels of bilingualism put learners at an advantage. While Cummins (2000) does caution that we must be mindful of how the threshold hypothesis is interpreted in shaping policy and practice in bilingual education (e.g., the reorganization of L1 and L2 instruction so that there is an inordinate focus on L1 and a delay in introducing L2), we would not see this as inconsistent with the central, important point that "children have not been found to suffer any disadvantages from learning and using two languages, even in academic settings, providing that *one of the languages is established to a level appropriate for children their age*" (Bialystok, 2001, p. 227, emphasis added). This point is particularly germane to the situation of the deaf child, as the requisite L1 proficiency is often not met in the case of deaf bilingual learners, providing a robust explanation for why they are at a definite disadvantage and have not been successful as literacy learners in bilingual programs, no matter the design of the educational setting.

But even for hearing learners, proficiency in L1, while necessary, is not sufficient for the development of literacy in L2. As we described in chapters 3 and 4, learning to read and write is mediated through the face-to-face form of the language of the text, and we would suggest that the activity of literacy learning in L2 is fundamentally the same process in this regard, meaning that a level of proficiency in the language of the text is necessary. The potential advantages for bilingual learners lie in the understandings and strategies from L1 that they can bring to bear on literacy development in L2 (notions of transfer). However, these are not unequivocal and play out in very particular and context-dependent ways. These will be discussed in more detail in the following sections, but at this point, we would like to highlight that the available empirical evidence indicates that the strongest correlations, relationships, and transfer occur between the ability to read and write in L1 and the ability to read and write in L2 (e.g., Treger & Wong, 1984; Canale, Frenette, & Belanger, 1987; Cumming, 1989), even in the case of young bilinguals (e.g., Buckwalter & Lo, 2002; Carlisle, Beeman, Davis, & Spharim, 1999; Geva, Wade-Woolley, & Shany, 1997; Muter & Diethelm, 2001; Nathenson-Mejia, 1989; Zutell & Allen, 1988). There is no demonstrated, equivalent correlation between the ability to communicate face-to-face in LI and the subsequent ability to read and write in L2.

Cummins (2000) suggests that there have been misunderstandings and misinterpretations in the application of the linguistic interdependence model, specifically as it pertains to notions of transfer and the development of L2 literacy and the conditions under which they occur. In explaining his concern, he cites the work of Hulstijn (1991), who argues that "L1 reading performance can only begin to correlate substantially with L2 reading after knowledge of L2 has attained a threshold" (as cited in Cummins, 2000, p. 177), and Bernhardt and Kamil (1995), who contend that "In order to read in a second language, a level of second language linguistic ability must be achieved. . .. Firm first language reading skills could not help readers compensate when reading in a second language. A lack of second language linguistic knowledge ultimately 'short-circuited' the first language reading knowledge" (as cited in Cummins, 2000, p. 177).

In other words, even when L1 literacy is well developed, this proficiency alone is not sufficient for development of literacy in L2. Irrespective of how much transfer of reading and writing skills occurs between L1 and L2, language-specific skills in L2 are still necessary. What this makes clear is that a threshold level of proficiency in L2 is required, representing a necessary condition for any transfer to be realized. What this means in practice for deaf learners in sign bilingual settings is that it is not possible to circumvent developing proficiency in a face-to-face form of the second language (e.g., communicative competence in English) in order to learn to read and write it.

With respect to a pedagogical model, Cummins (1981) argued: "To the extent that instruction in Lx is effective in promoting proficiency in Lx, transfer of this proficiency to Ly will occur provided there is adequate exposure to Ly (either in school or environment) and adequate motivation to learn Ly" (p. 29). However, we would suggest that this model must be interpreted in terms of the aforementioned understanding that "exposure to L2" entails developing a threshold proficiency in its face-to-face form. Proponents of sign bilingual models of literacy education have argued for "teaching a natural sign language to deaf children as their primary face-to-face language [L1] and teaching English [or some other spoken language] as a second language through literacy" (Erting 1992, p. 105). The implication is that via interactions with print, children will not only learn to read and write but will learn the language itself (Mayer & Akamatsu, 2011). Although print as a visual mode is fully accessible, it is not comprehensible unless it is mediated through, and understood in terms of, the language it represents (Mayer, 2007). To imply that the requirement for adequate exposure in order to develop L2 proficiency can be achieved via print, when it is this language that is necessary to mediate learning to read and write in the first place, seems a circular argument and inherently problematic (Mayer & Leigh, 2010).

Before leaving the topic of language proficiency, we consider the issue of vocabulary development in both L1 and L2, given that the importance of this factor is well established in literacy learning in a first language. Overall, the research indicates that when compared with their monolingual peers, bilingual learners know fewer words in both of their languages. Despite individual variations among learners and the challenge of designing properly controlled studies (that account for not only size but also conceptual coverage and linguistic sophistication), bilingual children demonstrate a generally slower acquisition of vocabulary, although this does not have a concomitant negative impact on their ability to communicate (see Bialystok, 2011, for a review and discussion). While there are decrements in vocabulary size as a consequence of learning two languages, there are other advantages to being bilingual that operate as a compensatory trade-off, so that the impact of a smaller lexicon is ameliorated. The nature of these advantages and constraints will be expanded on in the upcoming section on metalinguistic awareness.

However, it is worth noting that this issue has not been explored directly in the context of young deaf bilinguals and would be an especially worthwhile line of investigation in a sign bilingual context given the differences in modality (i.e., auditory-oral versus visual-gestural) and the substantial differences in size of lexical corpus between spoken and signed languages, with spoken languages having a far greater number of discrete words in their vocabularies. Even this observation can be misleading, as it is not entirely appropriate to equate words and signs as equivalent constructs, although they both function as meaning units in their respective languages.

PRINT CONCEPTS

As noted above, the transfer of skills between reading and writing in L1 and L2 is striking, representing one of the most robust examples of linguistic interdependence and holding true even when face-to-face proficiency in one of the languages is relatively weak. In a study of first and second grade children learning to read in both Hebrew and English, it was found that despite differences in the orthographic system, children were able to make use of what they knew about reading in one language to make sense of the other, with differences in performance attributed to varying individual abilities irrespective of language (Geva, Wade-Woolley, & Shany, 1997). The same has been found to be true for bilingual writers, for whom knowledge and skills also transfer across languages (Barletta, Klinger, & Orosco, 2011; Fitzgerald, 2006). Edelsky (1986) describes this process as one in which bilingual children have an available repertoire of literacy skills on which they can draw to make use of one system while addressing the gaps in the other. As Bialystok (2004) points out, it is almost as if bilingual children only need to learn to read and write in one language, giving them a buy-in to literacy in all other languages.

However, as is the case in all of aspects of bilingual and biliterate development, the reality is much more complex. A notion of simple transfer across languages, especially when the writing systems of the two languages are different, is misplaced, and the evidence suggests that there is less transfer of literacy skills from LI to L2 when the orthographies of the two languages are dissimilar (Cummins et al., 1984; see Bialystok, 2002, 2004, for a discussion). Bilingual children, as a consequence of interacting in two languages, do have an advantage with respect to developing concepts of print, particularly in coming to see how meaning is captured and represented in the symbols of the written language. However, beyond this understanding, the concepts of print needed for reading and writing are also determined by the target language and the writing system used to represent it.

These writing systems can be divided into two broad categories: meaning-based systems and sound-based systems. Meaning-based systems represent language at the level of the morpheme via logographic orthographies (e.g., Chinese). Sound-based systems represent language at the level of syllable (e.g., Tibetan) or phoneme (e.g., English, Spanish) and in the case of the phoneme using either an alphabetic (e.g., Greek, Roman) or consonantal (e.g., Hebrew, Arabic) script (Edwards, 2009). The systematic relationships between language and text are unique to each language, and even within languages using the same script (e.g., two alphabetic languages such as English and Finnish), there are differences with respect to the transparency of these relationships. Some alphabetic languages have a shallow, more transparent orthography in which the relationship between phoneme and grapheme is predictable and consistent (e.g., Finnish, Maltese), while others are less transparent, with a deeper, more opaque orthography in which the phoneme-grapheme relationships are unpredictable and inconsistent (e.g., English) (Seymour, Aro, & Erskine, 2003). Given this complexity, it should not be surprising that transfer will be affected by the nature of the language pairs and the contrast in their writing systems.

As Bialystok (2004) concludes, there is no easy, automatic transfer of skills across languages, especially if they use different writing systems and given that different phonological and linguistic concepts are relevant in mediating text, with different scripts causing the correspondences between talk and text to be relatively easier or harder to detect (i.e., shallow versus deep orthographies). "Therefore, predicting what kind of transfer might take place for children's literacy skills requires comparing the languages, the writing systems and the orthographies" (p. 593).

As already noted, in the context of sign bilingualism, there is no opportunity for transfer between the written forms of L1 and L2, as widely accepted written forms of L1 (e.g., ASL, BSL) do not exist, and thus there is nothing to be compared. This clearly obviates any transfer of print-related concepts. Recently, there have been moves in some contexts to develop written forms for aspects of signed languages for pedagogical purposes, perhaps with the view to exploiting the strength of the interdependence between the written forms of L1 and L2 (e.g., see Supalla & Blackburn, 2003, for a description of the ASL-phabet). However, to date, there is no research evidence to suggest that these approaches are effective in supporting linguistic transfer between a signed and a spoken language.

METALINGUISTIC AWARENESS

The processes of reading and writing are inherently metalinguistic in that they require the learner to extract meaning from text via conscious application of language-related and code-related knowledge and skills. It is in this domain that arguments are often made for a bilingual advantage, as the process of learning two languages heightens awareness of linguistic elements in both, particularly for those children who have a level of fluency in both languages (August & Shanahan, 2006; Bialystok, 1987, 2001; Koda, 2005; LeSaux & Siegel, 2003). We will focus on two areas that are of particular relevance when considering the impact of metalinguistic concepts on the development of early biliteracy: word awareness and phonological awareness (see Bialystok, 2004, for discussion).

Word awareness is a domain in which bilingual children have consistently shown superior understandings relative to their monolingual peers. It is typified by the ability to understand the abstract, arbitrary relationships between spoken and/or signed words and their meanings. In making sense of this relationship, two related insights are necessary: to understand that the stream of face-to-face language can be segmented into meaningful units (i.e., words, signs) and that these units can function to carry meaning. These insights are inextricably intertwined; the child must first be able to identify the relevant segments of the language (e.g., hear/see individual words/signs) in order to attach meaning to them. But if no meaning can be attached, it would not be possible to pull the word/sign from the language stream to begin with. As Vygotsky (1962) puts it, "A word without meaning is an empty sound; meaning therefore is a criterion of 'word' [or sign], its indispensable component" (p. 120).

A concept of word in any language is an arbitrary category, and languages vary in the ways in which word boundaries are realized. Consider the discrete lexical units of English (e.g., *to go on*) in contrast with the agglutinative nature of German words (e.g., *weitergehen*) which allows for the capture of multilayers of meaning in one word. The difference is even more pronounced for logographic languages such as Chinese, in which a notion of a word boundary does not apply in the same sense, given that the basic unit of meaning is the morpheme, with the character being the building block for multimorphemic words. In contrast with writing systems that make phoneme-grapheme (e.g., Italian) or phoneme-syllable (e.g., Cherokee) correspondences, logographic writing systems are described as morphosyllabic, but this does not mean that there is no relationship between talk and text in this writing system. Although readers and writers of these languages share a script (i.e., use the same characters), they pronounce the words differently in accessing the meaning (Perez, 2004).

It could be argued that it is really only for the purposes of learning to read and write that these notions of word boundaries are significant. For example, beginning writers construct a text piecemeal by writing down what they have first composed in their face-to-face language word by word, a process that necessitates knowledge of word boundaries. It is in this process of committing spoken word to paper that Olson (1994) argues children come to see their language in a new way, that they gain insights into the nature and structure of their language that would not have been realized if they had not written it down (e.g., developing concepts of letter, word, and sentence) (see also the discussion in chapter 4).

It would not be surprising that bilingual children would generally have more robust insights in this regard, as they have learned how to segment and make meaning of the spoken stream in two languages, affording them more linguistic flexibility. This raises questions about whether and how there is a relationship between segmenting signs from a visual language stream and identifying words in a spoken language. A fundamental difference between a signed and a spoken language is in their surface organization, in which signed languages evidence a co-occurring, layered, as opposed to a linear arrangement. In contrast with the more segmental/sequential nature of spoken languages, natural signed languages make much greater use of simultaneous options for making meaning (e.g., co-articulation, use of classifiers) (Wilbur, 2011). There is no research that we are aware of that has investigated the relationships between signs and spoken words from the perspective of how they are segmented from the language stream by young learners, so whether there is an advantage or any transfer between signed and spoken languages in this respect remains an open question.

Of all the components of metalinguistic awareness that are implicated in literacy development, it could be argued that the most critical is phonological awareness, especially for those children learning to read and write an alphabetic language. It is also one of the more challenging metalinguistic skills to master. That being the case, it is surprising how little research has focused on this aspect of early literacy learning, even in hearing bilingual children. The availability of research is also confounded by the fact that sample sizes are small, that a balanced level of bilingualism is often not in evidence, that the concept of phonological awareness can be defined in various ways (see the discussion of this point in chapter 3), and that any advantages identified for bilingual children in kindergarten seem to disappear by first grade (Bialystok, 2004).

In addition to this lack of clarity on the nature of any transfer between languages with regard to phonological awareness, complex relationships exist between phonological awareness and literacy learning that are intermediated by the nature of the writing system. As described above, different languages use different systems for representing spoken language in text, and it has been demonstrated that interdependence is greater when languages have similar writing systems (e.g., both are alphabetic languages). While a level of phonological awareness is required to read and write any script, even character-based scripts such as Chinese (Chan, 1998), it is particularly urgent in early literacy learning in alphabetic languages. In these languages, the ability to use phonological awareness to make sense of how the sounds of the language are captured in the written symbols is paramount (i.e., phoneme-grapheme correspondence). Given the iterative nature of the process, as children learn to read and write, they develop a more finely tuned sense of the phonological awareness necessary for the activity. Those children learning to read and write in syllabographic or logographic languages do not rely on a phoneme-grapheme analysis, as making the relationship between spoken and written language in this way is not required.

The central point is that the writing systems dictate the nature of the decoding and encoding strategies that are required to learn to read and write, and they place different demands on the literacy learner. Therefore, it is not surprising that research indicates more robust transfer between languages that share a writing system than those that do not. This can be accounted for by the fact that once a learner has sorted out how to make the relationships between talk and text particular to one language (e.g., a reliance on making phoneme-grapheme correspondences in English), he or she can use these insights most effectively in learning to read and write a second language that makes these relationships in a similar way (e.g., English and Spanish).

In the context of sign bilingualism, there is no written form for L1 (i.e., a natural signed language such as ASL or BSL); therefore, even though discrete signs can be broken down into their component parts (i.e., handshape, movement, and location) (Sutton-Spence & Woll, 1998; Valli, Lucas, Mulrooney, & Villanueva, 2011), there is no written form of the language onto which these can be mapped. When children attempt to represent these elements in the writing system of another language, they encounter a conflict in the representation systems, as there is no systematic correspondence to be uncovered between talk and text. Examples of this have been described in the literature (e.g., Mayer, 1998; Schleper, 1992), such as children attempting to use a visual-orthographic strategy to make the link between ASL sign and English, writing the ASL sign for *key* (made with an *x* handshape) as an English word that begins with an *x*. While these children are clearly applying a strategy, it does not get them to the same sort of invented spelling as would an auditory-orthographic strategy (see the discussion in chapter 4).

In sum, in considering the extent to which bilingualism can support the development of early literacy in any learner, it is clear that there is no simple answer. That said, the most general answer is in the affirmative, and in a number of ways, it is clear that bilingual children take advantage of and make use of what they know and understand in one language to make sense of the second. This is particularly evident in the areas of the cognitive and linguistic strategies that they bring to bear on the task (e.g., concept of word, print concepts across writing systems). However, these are not unequivocal and can be tempered by the child's language proficiencies in L1 and L2 and by the extent of the similarities in the two writing systems. Given that the impact of bilingualism changes with these circumstances, we would argue for the necessity of examining the particular circumstances that affect the literacy learning of the young deaf bilingual if we are to draw any conclusions that can meaningfully inform policy, research, and practice.

In the following sections, we will examine two bilingual situations for deaf children: the acquisition of two spoken languages and the acquisition of a signed and a spoken language. As explained previously, we would exercise caution in using the term *bilingual* indiscriminately when describing deaf children. At the risk of putting it too starkly, we would suggest that many of the deaf children who are characterized as bilingual are actually monolingual, or in some circumstances semi-lingual, given that they have no fully developed L1. The mere fact of introducing a second language into the child's environment does not confer bilingual status on the child. In these situations, any potential advantages or transfer of abilities as consequences of bilingualism will not be realized, consistent with what we know about the lessened benefits that accrue to hearing children who are limited bilinguals. In the examples below, we assume a threshold level of competence in L1 as a prerequisite for the development of L2 (whether simultaneous or sequential) and the development of biliteracy.

SPOKEN LANGUAGE BILINGUALISM AND EARLY LITERACY

Increasing numbers of deaf children grow up in homes in which the language of the family is not the majority language of the community or the schools. If the necessary language acquisition conditions are in place, the deaf child can acquire the spoken language of the home in a similar fashion to that of their hearing peers. Arguably the most critical condition to be met in the case of these deaf children is making the spoken language accessible. For many deaf children, this can be accomplished via the consistent use of hearing technologies (e.g., cochlear implants, BCHIs, hearing aids) and ensuring that parents and caregivers can effectively manage the equipment. These deaf children can develop L1 at home and acquire L2 at the onset of schooling or an educational program. As is true for hearing children, reading and writing development in L1 should be encouraged, as it will support literacy development in L2. In this case, at least in principle and provided language is accessible, the same circumstances or conditions that affect the nature of literacy development in hearing children will affect these deaf children. Given the increasing numbers of young deaf children who are becoming spoken language bilinguals, this is clearly an area that should be the focus of future research attention.

SIGN BILINGUALISM AND EARLY LITERACY

It would not be overstating the case to say that learning to read and write in the context of sign bilingualism presents a unique set of circumstances for considering the issue of bilingual development and the relationships between languages. The first issue that warrants attention is the fact that most deaf children do not acquire a natural signed language as their L1. With the exception of the few deaf children who come from homes with Deaf parents who are fluent users of a natural signed language (e.g., ASL, BSL), the requisite language acquisition conditions are not in place. The vast majority of deaf children (more than 95 percent) have hearing parents who do not sign or do not sign well enough to engage the child in meaningful linguistic interaction. Therefore, although visual-gestural languages are fully accessible, it would not be accurate to say that these languages are the natural L1 in most cases. Rather, it is typically the case that children begin schooling with limited or little proficiency in a signed L1 or, in some cases, any language at all, putting them at a decided disadvantage when they enter a sign bilingual education program, making it difficult to fully realize the intended benefits of such an approach (Mayer & Leigh, 2010).

Johnston, Leigh, and Foreman (2002) noted that one of the major difficulties in implementing a sign bilingual approach stemmed from the significant delay in the achievement of L1 skills (i.e., Auslan) by children in the program. Considering the same cohort, Leigh and Johnston (2004) investigated the specific level of achievement in Auslan by the children in the program. They found that only the children with parents who were Deaf sign language users achieved within the normal or "native-like" range on the tests of language ability. Although their skills improved over time, the children with hearing parents were delayed in their Auslan development. In examining the language scores for thirty-six children in the program, they found that on average, the children did not demonstrate age-appropriate levels of sign language ability, concluding that "the children in the program cannot be described as a population of children that bring an intact first language to the program—certainly not one that can be exploited immediately as a basis for learning a second language. Rather, the population under investigation are better described as a community of largely first language learners" (Leigh & Johnston, 2004, p. 4).

Given this reality, we would argue that the group of children who could truly be considered bilingual learners of a signed and a spoken language is very small. Even in cases where children have acquired some competence in a signed L1, we suggest that they would be in the same situation as their hearing peers who are characterized as limited bilinguals, a group that reaps lesser benefits from bilingualism.

However, as discussed previously, proficiency in L1 is not directly implicated in development of literacy in L2. The research evidence indicates that transfer is strongest between the written form of L1 and L2, and this is the basis on which parents are encouraged to use their L1 in the home not only in its spoken but also in its print form. As we have already noted, natural signed languages do not have written forms, and thus there is simply no print-to-print relationship to be exploited. While there are certainly aspects of L1 proficiency that can support literacy development in L2 (e.g., an understanding of narrative structure, a sense of word boundaries), interdependence is most robust in the relationships between the written forms.

But even if there were written forms for natural signed languages, this alone would not be sufficient for development of literacy in L2. Even in situations where there is maximal possible transfer between the written forms of two languages (e.g., Italian and Spanish), a level of proficiency in the spoken form of L2 is still necessary. This requirement cannot be bypassed and is a critical aspect of learning to read and write in L2. In the case of hearing bilinguals who are also in a circumstance where the L1 does not have a written form, L2 literacy is learned through developing proficiency in the spoken form of L2 (Mayer, 2009; Mayer & Wells, 1996).

In contrast with the situation of the young hearing bilingual, the challenge for the deaf child is that access to the spoken form of L2 for the purposes of acquiring it cannot be assumed. In any bilingual situation, questions arise regarding what constitutes adequate exposure to L2 so that a threshold level of proficiency can be developed. For the deaf child, this is complicated by the fact that the language is not fully accessible, even if opportunities for interaction in the language are provided. This access can often be achieved via hearing technologies alone (e.g., cochlear implants, hearing aids) or in combination with visual supports (e.g., signed forms of the spoken language, Cued Speech). But this can also be confounded, in that if the hearing technologies work well to provide meaningful access to a spoken language as L2, it is usually the case (i.e., if the parents are hearing) that the L1 will be a spoken language, even if this has been supplemented by visual input in the acquisition process.

This has certainly been true for the majority of babies and toddlers who have received cochlear implants. Although signed input may function as a support in developing spoken L1 for the children (Giezen, Baker & Escudero, 2014), the natural signed language will typically serve as L2 and not L1, if it is introduced into the child's life at all. It may even be that these parents will opt for a second spoken language if the choice is made to raise their child bilingually. We would suggest that these decisions are not "anti-sign" but are motivated by the parents' belief that two spoken languages make more sense and are more functional for the child given the parameters of the child's Umwelt, or life world (e.g., being able to communicate in Urdu with the family in the home and learn English at school). The group for whom signed L1 and spoken L2 bilingualism does reflect the reality of the child's lived experience is the small group of deaf children of Deaf parents who sign. They have the potential via improved hearing technologies to develop proficiency in the spoken form of L2 and to become balanced bilinguals in the process.

We have attempted to capture here some of the complexity that attaches to any discussion of sign bilingualism and literacy development and to raise questions about the nature and extent of any transfer between a signed L1 (that is often not an established L1 and that has no written form) and the written form of a spoken L2 for young deaf bilinguals. It is important to recognize this complexity, as it informs practice and provides direction for a research agenda.

IMPLICATIONS FOR PRACTICE

Perhaps the first and most fundamental observation that needs to be made with respect to practice is considering the extent to which we are actually talking about bilingualism or biliteracy in the context of literacy learning and young deaf children and the extent to which the understandings gained from hearing children apply. Suggestions have been made that it is instructive to consider deaf learners as another linguistic minority, as it has been shown that there are similarities between hearing and deaf bilinguals (Baker, 2006). However, the sociocultural context for deaf children represents a language acquisition and literacy learning scenario that is unique in many respects, and issues arise that are unlikely to be encountered when programming for hearing children. The pivotal point defining this difference has to do with the issue of development in an L1.

Our contention would be that for children who have no established L1, as is the case for some deaf children, it is premature to think about them as bilingual. The critical issue for these children is to create learning environments that will afford the best possible scenario for the development of a first language (i.e., the four necessary conditions described previously). A key feature of making this decision is determining what that L1 should be and whether it is reasonable to expect that parents can provide the adequate environment for the acquisition of a natural signed language as L1 if they cannot use it themselves. For hearing children, it is taken for granted that this L1 should be the language of the home, even if this is a natural signed language, as in the case of children of deaf adults (CODAs). Deaf parents who use a natural signed language as their L1 would not be expected to use a spoken language instead.

It seems that it is only in the case of deaf children of hearing parents that the suggestion is made that parents use a language in which they have little or no proficiency for communication and interaction with their child (e.g., using ASL when the home language is English). This is not unlike situations in which parents who speak a minority language (e.g., Spanish in the United States) may be advised to use only English in the home, although this is a language they cannot use fluently. We want to be clear that we are not suggesting that there is no role for signed language in the development of the spoken L1 (e.g., forms of sign-supported speech), but are underscoring that this is the use of sign to enhance access to the spoken form of the language, not the use of a different language entirely. While we acknowledge that this presents its own set of challenges in regard to how well parents can combine modes (spoken and signed), we would argue that these challenges are less than those of learning a new language, allow for the use of hearing technologies, and afford the option of using any spoken language for interaction, ultimately providing the best possible opportunities for the development of an L1.

It is only after an L1 foundation is established that we can go on to frame the issues for young deaf learners in terms of bilingualism and biliteracy, nuancing the discussion with regard to simultaneous or sequential development and relative proficiencies in L1 and L2, concerns that apply to all bilingual contexts. The following implications follow from this premise.

1. **While proficiency in L1 is necessary, it is not sufficient for developing literacy in L2. In order to learn to read and write in a second language, children need to develop proficiency in its face-to-face form.**

"For education to profit from children's bilingualism or escape impairment because of it, the absolute proficiency level of at least one language is crucial" (Bialystok, 2001, p. 228). Throughout this chapter, and indeed throughout this book, we have stressed that language underpins the development of literacy. A language foundation is the price of admission to learning to read and write in one and/or two languages. Therefore, ensuring that this language foundation is in place is the first consideration in planning a program for young deaf literacy learners. However, it is not the case that simply knowing one language (even being able to read and write it) is sufficient for learning to read and write in L2. As discussed earlier, developing proficiency in the face-to-face form of L2 is also necessary and cannot be bypassed.

In many models of sign bilingual education for young deaf children, it has been suggested that this L2 proficiency in a spoken and/or signed form is not required and that children can acquire the language through interactions in only the written form of the spoken language. The argument for this position seems to be that knowledge and skills will transfer from L1 to L2, precluding the need for proficiency in L2 to mediate literacy learning. There is a sense that children will learn to read and write through the act of reading and writing, circumventing any need for language to facilitate the process. In contrast with this view, we would strongly argue that developing proficiency in the second language is fundamental to learning to read and write it, and this needs to be a focus of instruction for all young deaf learners in bilingual programs.

2. The nature and quality of the instructional program play a significant role in the development of L2 literacy.

The literacy programs that have proven to be most successful for bilingual learners are those that provide instructional support for the development of the second language along with high-quality reading and writing instruction (August & Shanahan, 2006). There is no reason to think that this would not also hold true for deaf children, and we would argue for the implementation in bilingual programs of the instructional strategies described in chapters 3 and 4 that focus on the development of both code-related and language-related abilities.

An aspect of implementing this instruction is the need to think about how the languages are sequenced across the curriculum, how much time will be devoted to developing each language, and in which situations each language will be used. There is no set formula for making these programmatic decisions, nor is there any specific configuration of L1/L2 instruction that is determined by the application of a linguistic interdependence model (e.g., initial instruction only in L1, simultaneous use of both languages). There is also no hard and fast rule or sacrosanct principle that requires keeping the languages instructionally separated within a bilingual program (Cummins, 2000). The implication for deaf children is that we consider more fluid programmatic models that better address how each language serves different goals within the program (e.g., which language best mediates literacy learning) and employ the language that best meets those needs.

3. Instructional strategies can be differentiated to take advantage of the understandings children have in L1 to learn to read and write in L2.

If children are developing biliteracy, there appears to be no need for young bilingual readers and writers to relearn, or, more important, to be retaught, certain aspects of literacy development in their L2 (Reyes, 1992; Zecker, 2004). The instructional program should reflect the fact that children have already mastered in their L1 some of the abilities and skills that are supportive of learning to read and write in L2 (e.g., making phoneme-grapheme correspondences). This is not to suggest that literacy-specific instruction in L2 is not also required but to propose that we should be mindful that this learning could be buttressed by what the child has already mastered in L1. However, it must also be remembered that this is not a wholesale transfer of abilities, that L2 language proficiency plays a central role, and that it is between the written forms of L1 and L2 that more transfer occurs. With these caveats in mind, we need to consider the extent to which deaf bilingual children can make use of their L1 in learning to read and write in L2 and particularly how this differs in the context of sign bilingualism.

Another aspect of L2 instruction that is seen as efficacious for bilingual learners is in the area of what could be broadly described as metalinguistic activity. This is when children's attention is drawn to the differences and similarities between their first and second languages as a means of helping them develop a more conscious awareness of how the languages operate and thus support literacy development in L2. On the face of it, there is nothing untoward in having young literacy learners reflect on their language and view it as an object for consideration. For example, it can be helpful to understand that in one language, nouns can be masculine, feminine, or neuter, while in another language, there is no such construct. That being said, it would never be argued that these metalinguistic understandings alone would suffice as an avenue for learning to read and write in L2. Yet the pedagogical design of some sign bilingual programs and curricula have been driven by such understandings, with the claim being made that literacy can be learned through engaging in the use of L1 to understand L2 (e.g., see Fairview Learning, 2013). We would argue that this is vastly overreaching any notion of what metalinguistic activity can afford a learner, particularly in the case of young children who developmentally and cognitively are still limited in this regard. In effect, these approaches turn the activity of learning to read and write into translation activities, and these approaches are not effective with young bilinguals.

IMPLICATIONS FOR RESEARCH

In considering the situation as it relates to deaf learners, we would concur with Cummins (2000) in his observation that "both advocates and opponents of bilingual education have sometimes conflated the threshold and interdependence hypothesis and drawn inappropriate conclusions as a result" (p. 193). There has been a considerable amount of theorizing and rhetoric regarding whether deaf children must or should be bilingual, in which languages they should be bilingual, and what constitutes an effective pedagogical approach. There continues to be more debate than consensus on many of these issues.

To address these questions, and consistent with what we have advocated in the previous chapters, there is a pressing need for more research on bilingualism in deaf children and on the development of early literacy in particular. Applying dynamic research frameworks that take into account the sociocultural construction of language and knowledge and how it plays out in the context of the young deaf learner is paramount in the research agenda (Zecker, 2004). This is a heterogeneous group of learners, and that must be reflected in our consideration of the issues. It would also be important to include robust measures of both spoken and signed language (see Haug, 2005, for discussion of sign language assessment instruments) and literacy development (see chapter 6) in study designs and to undertake projects that track children over time to determine the extent to which we can claim with any certainty that deaf children have achieved bilingualism or biliteracy.

REFERENCES

Allen, V. (1991). Teaching bilingual and ESL children. In J. Flood, J. M. Jensen, D. Lapp, & J. R. Squire (Eds.), *Handbook of research on teaching the English language arts* (pp. 356–364). New York, NY: Macmillan.

August, D., & Shanahan, T. (2006). *Executive Summary—Developing Literacy in Second-Language Learners: Report of the National Literacy Panel on Language-Minority Children and Youth.* Mahwah, NJ: Erlbaum.

Baker, C. (2006). *Foundations of bilingual education and bilingualism* (4th ed.). Clevedon, United Kingdom: Multilingual Matters.

Barletta, L. M., Klinger, J. K., & Orosco, M. J. (2011). Writing acquisition among English language learners in U.S. schools. In A. Y. Durgunnoğlu & C. Goldenberg (Eds.), *Language and literacy development in bilingual settings* (pp. 210–241). New York, NY: Guilford Press.

Bernhardt E. B. & Kamil, M. L. (1995). Interpreting relationships between L1 and L2 reading: Consolidating the linguistic threshold and linguistic interdependence hypotheses. *Applied Linguistics 16*(1), 15–34.

Bialystok, E. (1987). Levels of bilingualism and levels of linguistic awareness. *Developmental Psychology, 24*, 560–567.

Bialystok, E. (2001). *Bilingualism in development: Language, literacy and cognition.* New York, NY: Cambridge University Press.

Bialystok, E. (2002). Acquisition of literacy in bilingual children: A framework for research. *Language Learning, 52*(1), 159–199.

Bialystok, E. (2004). The impact of bilingualism on language and literacy development. In T. K. Bhata & W. C. Ritchie (Eds.). *The handbook of bilingualism* (pp. 577–601). Malden, MA: Blackwell.

Bialystok, E. (2006). Bilingualism at school: Effect on the acquisition of literacy. In P. McCardle & E. Hoff (Eds.), *Childhood bilingualism: Research on infancy through school age* (pp. 107–124). Clevedon, United Kingdom: Multilingual Matters.

Bialystok, E. (2011). Language proficiency and its implications for monolingual and bilingual children. In A. Y. Durgunnoğlu & C. Goldenberg (Eds.), *Language and literacy development in bilingual settings* (pp. 121–138). New York, NY: Guilford Press.

Buckwalter, J. K., & Lo, Y. G. (2002). Emergent biliteracy in Chinese and English. *Journal of Second Language Writing, 11*, 260–293.

Canale, M., Frenette, N., & Belanger, M. (1987). Evaluation of minority students writing in first and second languages. In J. Fine (Ed.), *Second language discourse: A textbook of current research.* Norwood, NJ: Ablex.

Carlisle, J. F., Beeman, M., Davis, L. H., & Spharim, G. (1999). Relationship of metalinguistic capabilities and reading achievement for children who are becoming bilingual. *Applied Psycholinguistics, 20*, 459–478.

Chan, L. (1998). Children's understandings of the formal and functional characteristics of written Chinese. *Applied Psycholinguistics, 19*, 115–131.

Cumming, A. (1989). Writing expertise and second-language proficiency. *Language Learning, 39*, 81–141.

Cummins, J. (1979). Linguistic interdependence and the educational development of bilingual children. *Review of Educational Research, 49,* 222–251.

Cummins, J. (1981). The role of primary language development in promoting educational success for language minority students. In California State Department of Education (Ed.), *Schooling and language minority students: A theoretical framework* (pp. 3–49). Los Angeles, CA: Evaluation, Dissemination and Assessment Center, California State University.

Cummins, J. (1989). A theoretical framework of bilingual special education. *Exceptional Children, 56,* 111–119.

Cummins, J. (1991). Language development and academic learning. In L. M. Malave and G. Duquette (Eds.), *Language, culture and cognition.* Philadelphia, PA: Multilingual Matters.

Cummins, J. (2000). *Language, power and pedagogy: Bilingual children in the crossfire.* Clevedon, United Kingdom: Multilingual Matters.

Cummins, J., Swain, M., Nakajima, K., Handscombe, D., Green, D., & Tran, C. (1984). Linguistic interdependence among Japanese and Vietnamese immigrant students. In C. Rivera (Ed.), *Communicative competence approaches to language proficiency assessment: Research and application.* Clevedon, United Kingdom: Multilingual Matters.

Edelsky, C. (1986). *Writing in a bilingual program: Había una vez.* Norwood, NJ: Ablex.

Edwards, V. (2009). *Learning to be literate: Multilingual perspectives.* Bristol, United Kingdom: Multilingual matters.

Erting, C. (1992). Deafness and literacy: Why can't Sam read? *Sign Language Studies 7,* 97–112.

Fairview Learning. (2013). *The Fairview Program.* Available at http://www.fairviewlearning.com

Fitzgerald, J. (2006). Multilingual writing in preschool through 12th grade: The last 15 years. In C. A. MacArthur, S. Graham, & J. Fitzgerald (Eds.), *Handbook of writing research* (pp. 337–354). New York, NY: Guilford Press.

Garcia, O. (2009). *Bilingual education in the 21st century: A global perspective.* Malden, MA: Wiley Blackwell.

Geva, E., Wade-Woolley, L., & Shany, M. (1997). Development of reading efficiency in first and second language. *Scientific Studies of Reading, 1,* 119–144.

Giezen, M. R., Baker, A. E., & Escudero, P. (2014). Relationships between spoken word and sign processing in children with cochlear implants. *Journal of Deaf Studies and Deaf Education, 19(1),* 107–125. doi:10.1093/deafed/ent040

Haug, T. (2005) Review of sign language assessment instruments. *Sign Language & Linguistics, 8(1–2),* 59–96.

Hulstijn, J. H. (1991). How is reading in a second langauge related to reading in a first language? In J. H. Hulstijn & J. F. Matter (Eds.), *Reading in two languages* (pp. 5–14). Amsterdam: AILA.

Johnston, T., Leigh, G., & Foreman, P. (2002). The implementation of the principles of sign bilingualism in a self-described sign bilingual program: Implications for the evaluation of language outcomes. *Australian Journal of Education of the Deaf, 8,* 38–46.

Kenner, C. (2000). Children writing in a multilingual nursery. In M. Martin-Jones & K. Jones (Eds.), *Bilingualism in the primary school.* London, United Kingdom: Routledge.

Kenner, C. (2004a). *Becoming literate: Young children learning different writing systems.* Stokoe on Trent, United Kingdom: Trentham.

Kenner, C. (2004b). Living in simultaneuos worlds: Difference and integration in bilingual script learning. *International Journal of Bilingual Education and Bilingualism 7(1)*, 43–61.

Klossner, C., & Crain, K. L. (2010). Cued Spanish as L1: Teaching *la palabracomplementada* to Spanish-speaking parents of deaf children in the United States. In C. LaSasso, K. L. Crain, & J. Leybaert (Eds.), *Cued speech and cued language for deaf and hard of hearing children* (pp. 407–425). San Diego, CA: Plural.

Koda, K. (2005). *Insights into second language reading.* New York, NY: Cambridge University Press.

Leigh, G., & Johnston, T. (2004). First language learning in a sign bilingual program: An Australian study. *NTID Research Bulletin 9(2/3)*, 1–5.

LeSaux, N. K., & Siegel, L. S. (2003). The development of reading in children who speak English as a second language. *Developmental Psychology, 39(6)*, 1005–1019.

Mayer, C. (1998). Deaf children learning to spell. *Research in the Teaching of English, 33*, 158–180.

Mayer, C. (2007). What matters in the early literacy development of deaf children. *Journal of Deaf Studies and Deaf Education, 12*, 411–431. doi:10.1093/deafed/enm020

Mayer, C. (2009). Issues in second language literacy education with learners who are deaf. *International Journal of Bilingual Education and Bilingualism 12(3)*, 325–334.

Mayer, C., & Akamatsu, C. T. (2011). Bilingualism and literacy. In M. Marschark & P. Spencer (Eds.), *The Oxford handbook of deaf studies, language, and education* (2nd ed., Vol. 1, pp. 144–155). New York, NY: Oxford University Press.

Mayer, C., & Leigh, G. (2010). The changing context for sign bilingual education programs: Issues in language and the development of literacy. *International Journal of Bilingualism and Bilingual Education, 13(2)*, 175–186.

Mayer, C., & Wells, G. (1996). Can the linguistic interdependence theory support a bilingual model of literacy education for deaf students? *Journal of Deaf Studies and Deaf Education, 1(2)*, 93–107.

Meisel, J. (2004). The bilingual child. In T. K. Bhata & W. C. Ritchie (Eds.). *The handbook of bilingualism* (pp. 91–113). Malden, MA: Blackwell.

Muter, V., & Diethelm, K. (2001). The contribution of phonological skills and letter knowledge to early reading development in a multilingual population. *Language Learning, 51*, 187–219.

Nathenson-Mejia, S. (1989). Writing in a second language: Negotiating meaning through invented spelling. *Language Arts, 66*, 516–526.

Olson, D. (1994). *The world on paper.* Cambridge, United Kingdom: Cambridge University Press.

Peal, E., & Lambert, W. (1962). The relation of bilingualism to intelligence. *Psychological Monographs, 76 (546)*, 1–23. Reprinted 1972 in R. Gardner & W. Lambert (Eds.), *Attitude and motivation in in second language learning.* Rowley, MA: Newbury House.

Perez, B. (2004). Writing across writing systems. In B. Perez (Ed.), *Sociocultural contexts of language and literacy* (2nd ed., pp. 57–75). Hillsdale, NJ: Erlbaum.

Reyes, M. L. (1992). Challenging venerable assumptions: Literacy instruction for linguistically different students. *Harvard Educational Review, 62*, 427–446.

Schleper, D. (1992). When "F" spells "Cat": Spelling in a whole language program. *Perspectives in Deaf Education, 11*, 11–14.

Seymour, P. H. K., Aro, M., & Erskine, J. M. (2003). Foundation literacy acquisition in European orthographies. *British Journal of Psychology, 94*, 143–174.

Small, A., & Mason, D. (2008). American Sign Language (ASL) bilingual bicultural education. In N. Hornberger (Ed.), *Encyclopedia of language and education* (Vol. 5, pp.133–150). Boston, MA: Springer.

Supalla, S., & Blackburn, L. (2003). Learning how to read by bypassing sound. *Odyssey, 5(1)*, 50–55.

Sutton-Spence, R., & Woll, B. (1998). *Linguistics of British Sign Language*. New York, NY: Cambridge University Press.

Treger, B., & Wong, B. K. (1984). The relationship between native and second language reading comprehension and second language oral ability. In C. Rivera (Ed.), *Placement procedures in bilingual education: Education and policy issues.* Clevedon, United Kingdom: Multilingual Matters.

Valli, V., Lucas, C., Mulrooney, K. J., & Villanueva, M. (2011). *The linguistics of American Sign Language* (5th ed.). Washington, DC: Gallaudet University Press.

Vygotsky, L. S. (1962). *Thought and language*. Cambridge, MA: MIT Press.

Wilbur, R. (2000). The use of ASL to support the development of English and literacy. *Journal of Deaf Studies and Deaf Education 5*, 81–104.

Wilbur, R. (2011). Modality and the structure of language: Sign languages versus signed systems. In M. Marschark & P. Spencer (Eds.), *Oxford handbook of deaf studies, language, and education* (pp. 350–366). New York, NY: Oxford University Press.

Zecker, L. B. (2004). Learning to read and write in two languages: The development of early biliteracy abilities. In C. A. Stone, E. R. Silliman, B. J. Ehren, & K. Apel (Eds.), *Handbook of language and literacy: Development and disorders* (pp. 248–265). New York, NY: Guilford Press.

Zutell, J., & Allen, V. (1988). The English spelling strategies of Spanish-speaking bilingual children. *TESOL Quarterly, 22*, 333–340.

6

Assessment of Early Literacy

As discussed throughout this book, much is known about the precursor abilities that are consistent and reliable indicators of early literacy development and subsequent conventional literacy achievement (e.g., National Early Literacy Panel, 2008). Children who have acquired the foundational requisites in the language-related and code-related domains prior to the onset of formal literacy instruction in kindergarten tend to thrive, grow academically, and go on to become skilled readers and writers. In contrast, those considered at risk in acquiring these abilities and skills are often less fortunate and many times do not continue along the path of literacy development and achievement in the same manner as their more advantaged peers (see Stanovich, 1986). Because the "developmental antecedents that underlie the acquisition of reading [and writing] are found early and prior to the onset of formal schooling" (Lonigan, Allan, & Lerner, 2011, p. 489), using assessments that pinpoint strengths and weaknesses in the areas most consistently associated with early literacy skill development can be useful in creating a system of identification and intervention for at-risk learners.

Given the risk factors often associated with the presence of a hearing loss, we would assert that this approach is germane to discussions of early literacy assessment for young deaf children and can assist educators and researchers in the process of improving the early literacy outcomes for this population of students. It has been suggested that there are three essential questions to consider when selecting early literacy assessments for young children: (1) why we are assessing, (2) what we are assessing, and (3) how we are assessing (Snow & Oh, 2011). Therefore, these questions will serve as a framework to guide our discussion of assessments of early literacy assessment presented in later sections of this chapter.

WHY ARE WE ASSESSING?

In addition to identifying students who are potentially at risk, the need to administer measures *for* and *of* learning has been emphasized in several recent governmental reports and policy papers (e.g., Commonwealth of Australia, 2005; Kennedy et al., 2012; Snow & Van

Hemel, 2008). Employing a variety of measures, teachers assess *for* learning to determine children's prior knowledge in particular skill areas and to monitor progress as a result of interventions. These assessments are typically formative in nature, can serve a screening purpose, and are used to plan, implement, and evaluate instruction. Assessments *of* learning, on the other hand, are summative measures that are intended to measure growth over time (usually one year), are often used to determine overall instructional effectiveness, and may be employed as measures of program accountability (Invernizzi, Landrum, Teichman, & Townsend, 2010). For children receiving special education services, including deaf learners, assessments are also routinely administered to determine (1) eligibility for services, (2) ability to access the general education curriculum, (3) appropriate educational placement options, and (4) present level of performance to guide the development of goals and objectives for annual individualized education programs (IEPs).

Even though there is general consensus regarding *why* we administer early literacy assessments, according to Snow and Oh (2011), the selection of specific assessments reflects one's theory of literacy development, a position that was also recently extended to the discussion of assessments used with young deaf children (Andrews, 2013). Consistent with the theoretical orientation of early literacy development and instruction discussed in earlier chapters, in regard to *what* is assessed, we promote the use of assessments that measure the critical foundational requisites in both the language-related (e.g., vocabulary, syntax) and code-related (e.g., phonological sensitivity, alphabet knowledge) domains. While the assessments we discuss and describe in this chapter were developed for hearing children, they have also been effectively utilized with subgroups of early literacy learners, including children of low SES, English language learners (ELLs), and those identified with language impairments and other disabilities, including deaf children.

In concert with the viewpoint presented throughout this book, we recognize that when utilizing these assessments with some deaf children, the administrative procedures and response modes may need to be differentiated in order to make the measures accessible. Given the heterogeneity of the population, some deaf children will require accommodations, whereas others may not. Therefore, it is essential for educators and researchers to thoroughly understand the abilities and skills being assessed through each individual assessment, along with a child's proficiency in that related area, in order to select appropriate accommodations that maintain the validity and reliability of measures (see Cawthon & Leppo, 2013, for discussion). We recognize that some of the assessments we are proposing may be disputed, particularly given the tradition of special norming samples and the types of test accommodations that have historically been employed when using standardized measures of achievement with deaf learners. Therefore, before we describe specific early literacy assessments and strategies for differentiation, we will briefly examine the history of assessment procedures used in the field, explore the implications of these factors in the current era of accountability, and comment on their relevance to selecting measures of early literacy abilities to be used with young deaf children.

HISTORY OF ASSESSMENT ACCOMMODATIONS FOR DEAF LEARNERS

The most common achievement test historically utilized with deaf learners in North America is the Stanford Achievement Test (SAT). The first large-scale use of this assessment with this population occurred in 1965, when the fifth edition of the SAT was administered to approximately twelve thousand students. Because the general version of the SAT required students to take an assessment corresponding to their grade placement (e.g., a fifth grade student was administered fifth grade level tests), a special version of the sixth edition of the SAT was created especially for deaf students in 1974, titled the Stanford Achievement Test for Hearing Impaired (SAT-HI). To accommodate those deaf students achieving below grade level, the SAT-HI introduced a screening measure that would allow educators to match the subtests of the assessment to students' current level of educational performance. This screening assessment also permitted educators to choose specific levels by test area. For example, a student enrolled in fifth grade may be administered the second grade level reading test but the fifth grade level math assessment. Additionally, practice test items were developed to familiarize students with the testing procedures, and directions that were typically read aloud were printed within the test booklets. The SAT developers included both the practice items and written directions for general use by all students in subsequent versions of the assessment (see Qi & Mitchell, 2012, for discussion).

In addition to the aforementioned test accommodations, the development of the SAT-HI also marked the first time normative data were calculated exclusively for deaf students and based on the results obtained from a nationally representative sample of approximately seven thousand participants (see Trybus & Karchmer, 1977). Since the introduction of the SAT-HI, special norms have been developed for the four subsequent editions of the SAT, with samples including as many as eight thousand participants in 1983 for the seventh edition and, for the most recent edition of the assessment (the tenth), including approximately thirty-five hundred students (see Qi & Mitchell, 2012, for discussion; see also Allen, 1986; Holt, Traxler, & Allen, 1992, 1997; Mitchell, Qi, & Traxler, 2007). It is important to note that the presentation of test items (i.e., written) and response mode (i.e., multiple choice) of the SAT was not altered from its original form when creating the SAT-HI for use with deaf learners. Rather, the results obtained for students on the SAT-HI could simply be compared with those for other deaf students who were administered the same assessment.

While this practice of special norming has continued for nearly forty years, we question its usefulness and applicability in the current educational context. When this special assessment and norming sample was originally developed, many more deaf children attended residential schools or special congregated programs housed in public school settings, and perhaps this comparison was more relevant at that time. This stands in contrast with the current situation, as the most recently reported statistics indicate that approximately half of all deaf children in the United States spend more than 80 percent of their day in the general education classroom, and only about 13 percent are educated in separate schools or other specialized settings (US Government Accountability Office, 2011). The statistics offered in a recent report evidence a similar pattern of educational placements in the United Kingdom (Consortium for Research in Deaf Education, 2013). Because of this instructional arrangement, deaf educators serving children in general education environments are often held to the same accountability standards as all teachers, and they are required to administer annual assessments mandated by the state/province and to frequently monitor student progress to determine eligibility for interventions based on benchmark assessment cut scores (e.g., National Center on Response to Intervention, 2010).

We also question whether these special normative samples adequately represent the achievement performance across the full range of deaf learners. For example, the most frequently cited research study reporting the literacy performance in this population of students summarizes the norming and performance standards for deaf and hard-of-hearing (DHH) students on the SAT ninth edition (Traxler, 2000). Of the normative sample represented in this study, 28 percent had a hearing loss less than severe, 21 percent had severe hearing loss, and 51 percent had profound hearing loss. According to the most recent statistics available from the Gallaudet Research Institute's survey of DHH children and youths (2008), 58.7 percent reportedly had a hearing loss less than severe, 13.8 percent had severe hearing loss, and 27.5 percent had profound hearing loss. For that reason, we suggest that the current sample actually overrepresents the profoundly deaf group and does not mirror the demographics of the majority of deaf students being educated in schools today.

Because of increased accountability measures for schools serving students with disabilities, many deaf children are now assessed using the same standardized academic achievement measures as those used for their hearing peers (see Qi & Mitchell, 2012, for discussion). Cawthon and Leppo (2013) pointed out that in making decisions about administering these measures to deaf learners, it is important to keep in mind the distinction between test accommodations and test modifications when altering the administration procedures of standardized assessments. Because the primary purpose of test accommodations is to increase students' access to the measure, these adjustments still allow for the resulting scores to be interpreted in the same manner. In other words, test accommodations do not change the constructs under investigation, so the validity of the assessment is maintained. The most common accommodations reportedly used for students with disabilities include extended time, tests administered in an alternative setting (e.g., a separate room), and having test instructions and items read aloud (Cawthon & Leppo, 2013).

Even though only 11 percent of deaf students are reportedly educated using sign language only (US Government Accountability Office, 2011), much discussion in the field has centered on the use of a natural sign language (e.g., ASL) as a test accommodation in standardized assessment administration. While the aforementioned accommodations for students with disabilities also extend to deaf learners, translating test directions, presenting test passages and items using a signed system or sign language, and using a scribe (the student provides an answer in sign language, and the response is translated into written English by an adult) have also been done. Not only has the intent (accommodation versus modification) of these practices raised questions in relation to maintaining the validity of the original measures, but results of several studies also have indicated that signed presentations of assessments do not have a significant impact on student outcomes (e.g., Cawthon, Winton, Garberoglio, & Gobble, 2011; Maihoff et al., 2000; Marschark et al., 2009). Additionally, depending on the construct being assessed, test modifications such as translated items may result in more significant changes that in fact alter the construct being measured, thereby resulting in invalid scores.

In regard to literacy assessments specifically, we contend that translating test items using ASL or another natural sign language definitely compromises the validity of the measures. As Qi and Mitchell (2012) suggest, the purpose of test accommodations is to remove "obstacles to successful test performance that are unrelated to the traits or constructs being measured" (p. 11). Because literacy measures are specifically designed to evaluate traits of the English language (e.g., vocabulary, syntax, alphabet knowledge), we argue that a translation would be characterized as a modification that changes the construct being assessed (see Cawthon & Leppo, 2013; Qi & Mitchell, 2012, for discussions). For example, comprehension of written English would not be the construct measured if a reading passage and associated questions from a reading comprehension assessment were signed *to* a student and not independently read *by* the student (Qi & Mitchell, 2012). In other words, this modification would essentially result in an assessment of sign language comprehension rather than reading comprehension. Support for this position can be drawn from provisions applied to the assessment of English language learners, in which regulations indicate that items on math and other subject area assessments can be translated, but those on measures of reading cannot (see Liu, Anderson, Swierzbin, & Thurlow, 1999, for discussion).

A final point in regard to historical issues surrounding assessment measures and procedures utilized with deaf learners relates to test bias. Questions of test bias were raised over the last several decades in relation to the use of verbal tests of intelligence (see Braden, 1994, for discussion) and have recently resurfaced in regard to measures of phonological sensitivity (see Luckner, 2013; Qi & Mitchell, 2012). Our position is that assessments of English language and literacy skills, when administered with appropriate accommodations, are not biased against deaf learners any more than they are biased against other subgroups of children who may perform poorly on these measures, such as children with dyslexia or language impairments. Rather, children's low scores on these assessments may simply reflect delayed abilities in the areas being measured. This position will be expanded on later in this chapter, where we describe areas to be assessed and strategies that can be used to provide differentiated access to assessments that allow examiners to maintain the validity of the measures.

WHAT ARE WE ASSESSING?

Results of a meta-analysis of available early literacy research conducted by the NELP (National Early Literacy Panel, 2008) revealed six precursor skills (phonological awareness, alphabet knowledge, phonological memory, rapid automatic naming of letters and/or digits, rapid automatic naming of objects or colors, writing) with medium to large relations to later measures of literacy development. An additional five areas (concepts of print, print knowledge, reading readiness, visual processing, and oral language[1]) were also identified as promising correlates (see also chapter 3) of early and conventional literacy skills. Given the critical role of these requisite abilities, administering assessments that measure children's aptitude and achievement in these areas has implications for both practice and research. As indicated earlier in this chapter, early literacy assessments are administered both *of* and *for* learning.

---

[1] When the term *oral language* is used, it reflects the terminology employed in the original source (e.g., NELP, a published study, etc.). This term is often used synonymously with *spoken language* in the broader literature in the field of literacy. It is only in the field of deafness that the distinction between oral and spoken language merits attention.

In the following sections, we will address the second key question in relation to early literacy assessments (what we are assessing?) by providing general descriptions of early literacy constructs and how they are measured. Supplying these explanations will also provide insights into instructional activities that can be used to foster skill development in each of these areas. We will categorize measures in four broad domains of early literacy development and instruction: (1) language-related abilities, (2) code-related skills, (3) consolidated code-related and language-related abilities, and (4) concepts of print.

Language-Related Abilities

Receptive and expressive vocabulary and semantics, syntax, and oral language comprehension are constructs within the language-related domain. Basic receptive vocabulary is usually measured using assessments that require examinees to point to the correct picture (typically out of a group of four) that corresponds to an individual word presented by the examiner. It has been suggested that assessments of receptive vocabulary may underestimate children's overall lexical knowledge, thereby influencing the strength of the relationship that can be demonstrated between vocabulary and subsequent reading abilities. These findings have led some researchers to propose the use of expressive language assessments to gauge vocabulary knowledge, as these measures typically also tap into semantic depth and organization and result in stronger correlations with later reading achievement than those documented for receptive language measures (see Sénéchal, Ouellette, & Rodney, 2006 for discussion).

In the area of expressive language, vocabulary is usually measured by asking children to view a single picture and to name what is illustrated. As the NELP meta-analysis revealed, measures of complex language abilities (e.g., definitional vocabulary, listening comprehension, grammar) were stronger predictors of conventional literacy skills than measures of vocabulary alone (see also chapter 3). Therefore, it is recommended that more complex measures of language abilities be utilized with young children to simultaneously assess syntactic abilities and overall language comprehension. These include assessments that require children to engage in tasks such as defining individual words, describing relationships among words, following directions, recalling items and sentences in the correct order, and/or formulating sentences or stories in response to pictures or verbal prompts from the examiner.

Consistent with our assertion that the development of implicit phonological awareness (e.g., recognizing rhyme and syllables) occurs in the process of language acquisition (see chapter 2), this construct is purposely being discussed within the language-related domain. Measures used to assess implicit phonological awareness usually involve both recognition and production tasks, further reflecting the relationship of these abilities to receptive and expressive language. For example, in rhyme identification tasks, children must indicate whether pairs of orally presented words (*funny/bunny, desk/soup*) rhyme (receptive language), whereas in rhyme production activities, children must generate a word that rhymes with one presented by the examiner (expressive language). Measures of syllable manipulation abilities are also associated with both receptive and expressive language and include tasks that require children to identify the number of syllables in words (*bed* = 1, *bedroom* = 2), blend syllables to form words (*pa/per* = *paper*), and delete syllables within words to create new words (*downtown* – *town* = *down*; *candy* – *dy* = *can*). Finally, assessment activities that ask young children to repeat orally presented words and nonsense words and strings of digits (typically two to seven) can be used to measure phonological memory or the ability to code information phonologically for temporary storage in short-term memory (see chapter 3 for discussion).

Code-Related Abilities

Measures of code-related constructs include those associated with phonemic awareness skills, letter knowledge, the alphabetic principle, phonemic decoding and encoding, and word recognition. Assessments that gauge children's development of phonemic awareness, or the explicit understanding that words are composed of sound units smaller than a syllable, use a variety of measures of increasing difficulty. For example, phoneme isolation activities that ask children to identify the initial sound in orally presented words (/b/ in *ball*) are considered the most basic, followed by those requiring final sound identification (/sh/ in *wish*). Similarly, phoneme blending abilities, those that require children to blend a series of orally presented phonemes to form a word (examiner presents /s/, /t/, /o/, /p/, examinee responds with *stop*), are viewed as less challenging than those that require them to segment a word into individual phonemes (examiner presents *ship*, examinee responds with /sh/, /i/, /p/). Finally, phonemic awareness activities that require children to delete phonemes to form new words (*train* without the /n/ is *tray*), substitute individual phonemes to create new words (say *tall*; now change the /t/ to /b/; what's the new word?), or reverse phonemes in words (say /m/ /a/; now say /m/ /a/ backward: *am*) are considered the most difficult. It is important to reiterate that while picture prompts may be used, phonemic awareness assessments are administered without the aid of print (see chapter 3 for discussion).

Measuring letter knowledge involves using assessments that determine children's ability to name upper- and lower-case letters of the alphabet when presented in a random order. Because these assessments typically involve a one-minute limit or require the examiner to record the number of seconds needed to correctly name letters to calculate a score, they can also be simultaneously used to measure another construct, rapid automatic naming (RAN). However, it is important to note that assessments of RAN that require examinees to name letter and digits may not be valid when used with preschool children who have yet to learn the names of letter and numbers. Therefore, assessments that require color or object/picture naming may be more appropriate for younger children (see Lonigan, 2006). Testing configurations similar to those used to measure letter knowledge are also used to assess children's ability to associate phonemes with printed graphemes, thereby tapping their knowledge of the alphabetic principle.

In terms of measuring phonemic decoding abilities, assessments can be used that require examinees to blend phonemes to read words with increasingly difficult phonological structures, moving from words with consonant-vowel-consonant patterns (*man*), to those containing diagraphs in the initial (*chin*) and final (*rich*) positions, to those words containing blends in the initial (*brag*) and final (*dust*) positions. Nonsense words are often employed in these decoding measures to ensure that the ability to relate phonemes to graphemes is the construct being assessed rather than the ability to recall words holistically. These same categories of words and pseudowords are often applied in measures of early encoding (i.e., spelling) abilities. As discussed in chapter 4, evaluating children's use of invented spellings can also provide insights into the development of both phonemic encoding and decoding abilities. Finally, tests requiring children to read high-frequency, phonetically irregular words (*was, said*) are often administered as an additional assessment of word recognition abilities.

Consolidated Code-Related and Language-Related Abilities

The end of kindergarten typically marks the point when early literacy measures start to reflect the application of prerequisite skills to conventional reading and writing tasks and begin to evidence the interaction between code-related and language-related abilities. Assessments introduced at this juncture require children to read and write sentences and short passages. In terms of reading, once children are introduced to these selections, basic measures of reading comprehension such as answering wh-questions and/or retelling the story can also be added. Some reading comprehension assessments utilize a cloze or maze procedure that requires the reader to fill in the blanks for words that have been systematically deleted from the written selection, most often every fifth or seventh word. Evaluating children's written language samples at this stage can provide valuable information about their growing knowledge of grammatical structures and syntax. As a final point, the relationship between code-related and language-related abilities and performance may differ depending on the specific type of reading outcome measure employed. For example, code-related skills appear to be more strongly associated with measures of reading accuracy, whereas language-related abilities align more closely when assessments of reading comprehension are used (see Gillon & Dodd, 1994).

Concepts of Print

Based primarily on the work of Clay (2000), who described concepts of print as the "rules of the road" for both reading and writing, measuring concepts of print involves assessing several areas: (1) book concepts, such as front and back cover and title; (2) reading concepts, or the understanding that print, not pictures, communicates the story; (3) text concepts, including left to right orientation of print and tracking between lines of text; and (4) print concepts, such as recognizing upper- and lower-case letters, words, word boundaries, high-frequency words, and punctuation. To access concepts of print, the examiner reads a preselected, engaging early level text to the examinee and assesses his or her knowledge using probes and questions, such as *Show me the title of the book. Point to the pictures. Where are the words? Show me where I start reading. Point to a letter. Show me one word. Show me two words. Point to the word* was. While concepts of print assessments are typically administered in relation to reading, many of these concepts can also be easily assessed as children engage in writing tasks, completed independently or in collaboration with an adult using strategies such as interactive writing (see Williams, 2011).

HOW ARE WE ASSESSING?

For children considered at risk, identifying barriers to successful early literacy skill acquisition is critical. Because there are numerous factors within both the language-related and code-related domains that influence skill development, it is essential to determine specific areas of concern so that efficacious instructional approaches and strategies can be implemented to minimize the effect of delays on early literacy skill development and their subsequent impact on conventional reading achievement. Therefore, identifying reliable and valid measures of essential early literacy constructs becomes the first step in developing a system of early identification and intervention. Three main categories of early literacy assessments can be utilized in this process: (1) informal assessments, (2) screening/progress monitoring assessments, and (3) diagnostic assessments (Lonigan et al., 2011). In the following sections, we describe each category of measures and explore research findings salient to the discussion of early literacy assessment practices employed with young deaf children.

Informal Assessments

Informal assessments typically involve having parents and/or teachers observe children's early literacy behaviors and complete checklists, rating scales, or questionnaires to summarize their perspectives on overall development. Constructing portfolios of children's work samples is also considered an example of an informal measure. While the majority of research regarding the use of informal literacy assessments has involved children engaged in conventional literacy instruction in first or second grade, several studies reporting the use of this assessment practice by both parents and teachers of preschool children are beginning to emerge (see Lonigan et al., 2011, for discussion). The findings of the investigations most pertinent to discussions of young deaf learners are described briefly below.

Based on the results of previous studies that revealed strong correlations between parent reports and measures of early literacy development (e.g., Colligan, 1976; Dickinson & DeTemple, 1998), Boudreau (2005) conducted a study to compare the information reported by parents of preschoolers with (seventeen children) and without (twenty children) identified language impairments to the results of formal measures of early literacy development obtained for these children. Parents were asked to complete a thirty-one-item questionnaire to rate their children's early literacy behaviors in several topic areas, such as orientation to literacy, interactions with books, response to environmental print, alphabet knowledge (letter names and sounds), phonological awareness (e.g., rhyming), and writing. Formal assessments of literacy administered to the children included measures of phonological awareness, letter and alphabet knowledge, concepts of print, and retelling of a wordless book that was analyzed for elements of story grammar to measure narrative abilities.

Results of this investigation indicated that reports provided by parents of children with language impairments were highly correlated with measures of phonological awareness, environmental print, and alphabet knowledge but not with measures of narrative abilities. In contrast, information offered by the parents of typically developing children evidenced overall weaker relationships. The researcher surmised that the behaviors described in the questionnaire in relation to storybook engagement may not have been as closely associated with narrative development as originally thought, thus resulting in a weaker relationship between parent reports and the formal assessment of this construct. In regard to the differences noted between the two groups of parents, the researcher suggested that parents of children with language impairments may have more experience describing their children's limitations and/or are more accustomed to reflecting on development and therefore were more accurate in rating abilities in the domains assessed than parents of typically developing children (Boudreau, 2005).

In a study of the accuracy of teachers' ratings, educators serving 209 children from forty-four federally funded preschool programs in one state evaluated their students' skills within the print knowledge domain (Cabell, Justice, Sucker, & Kilday, 2009). Using an abbreviated twelve-item version of the teacher rating scale from the Clinical Evaluation of Language Fundamentals—Preschool assessment (Semel, Wiig, & Secord, 2004), children's abilities in the areas of print concept knowledge, alphabet knowledge, and emergent writing were evaluated. Teacher ratings collected midway through the school year were then compared to results of formal measures of these constructs administered between two and three months later. While findings of this investigation indicated that teacher ratings were positively correlated with the results of formal assessments, results of the study also revealed that teacher participants were more accurate in identifying students who were not at risk (those performing at higher than the 26th percentile) as compared with those who performed most poorly at the end of the year.

The differential impact of teacher training on the ability to accurately rate the early literacy abilities of prekindergarten children (Begeny & Buchanan, 2010) was explored in a study of five teachers, five teaching assistants, and eighty children. As part of this investigation, half of the adult participants received training regarding the various subtests of the Early Literacy Skills Assessment (DeBruin-Parecki, 2004), which assesses oral language comprehension, phonological awareness, letter and alphabet knowledge, and concepts of print. Results of these measures are subsequently used to classify children as early emergent, emergent, or competent emergent in each of the four areas. All ten adult participants were asked to characterize the early literacy achievement (emergent, emergent, or competent emergent) of eight children in their class using the child summary sheet included in the assessment. Findings of these ratings were then compared with the actual results obtained when the assessment was administered to the children by the researchers. Results of this study suggested that teachers who received training provided better judgments regarding children's performance than teachers who did not. An additional finding was that both groups of teachers tended to overestimate children's comprehension abilities and underestimate their phonological awareness capabilities.

Screening/Progress Monitoring Assessments

Unlike informal assessments, screening/progress monitoring assessments of early literacy development are considered standardized measures; therefore, consistent stimulus materials and administration procedures characterize these types of tests. Specific scoring methods are detailed for teachers administering these assessments, and the results obtained are compared with criterion-referenced target scores calculated from a normative sample (Lonigan et al., 2011).

These assessments often provide cut-point scores for three different time points during the year (fall, winter, spring) to evaluate children's risk in specific areas assessed and to categorize their performance as either at, below, or well below the reported benchmark. Another common feature of screening/progress monitoring assessments is that they are designed to measure increasingly difficult aspects of early literacy in a developmental sequence. For example, widely used in the United States, the Dynamic Indicators of Basic Early Literacy Skills (DIBELS) assessment includes measures of first sound fluency, letter naming fluency, phoneme segmentation fluency, and nonsense word fluency at the kindergarten level. By second grade, measures of nonsense word fluency, oral reading fluency, and story retelling are administered, illustrating the progression of skill development expected (Good & Kaminski, 2002). Provisions for administering measures to children at levels other than their current grade placement (e.g., a second grade student assessed with kindergarten probes) are also typically outlined in the administration procedures of screening/progress monitoring assessments in order to accommodate the needs of children performing below grade level expectations.

The use of the term *fluency* in the title of the majority of subtests included in the DIBELS measure reflects another attribute of these kinds of tests. When screening/progress monitoring assessments are administered, each subtest usually has a one-minute time limit; therefore, administering the battery of measures to a kindergartener would take approximately five minutes. Parallel versions of the each subtest are usually available in the form of weekly probes, making them excellent measures to closely monitor children's progress in individual areas of early literacy. In addition to screening and progress monitoring functions, these assessments can also be used in a diagnostic capacity and to measure children's outcomes over the course of a year (Coyne & Harn, 2006).

Given that questions of test bias have been previously raised in the field of deaf education, reviewing the findings of a study examining predictive bias of screening/progress monitoring assessments for English language learners and ethnic subgroups (Betts et al., 2008) may buttress discussions presented later in this chapter regarding the use of these assessments with deaf learners. In this investigation, Betts and colleagues examined the results obtained from a screening/progress monitoring assessment administered to nearly two thousand kindergarten children in one school district in relation to scores reported on a subsequent standardized measure of conventional reading skill achievement administered in second grade. The screening/progress monitoring assessment contained subtests measuring several early literacy constructs, including letter and alphabet knowledge, phonemic segmentation, rhyming, alliteration, and preprimer passage reading, whereas the standardized assessment reportedly gauged students' general reading achievement. Findings of this study indicated a significant and moderately strong association between scores obtained on the kindergarten and second grade assessments for the entire group and for the various ethnic subgroups. Further analyses revealed that there was no evidence of predictive bias found for the approximately 30 percent of students identified as English language learners. It is important to note that because this investigation was intended to focus on general education students, scores for children identified with disabilities were not included in the analyses.

While the administration of screening/progress monitoring assessments typically coincides with the introduction to formal literacy instruction in kindergarten, measures of this type have been developed to assess the precursor abilities of preschool children, which also incorporate administration formats that are considered developmentally appropriate for this age group. For example, the Get Ready to Read! screening tool (Whitehurst & Lonigan, 2001) was designed to assess print knowledge and phonological awareness by having children point to pictures in response to questions posed by the examiner. Similarly, the Individual Growth and Development Indicators assessment (McConnell, 2002) contains subtests intended to measure alliteration, rhyming, and picture naming (see Lonigan et al., 2011, for discussion). The Phonological Awareness Literacy Screening for preschoolers (Invernizzi, Sullivan, & Meier, 2001) is another example of an assessment created for young literacy learners. Subtests of this measure include tasks related to letter and alphabet knowledge, phonological awareness, name writing, and print and word awareness (see also Invernizzi et al., 2010). Even though classroom teachers can administer this assessment, Lonigan and colleagues suggest that the extensive number of items and the length of time needed to administer it make it more closely aligned to characteristics typically exhibited in diagnostic assessments.

Diagnostic Assessments

The primary feature of diagnostic assessments that sets them apart from the other measures we have described is their in-depth coverage and evaluation of specific literacy constructs. In most instances, these individually administered, norm-referenced assessments provide a wide array of specific tasks that provide a thorough examination of a particular skill area. For example, the Woodcock Reading Mastery Tests (Woodcock, 2011) include five subtests to evaluate phonological awareness, three sections to assess word comprehension, two measures of RAN, and individual subtests dedicated to the areas of letter identification, word identification, word attack, listening comprehension, oral reading fluency, and passage comprehension. Because items within each subtest are arranged sequentially according to level of difficulty and the number of items presented by the examiner is determined by basal and ceiling rules rather than grade placement, these assessments can provide excellent information for children at various developmental levels, including those performing below grade level expectations (see Lonigan et al., 2011, for discussion).

Scores obtained on these diagnostic assessments can be interpreted using a variety of indices, including standard scores, percentile ranks, and age or grade equivalents. Examiners often have the option of interpreting scores by individual subtest or in related clusters. Using the Woodcock Reading Mastery Tests (Woodcock, 2011) as an example, results of the word identification and word attack measures can be viewed separately or when combined to form what the assessment characterizes as a readiness cluster. In comparison with assessments such as the SAT that utilize a paper-pencil format and rely on group test administration procedures, the diagnostic assessments described here are typically individually administered in a dynamic mode. This assessment configuration allows the examiner not only to directly monitor correct and incorrect responses but also to gain insights into why errors are occurring. Another key feature of this category of assessments is the qualifications required to administer them. While informal and screening/progress monitoring assessments are typically administered, scored, and interpreted by teachers, many diagnostic assessments require specialized training and/or a documented level of expertise in order to effectively administer them and evaluate the results (Lonigan et al., 2011).

It is important to note that all three forms of assessments (informal, screening/progress monitoring, diagnostic) can be used to evaluate the key constructs described in the previous section. For example, development in phonological awareness can be gauged by employing informal measures, screening/progress monitoring, and diagnostic assessments or a combination thereof. Progression through the three categories of assessment becomes increasingly formalized and specified. Depending on children's needs, measures from each category can be used individually or collectively to gain insights into the relative strengths and weaknesses of the young deaf literacy learner.

It is beyond the scope of this book to supply detailed reviews and/or offer specific recommendations regarding assessments, particularly given that both required and recommended assessment instruments tend to vary based on country, state/province, region, or individual school setting. However, there are resources available for selecting valid and reliable early literacy measures, including published articles (e.g., Lonigan et al., 2011), book chapters (e.g., Lonigan, McDowell, & Phillips, 2004), and free online sources such as the Florida Center for Reading Research (www.fcrr.org), Reading Rockets (http://www.

readingrockets.org), and the Southwest Educational Development Laboratory (http://www.sedl.org). As an additional resource for educators and researchers working with deaf learners, Luckner and Bowen (2006) summarized the findings of a survey of the assessment practices and materials employed by various professionals (e.g., teachers, administrators, counselors, psychologists, speech and language clinicians) in the field of deaf education. Of particular interest, frequency-of-use rankings for literacy assessment instruments (reading, writing, language) and also those in other subject areas (e.g., math, science), are provided.

IMPLICATIONS FOR PRACTICE AND RESEARCH

Because the primary purpose of administering assessments is to identify areas of strength and weakness to inform a system of identification and intervention (Lonigan et al., 2011), administering measures in the areas most consistently associated with early literacy skill development have implications for both educators and researchers working with young deaf learners. Of particular importance to this topic is ensuring that *test accommodations* intended to provide differentiated access to the constructs under investigation are employed, rather than *test modifications* that alter the construct being measured. Therefore, in our discussion of implications for practice and research, we will describe strategies that can be used when administering the previously described assessments to deaf learners that allow examiners to administer the measures with fidelity and maintain the validity of the findings.

1. **Strategies to provide differentiated access to assessments of language-related abilities must be carefully selected in order to maintain validity of the measures.**

Given the heterogeneity of the population of young deaf learners, some children will require accommodations for early literacy assessments, whereas others may not. We are therefore not advocating a one-size-fits-all approach to providing differentiated access to measures but rather promoting the use of strategies that reflect not only individual needs but also the demands of the assessment tasks themselves. Earlier in this chapter, we also discussed that the majority of these assessments are typically administered in the dynamic, face-to-face mode; therefore, guidelines for adhering to the use of the target language are critical to any discussion of providing differentiated access to measures of early literacy development for deaf learners.

For many deaf children, minimal accommodations will be needed to administer these assessments of early literacy with fidelity. According to the most recently available demographic data, 52 percent of deaf children reportedly use speech alone as the primary communication mode for instruction, 35 percent are educated using speech and sign, and 2 percent are taught with Cued Speech and other methods (US Government Accountability Office, 2011). From these statistics, it is apparent that for approximately 90 percent of the population, providing accessibility to these measures of English language-related abilities could be accomplished using strategies discussed in early chapters of this book, such as maximizing auditory input through the use of assistive listening devices, supplementing auditory input with a signed form of English, or using Cued Speech. For some language-related measures, such as those assessing phonological sensitivity, Visual Phonics may also be an appropriate accommodation tool (see chapter 3 for an in-depth discussion).

In working with pre- and in-service teachers, we have found that when they have opportunities to explore and administer measures of early literacy to deaf children, educators can begin to identify the areas of assessments that require accommodation strategies in order to ensure equitable access. For example, the challenge of conveying a sentence from a sentence structure subtest of an English language assessment may draw examiners' attention to emphasizing the -ed ending when presenting the prompt orally or using a morphological marker when presenting this task using a signed English system or simultaneous communication (speech and signed language). As discussed throughout this chapter, these types of accommodations simply remove barriers to successful test performance and do not significantly alter the construct being assessed; therefore, validity of the measure is maintained. Given that these solutions to providing differentiated access are relatively straightforward, we will focus the remainder of our discussion on a topic that has garnered much attention in the field and has led to significant controversy and continued discussion: the use of a natural sign language as an accommodation strategy for literacy skill assessments.

Measures of language-related abilities associated with the development of early literacy skills include those assessing constructs in the receptive and expressive vocabulary, syntactic, and listening comprehension domains. The specific tasks included in these assessments are intended to evaluate traits of the English language, so they must be administered in English in order for the results to be considered valid. For the sake of argument, this same rationale would extend to discussion of sign language assessments. For example, if the trait to be evaluated were ASL, the measure would need to be administered in ASL in order for the results to be considered valid. While it has often been recommended that measures of English literacy be translated into ASL for administration with some deaf children, we would ask why the suggestion has not also been made to translate assessments of ASL into English. In either case, this seems illogical, given that the construct being evaluated would be significantly modified by this approach. We would suggest that it is counterintuitive to assume that the validity of any language assessment would be maintained if it were translated into another language (e.g., a Spanish assessment translated into English).

A task from an assessment of English syntax may best illustrate this point. These types of measures often require an examinee to look at four pictures and point to the one that best illustrates the sentence presented by the examiner. For instance, an item from this type of measure might be *The mother gave the boy his hat.* As specifically designed, this item is intended to evaluate children's knowledge of English language features including morphology, semantics, and syntax. While translating the sentence into ASL would maintain the intended meaning of the sentence, the essential elements of the target language (English) would be lost. This example illustrates that the modification significantly alters the construct being assessed and essentially results in an assessment of features of ASL rather than English. In other words, the integrity of the measure has been compromised, and thus the results cannot be considered valid.

Given the importance of ensuring the appropriateness of accommodations to differentiate access to early literacy assessments, we strongly recommend that educators and researchers evaluate the effectiveness of various strategies that are based on the needs of individual children and apply them to informal measures before exploring their applicability to more formal testing situations (e.g., screening/progress monitoring and diagnostic assessments). In our experience, a one-size-fits-all approach is often adopted, particularly with those deaf children who are educated using a Total Communication approach that incorporates the use of simultaneous communication. Requiring some children in these environments to produce responses to assessment measures in simultaneous communication, when they could more efficiently and accurately respond in one mode or the other, can actually result in an assessment that is more challenging to complete than the original and/or that distracts the examinee from the intended tasks. Support for this position can also be gleaned from a recent study of using ASL as a test accommodation in a reading assessment in which the researchers suggested that this modification "may have been a distraction and not a way to increase access to test content" (Cawthon et al., 2011, p. 207). In sum, maintaining the integrity of the target language when selecting and administering assessments is the key to ensuring the validity of assessment findings to inform both practice and research.

2. **As with assessments of language-related abilities, strategies to provide differentiated access to assessments of code-related**

abilities must be carefully selected in order to maintain validity of the measures.

While many of the same issues associated with providing differentiated access to assessments of language-related abilities also apply to measures of code-related skills, a few additional comments are offered here. Even though direct assessments evaluating the consolidation of code-related and language-related abilities are not typically administered until the end of kindergarten, we want to reiterate that the relationship between code-related and language-related abilities is still apparent even in assessments of early code-related skills; therefore, the issue of maintaining the target language remains relevant. Ranging from the most basic phoneme isolation tasks to the most difficult phonemic segmentation tasks, the influence of lexical knowledge on the ability to complete these manipulation tasks is evident. For example, in order to be able to identify that the initial phoneme in the word *ball* is /b/, knowledge of the word *ball* in the target language of English is necessary. Similarly, to be able to look at a picture of a ship and provide the associated phonemes /sh/, /i/, /p/, children must first know the label for the picture in English. Assessment activities that require children to complete these tasks without the use of pictures may also present additional challenges, as these activities engage both receptive and expressive language abilities.

In terms of providing differentiated access to these tasks, we again recommend drawing on strategies that have been previously described, such as maximizing and supplementing auditory input, using a signed form of English, and employing Cued Speech. As with measures of phonological awareness, Visual Phonics may also be a suitable tool to differentiate access. The decision about whether Visual Phonics would provide an appropriate accommodation provides an excellent example of the importance of having a thorough knowledge of the skills and abilities being assessed by a particular measure in order to make informed choices regarding appropriate strategies for differentiated access. For example, in the task in which the examinee is presented with a picture of a ship and asked to segment the associated word, responding using the Visual Phonics hand cues to represent the phonemes /sh/, /i/, and /p/, would maintain the fidelity of the measure. However, if the assessment required the examiner to orally present the word *ship* and then ask the examinee to segment the word phoneme by phoneme, the examiner would modify the construct if he or she employed Visual Phonics to present the item. In other words, this adjustment would essentially result in a visual sequential memory task (remembering the sequence of phonemes presented visually by the examiner) rather than on measuring phoneme segmentation abilities. To maintain fidelity of the construct being measured in this case, the word *ship* would need to be presented orally, perhaps with supplemental sign language support.

As discussed in chapter 4 in relation to spelling and writing, mouth movements that represent specific English words used in conjunction with signed responses would also serve as an appropriate accommodation for many of the code-related assessments described here. This addition would also be particularly useful in maintaining the integrity of letter-naming assessments in which providing a fingerspelled response alone would not be considered valid. In this instance, Visual Phonics would also provide an appropriate tool for accommodating assessments of the letter-naming construct, as it provides a means of representing the letter name (e.g., /e/ /m/ for the letter *m*) phonetically (see chapter 3 for discussion).

While we see a number of acceptable accommodations for differentiated access to assessments of code-related skills, a recently conducted survey of experts in the field of reading and deafness yielded mixed opinions (Luckner, 2013). In this investigation, a panel of thirteen individuals was asked to offer their perspectives on the appropriateness of the various subtests of DIBELS assessment (Good & Kaminski, 2002) for use with deaf learners who use a variety of communication modes, including speech only, speech and sign language, and sign language only. Respondents were asked to indicate whether the measures fell into one of three categories (appropriate, not appropriate, or possibly appropriate) for students using each of the communication modes. In addition to the ratings, panel members were asked to provide descriptions of acceptable accommodations and/or recommendations for adaptations.

Several of the test accommodations recommended by the panelists echo the recommendations we have offered here, such as using Visual Phonics and Cued Speech. We also appreciated the suggestion that test sessions should be recorded or rated by two examiners simultaneously to ensure the fidelity of administration procedures and accuracy of scoring. While recommendations were made to allow a presentation of directions in signed language, it is unclear from the findings whether this implies the use of a signed form of English or a translation using a natural sign language such as ASL. The suggestion to permit fingerspelling may or may not be appropriate, depending on the particular subtest in which it is used (see Luckner, 2013).

While Luckner acknowledged limitations to the study, such as the use of a three-category communication continuum, lack of definition for the term *appropriate,* and the influence of findings based on the backgrounds of the particular panel members selected, we suggest that there may be additional factors affecting the findings. Missing from this study is an understanding of the theoretical orientation toward literacy development subscribed to by the panelists, which has been shown to influence the selection of assessments (Andrews, 2013; Snow & Oh, 2011). Additionally, it is uncertain from the report of study findings whether the selected experts had experience in administering these assessments or if they were simply commenting on the assessments from the materials provided (Luckner, 2013). These are questions that we would recommend exploring in future investigations of this type.

Despite agreeing with many of the panel's findings, we would suggest that several of the overall themes that emerged as a result of the survey mirror some of the historical issues discussed at the beginning of this chapter (special norming, test bias). First, in regard to the benchmark scores used to interpret findings of the DIBELS screening/benchmark assessment, it was stated that they "may not be appropriate for students who are deaf or hard of hearing and should be interpreted cautiously" (Luckner, 2013, p. 14). Second, possible test bias is implied by the statement indicating that the nonsense-word fluency subtest that requires children to read pseudowords "may not be appropriate for some students who are deaf or hard of hearing because they may lack the language skills to be able to determine what is and what is not a nonsense word" (p. 14). As the results of this survey suggest, the perspectives on the appropriateness and applicability of early literacy assessments for use with young deaf literacy learners continue to be controversial and debatable; therefore, it is apparent that there is a need for additional research in this area.

3. **Additional research is needed to determine the most effective means of assessing young deaf children's early literacy abilities in both the language-related and code-related domains.**

It should be clear from the information presented in this chapter, and thoroughly explicated in earlier chapters of this book, that we strongly advocate the use of early literacy assessments that measure the essential requisites in both the language-related and code-related domains. We recognize that this perspective is closely aligned to our theoretical orientation toward literacy development and to the assertion that deaf children must follow the same process from language to literacy as their hearing peers do if they are eventually to become proficient readers and writers. However, we also recognize that alternative viewpoints exist. Therefore, we recommend that future research explore issues of assessment from a variety of perspectives and systematically investigate both long-standing beliefs and emerging perspectives in the field.

For example, we would suggest that if questions of test bias continue to linger or have reemerged as the result of introducing new assessments to the field, this issue should be formally explored, as it was in the study conducted by Betts and colleagues (2008), who examined this issue with the subgroup of ELL. Investigations such as these would serve to provide the evidence necessary to either confirm or deny such claims. Furthermore, replicating studies such as those presented earlier in this chapter that compared the findings of informal measures such as parent and teacher observations with those obtained on formal measures of literacy development is also recommended.

Another area of research focus that we recommend centers on investigating the current assessment practices and accommodation strategies employed by practicing teachers in a variety of educational settings. Since the majority of deaf learners are currently being taught in the general education environment, studies conducted with this population of teachers and the children they serve would be especially informative. Finally, given the nuances in understanding appropriate accommodation strategies for providing differentiated access to language-related and code-related measures, studies that explore the impact of professional development on these practices would be advantageous and would inform both practice and research. Regardless of research methods employed, the goal of research related to the assessment of early literacy development for deaf learners should remain focused on identifying children's strengths and weaknesses so that findings can be used to implement efficacious interventions aimed at improving outcomes for this population of children.

REFERENCES

Allen, T. E. (1986). *Understanding the scores: Hearing-impaired students and the Stanford Achievement Test (7th ed.).* Washington, DC: Gallaudet Research Institute, Center for Assessment and Demographic Studies.

Andrews, J. F. (2013). Assessment and reading paradigms: A response to John Luckner [Letter to the editor]. *American Annals of the Deaf, 158(4),* 399–405.

Begeny, J. C., & Buchanan, H. (2010). Teachers' judgments of students' early literacy skills measured by the Early Literacy Skills Assessment: Comparison of teachers with and without assessment administration experience. *Psychology in School, 47(8),* 859–868. doi:10.1002/pits.20509

Betts, J., Reschly, A., Pickart, M., Heistad, D., Sheran, C., & Marston, D. (2008). An examination of predictive bias for second grade reading outcomes from measures of early literacy skills in kindergarten with respect to English-language learners and ethnic subgroups. *School Psychology Quarterly, 23(4),* 553–570.

Boudreau, D. (2005). Use of a parent questionnaire in emergent and early literacy assessment of preschool children. *Language, Speech, and Hearing Services in Schools, 36,* 33–47.

Braden, J. P. (1994). *Deafness, deprivation, and IQ.* New York, NY: Plenum Press.

Cabell, S. Q., Justice, L. M., Sucker, T. A., & Kilday, C. R. (2009). Validity of teacher report for assessing the emergent literacy skills of at-risk preschoolers. *Language, Speech, and Hearing Services in Schools, 40,* 161–173.

Cawthon, S., & Leppo, R. (2013). Assessment accommodations on tests of academic achievement for students who are deaf or hard of hearing: A qualitative meta-analysis of the research literature. *American Annals of the Deaf, 158(3),* 363–376.

Cawthon, S. W., Winton, S. M., Garberoglio, C. L., & Gobble, M. E. (2011). The effects of American Sign Language as an assessment accommodation for students who are deaf or hard of hearing. *Journal of Deaf Studies and Deaf Education, 16(2),* 199–211. doi:10.1093/deafed/enq053

Clay, M. M. (2000). *Concepts about print: What have children learned about printed language?* Portsmouth, NH: Heinemann.

Colligan, R. C. (1976). Prediction of kindergarten reading success from pre-school report of parents. *Psychology in the Schools, 13,* 304–308.

Commonwealth of Australia (2005). *Teaching reading.* Australian Government Department of Education, Science and Training, Canberra.

Consortium for Research in Deaf Education (2013). *UK: Education—CRIDE survey of educational provision for deaf children.* Available at http://www.ndcs.org.uk/professional_support/national_data/uk_education_.html

Coyne, M. D., & Harn, B. A. (2006). Promoting beginning reading success through meaningful assessment of early literacy skills. *Psychology in the Schools, 43(1),* 33–43. doi:10.1002/pits.20127

DeBruin-Parecki, A. (2004). *Early Literacy Skills Assessment.* Ypsilanti, MI: HighScope.

Dickinson, D. K., & DeTemple, J. (1998). Putting parents in the picture: Maternal reports of preschoolers; literacy as a predictor of early reading. *Early Childhood Research Quarterly, 13,* 241–261.

Gallaudet Research Institute. (2008). *Regional and national summary report of data from the 2007–08 Annual Survey of Deaf and Hard of Hearing Children and Youth.* Washington, DC: GRI, Gallaudet University. Available at http://research.gallaudet.edu/Demographics/2008_National_Summary.pdf

Gillon, G., & Dodd, B. J. (1994). A prospective study of the relationship between phonological, semantic and syntactic skills and specific reading disability. *Reading and Writing, 6,* 321–345.

Good, R. H., & Kaminski, R. A. (Eds.). (2002). *Dynamic Indicators of Basic Early Literacy Skills* (6th ed.). Eugene, OR: Institute for the Development of Educational Achievement. Available at http://dibels.uoregon.edu/

Holt, J. A., Traxler, C. B., & Allen, T. E. (1992). *Interpreting the scores: A user's guide to the 8th edition Stanford Achievement Test for educators of deaf and hard of hearing students (Gallaudet Research Institute Technical Report 92-1).* Washington, DC: Gallaudet University.

Holt, J. A., Traxler, C. B., & Allen, T. E. (1997). *Interpreting the scores: A user's guide to the 9th edition Stanford Achievement Test for educators of deaf and hard of hearing students (Gallaudet Research Institute Technical Report 97-1).* Washington, DC: Gallaudet University.

Invernizzi, M., Landrum, T. J., Teichman, A., & Townsend, M. (2010). Increased implementation of emergent literacy screening in pre-kindergarten. *Early Childhood Education Journal, 37,* 437–446. doi:10.1007/s10643-009-0371-7

Invernizzi, M., Sullivan, A., & Meier, J. (2001). Phonological Awareness Literacy Screening—pre-kindergarten. Charlottesville, VA: University of Virginia.

Kennedy, E., Dunphy, E., Dwyer, B., Hayes, G., McPhillips, T., Marsh, J., O'Connor, M., & Shiel, G. (2012). *Literacy in early childhood and primary education (3–8 years)*. National Council for Curriculum and Assessment, Dublin, Ireland.

Liu, K., Anderson, M. E., Swierzbin, B., & Thurlow, M. (1999). *Bilingual accommodations for limited English proficient students on statewide reading tests: Phase 1 (Minnesota Report No. 20)*. Minneapolis, MN: University of Minnesota, National Center on Educational Outcomes. Available at http://www.cehd.umn.edu/NCEO/onlinepubs/archive/AssessmentSeries/MnReport20.html

Lonigan, C. J. (2006). Conceptualizing phonological processing skills in prereaders. In D. K. Dickinson & S. B. Neuman (Eds.), *Handbook of early literacy research* (Vol. 2, pp. 77–89). New York, NY: Guilford Press.

Lonigan, C. J., Allan, N. P., & Lerner, M. D. (2011). Assessment of preschool early literacy skills: Linking children's educational needs with empirically supported instructional activities. *Psychology in Schools, 48*(5), 488–501. doi:10.1002/pits.20569.

Lonigan, C. J., McDowell, K. D., & Phillips, B. M. (2004). Standardized assessments of children's emergent literacy skills. In B. H. Wasik (Ed.), *Handbook of family literacy* (pp. 525–550). Mahwah, NJ: Erlbaum.

Luckner, J. (2013). Using the Dynamic Indicators of Basic Early Literacy Skills with students who are deaf or hard of hearing: Perspectives of a panel of experts. *American Annals of the Deaf, 158*(1), 7–19.

Luckner, J. L., & Bowen, S. (2006). Assessment practices of professionals serving students who are deaf or hard of hearing: An initial investigation. *American Annals of the Deaf, 151*(4), 410–417.

Maihoff, N., Bosso, E., Zhang, L., Eischgrund, J., Schulz, J., Carlson, J., & Carlson, J. E. (2000). *The effects of administering an ASL signed standardized test via DVD player/television and by paper-and-pencil: A pilot study*. Dover, DE: Delaware Department of Education.

Marschark, M., Sapere, R., Convertino, C., Mayer, C., Wauters, L., & Sarchet, T. (2009). Are deaf students' reading challenges really about reading? *American Annals of the Deaf 154*(4), 357–370.

McConnell, S. R. (2002). *Individual growth and development indicators*. Minneapolis, MN: University of Minnesota.

Mitchell, R. E., Qi, S., & Traxler, C. B. (2007). *Stanford Achievement Test, 10th edition: National performance norms for deaf and hard of hearing students: A technical report*. Unpublished manuscript. Washington, DC: Gallaudet University Press.

National Center on Response to Intervention (2010). *Essential components of RTI—A closer look at response to intervention*. Washington, DC: U.S. Department of Education, Office of Special Education Programs, National Center on Response to Intervention. Available at http://www.rti4success.org/sites/default/files/rtiessentialcomponents_042710.pdf

National Early Literacy Panel. (2008). *Developing early literacy: Report of the National Early Literacy Panel*. Washington, DC: National Institute for Literacy. Available at http://lincs.ed.gov/publications/pdf/NELPReport09.pdf

Qi, S., & Mitchell, R. E. (2012). Large scale academic achievement testing of deaf and hard-of-hearing students: Past, present, and future. *Journal of Deaf Studies and Deaf Education, 17*, 1–18. doi:10.1093/deafed/enr028

Semel, E., Wiig, E., & Secord, W. (2004). *Clinical Evaluation of Language Fundamentals—Preschool* (2nd ed.). San Antonio, TX: Pearson.

Sénéchal, M., Ouellette, G., & Rodney, D. (2006). The misunderstood giant: On the predictive role of early vocabulary to future reading. In D. K. Dickinson & S. B. Neuman (Eds.), *Handbook of early literacy research* (Vol. 2, pp. 173–184). New York, NY: Guilford Press.

Snow, C. E., & Oh, S. S. (2011). Assessment in early literacy research. In S. B. Neuman & D. K. Dickinson (Eds.), *Handbook of early literacy research* (Vol. 3, pp. 228–241). New York, NY: Guilford Press.

Snow, C. E., and Van Hemel, S (2008). *Early childhood assessment: Why, what, how.* Washington, DC: National Research Council.

Stanovich, K. (1986). Matthew effects in reading: Some consequences of individual differences in the acquisition of literacy. *Reading Research Quarterly, 21,* 360–407.

Traxler, C. (2000). The Stanford Achievement Test, 9th edition: National norming and performance standards for deaf and hard of hearing students. *Journal of Deaf Studies and Deaf Education, 5,* 337–348. doi:10.1093/deafed/5.4.337

Trybus, R. J., & Karchmer, M. A. (1977). School achievement scores of hearing impaired children: National data on achievement status and growth patterns. *American Annals of the Deaf Directory of Programs and Services, 122,* 62–69.

US Government Accountability Office. (2011). *Deaf and hard of hearing children: Federal support for developing language and literacy.* Available at http://www.gao.gov/new.items/d11357.pdf

Whitehurst, G. J., & Lonigan, C. J. (2001). *Get ready to read! Screening tool.* New York, NY: National Center for Learning Disabilities.

Williams, C. (2011). Adapted interactive writing instruction with kindergarten children who are deaf or hard of hearing. *American Annals of the Deaf, 156,* 23–34. doi:10.1353/aad.2011.0011

Woodcock, R. W. (2011). Woodcock Reading Mastery Tests (3rd ed.). San Antonio, TX: Pearson.

Afterword

It becomes immediately apparent in this account of early literacy development in deaf children that what we have learned and what we know is far less than what remains to be understood and examined. However, the reality is that the babies, toddlers, and children we work with cannot wait for the research evidence to be developed that unequivocally supports every pedagogical or educational claim. We need to take action on the basis of what we *do* know, at least to the best of our current understandings. Our argument in this book has been that these understandings should be informed by what we know about the early literacy development of both hearing *and* deaf children, particularly as the evidence base for the latter group is so thin. However, in the process, we must also be mindful of the fact that simply applying what we know about hearing children to the case of deaf learners must be done carefully and thoughtfully, in an attempt to avoid assumptions and overgeneralizations. We believe that identifying areas and issues where we have questions about application of knowledge across contexts provides a rich avenue for future research. Therefore, we conclude this text by revisiting the implications sections of each chapter and summarizing what we would see as the most critical issues to be considered for both research and practice.

Perhaps the most obvious conclusion drawn from the review of the research of the early literacy development of deaf children is that more research is needed in all areas that we have considered: reading, writing, bilingualism, and assessment. We would suspect that few would disagree with us in this observation. Beyond amassing a larger quantity of research evidence, attention needs to be directed to the quality of this research in a number of respects. First, we would underscore the need for more longitudinal studies that follow children over time and that include clear outcome measures so that we can ensure that children have learned what we have attempted to teach. Research of this type is particularly important in investigations of early literacy, as tracking children through the developmental process is the only way to clearly understand the nature of this development and to ensure that pedagogical interventions are efficacious.

We would also advocate a broad range of research designs, both qualitative and quantitative, undertaken not for the sake of expediency or convenience, but in order to address the research question via the most meaningful and relevant approach. Without one type of research being privileged over another, there is a relative lack of empirical evidence in almost all aspects of early literacy learning. This may be exacerbated by the fact that there is disagreement in the field regarding what measures are appropriate for assessing language, reading, and writing in deaf children, with suggestions of test bias in using instruments designed for hearing children, particularly as this relates to how measures will be administered (e.g., the tension between making the test accessible via a signed language and compromising the validity of the test).

However, if we do not make use of robust measures with strong psychometric properties that have demonstrated efficacy with hearing children, we will continue to face challenges in designing studies that have the potential to make well-substantiated claims. This challenge also extends to assessing children's proficiency in a natural signed language. While there have been some developments in this area, these measures are still limited in number and scope (e.g., focusing primarily on receptive language), particularly when contrasted with measures of spoken language proficiency. That said, it must also be remembered that this concern pertains to a small minority of the population (i.e., sign bilingual learners), as most deaf children will be assessed via spoken language, albeit with accommodations to address issues of access.

In concert with increasing the range of research designs employed is the challenge of engaging in research that includes greater numbers of participants. While case studies of individuals or small cohorts can and do yield important insights, there is a particular need to increase the N if we are to make broader, more generalizable claims. Beyond the call for increased numbers of participants, we would argue for more focus on the majority group, those children with less significant hearing losses, even though they can be harder to locate, as they are typically taught in mainstream, general education situations. While recognizing the continued need to focus on those children with more profound hearing loss in schools for the deaf and other congregated or specialist settings, we emphasize the need to carry out investigations of the cohort that has been traditionally understudied, especially as this group is the fastest growing.

It would also be important to focus research on the questions that have been shown to be especially important in the development of early literacy. This is where insights from the literature on hearing children are particularly germane. For example, much has been made of the transfer between languages in bilingual development, but we know very little about the nature of interrelationships between a signed L1 and a spoken L2. In the case of learning to read and write, we are only beginning to build the evidence base for the contribution of phonological awareness in young deaf children. One productive research direction would be to replicate studies that have been conducted with hearing children to determine whether the same conclusions apply.

As in the case of research, we recommend that our understandings of practice be informed by what we know to be effective approaches, strategies, and interventions for teaching reading and writing to young hearing learners, not on practices that have no demonstrated efficacy and often seem counter to what we know is effective pedagogy for hearing learners (e.g., bypassing a focus on phonology in the teaching of reading, translation approaches in bilingual programs). As we have argued throughout this book, in the activity of literacy learning, deaf children must master the same fundamental language-related and code-related requisites as their hearing counterparts. In our view, the nature of the process is not different, although the instruction may need to be differentiated to address the particular needs and challenges the deaf child faces in engaging in the process, particularly as these relate to issues of access to language. However, differentiation, as is also the case for hearing children, can be realized in numerous ways: the rate and pace of instruction, time on task, and implementation of particular curricula. There would be no reason to expect that these sorts of adaptations would not also apply to deaf children.

Related to any discussion of differentiating instruction is the issue of assessment. It is only possible to identify gaps and areas of relative weakness by evaluating performance from the perspective of both outcomes and process (i.e., summative and formative assessments). We would advocate the use of a broader range of measures to track development in young deaf literacy learners, making use of those assessments that have yielded valuable information in teaching hearing children. With respect to assessing reading and writing, there would be no need to develop different tests or establish special norming samples, as we are measuring the same constructs in the same language. Providing accessibility to assessments must be thoughtfully considered to ensure that the fidelity of traits and validity of findings is maintained.

One overarching theme in any consideration of practice is the central role that language plays in the early literacy learning process, and by that we mean a level of proficiency in the *face-to-face language of the text*. As we have argued, although this proficiency in a spoken language is most easily achieved via ear (e.g., auditory access for deaf learners through hearing technologies), this can be supported by visual strategies (e.g., speechreading, signed forms of the spoken language, Cued Speech). The critical point is not *how* (modality) but rather *that* the language is acquired, and attempting to teach literacy in the absence of this language foundation is a futile endeavor.

In all of this, we need to take into account the sociocultural situation, the life world of the deaf child. Just as SES and language of the home play a role in the early literacy development of hearing children, they are equally implicated in the process for deaf children. These issues need to be considered in designing early literacy programs so that unrealistic expectations are not placed on parents/caregivers and families (e.g., having them read to a child in a language they do not know). These factors also need to be considered in determining the child's first or second language and whether and how development of these languages can be supported in the child's environment.

The foundation for learning to read and write well as an adult is laid down in the early years. A focus on what happens during this critical period from birth to the onset of formal literacy instruction is key in effecting a positive change in outcomes for deaf learners, so that it becomes the many, and not the few, who achieve outcomes commensurate with hearing age peers, not just outcomes that are seen as "good for a deaf child." The good news is that the possibilities have never been better: the implementation of UNHS and advances in hearing technologies have allowed for the development of the language that is fundamental to the development of early literacy. There are challenges, too: how to serve the growing number of deaf children in mainstream general education settings, those with complex needs, and those from homes in which minority, spoken languages are used. It is our hope that this book can play a supportive role in meeting the research and practice challenges of the coming years, impact the education of both pre- and in-service educators, and make a positive difference in the early literacy learning lives of deaf children.

Index